Educating Professional Psychologists

HISTORY AND GUIDING CONCEPTION

■

Donald R. Peterson

AMERICAN PSYCHOLOGICAL ASSOCIATION ■ WASHINGTON, DC

Published by
American Psychological Association
750 First Street, NE
Washington, DC 20002

Copies may be ordered from
APA Order Department
P.O. Box 92984
Washington, DC 20090-2984

In the United Kingdom and Europe, copies may be ordered from
American Psychological Association
3 Henrietta Street
Covent Garden
London WC2E 8LU
England

Typeset in Goudy by GGS Information Services, York, PA

Printer: Kirby Lithographic Company, Inc., Arlington, VA
Cover designer: Berg Design, Albany, NY
Technical/production editor: Valerie Montenegro

Library of Congress Cataloging-in-Publication Data
Peterson, Donald R. (Donald Robert), 1923–
Educating professional psychologists : history and guiding conception / Donald R. Peterson.
p. cm.
Includes bibliographical references and index.
ISBN 1-55798-420-4 (pbk. : acid-free paper)
1. Psychologists—Training of—United States. I. Title.
BF80.7.U6P48 1997
150′.71′173—dc21 97-14077
CIP

British Library Cataloguing-in-Publication Data
A CIP record is available from the British Library.

Printed in the United States of America
First edition

CONTENTS

PART III: QUALITY CONTROL IN PROFESSIONAL EDUCATION

PART IV: THE FUTURE OF PROFESSIONAL PSYCHOLOGY

FOREWORD

Professional Psychology and the Contributions of Donald R. Peterson

In a concert, the American folk singer Tom Paxton told a story of happening upon a London street singer who was singing a song that Paxton had written. He asked, "Do you know who wrote that song?" Quickly and with great assurance, the street singer answered, "It's traditional, don't ya know." Paxton said he first felt hurt that his work was not universally known as his, but then he experienced an odd satisfaction that he had been absorbed into the culture, and he walked on without further comment. Donald Peterson must feel a bit like that when he hears repeated back to him ideas that he introduced to the professional psychology culture a decade or two earlier. Across the country, psychologists are singing Don's songs without quite knowing where they heard them first.

This is a story of the development of professional psychology. As the work of a person who has been deeply involved in professional psychology throughout its most vigorous half-century existence, and the only person in the world who has directed a research-oriented scientist–practitioner program, a professional program in an academic department, and a professional school in a major research university, it is a story that Donald Peterson is uniquely qualified to tell. In part, the account is personal and local, as all narratives must be, but, taken as a whole, it is also broadly general. It begins with Don's entry into clinical psychology just as organized psychology, for the first time in its history, officially acknowledged that it *was* a profession as well as a science, just as the scientist–practitioner model of education was being formalized and widely accepted, and just as the largest surge of growth in the history of clinical psychology was getting underway. It continues into his career as a researcher, practitioner, and teacher of psychology, and, later, as an administrator and designer of programs for educating professional psychologists. There he tells of his appreciation of the scientist–practitioner concept and also of the distress over its limitations that led him, as director of clinical training at the University of Illinois, to organize the first Doctor of Psychology

(PsyD) program in the United States. The account proceeds through Don's experiences as a leader in the professional school movement and presents, in cogent order, the most decisive of the many papers he has written on the nature of professional psychology and education for practice in our field. Written over a span of 20 years, the papers are landmarks in the development of professional psychology. The papers in the final section of the book—all written within a 3-year period after Don had officially retired as dean of the Graduate School of Applied and Professional Psychology at Rutgers University—offer the wealth of his experience as well as his mature thought on the nature of our profession and on preparation for the challenges that professional psychologists, now and in the future, will encounter throughout their careers.

Organized now as chapters in a book, the papers define the basic issues with which all professional psychologists must be concerned. Embedded in a rich understanding of the history of psychology, they provide a coherent ideology for professional psychology and education of its practitioners. In its entirety, the statement embraces commentary on the epistemological foundations of our discipline, an outline of its substantive content, means for continuing appraisal and improvement of professional education, and proposals for improving the functional value of the profession in meeting the needs of the larger society.

On the first page of the first chapter of the book, Don characterizes the pioneers of psychology as people who "dug right in," who saw human problems, did their best to solve them, and in the process "developed the conceptions and encouraged the research needed to place their work on a progressively more systematic, scientifically informed foundation." This book exemplifies the spirit of the pioneers. Many of the papers in it have long been required reading for students of psychology. Here as chapters in a story of the development of professional psychology, the papers take on new meaning and will be all the more valuable to people who want to understand their discipline fully and deeply. Teachers of professional psychologists, in professional schools and academic departments alike, should find the book useful, and many will regard it as essential matter for courses in professional issues. It will be especially appealing as a synoptic introduction to professional psychology. For introductory graduate courses and advanced undergraduate courses that include material on the profession of psychology, the book offers a clear, readable view of the field. Undergraduate students and others who ask about education in professional psychology can now be referred to a convenient source. As a complement to more general statements, the book will enrich study of the history of psychology and provide necessary content for those seeking a thorough understanding of professional psychology. Scholars concerned more broadly with the development of professions will also find much to inform them in this volume. Indeed, this book should be required reading for those on the "scientific" side of psychology who persist, without data or any other evidence of scholarly probity, in treating professional schools and the professional degree as devoid of scientific content. However passionately some critics may deplore the growth of practitioner programs and professional schools, the schools are here to stay. Responsible critics can no longer dismiss them as inconsequential, or deride them, without inquiry, as educational aberrations. Much of the wisdom in the pages to follow is highly distilled. For some scholars, this book is likely to become one of those well-thumbed volumes that invites periodic rereading as issues are reexamined and understanding deepens.

Donald Peterson's voice is American and midwestern—empirical, reasoned, pragmatic, socially responsible, skeptical of fads and "sun science." It embodies some of the unusual combination of the conservative and the revolutionary associated with the populist politics of Minnesota where Don grew up. The professional psychology he espouses is conservative in its attention to systematic study, rigorous standards in the quality of training, and the conviction that the solution of social problems requires keen intelligence, thorough education, sound conceptualization, systematic assessment, and unwavering respect for data. As an interpersonalist and contextualist, Don believes that professional psychologists should be in the front lines of those grappling with our community's most intransigent human problems, and that our engagement with those problems should organize our training, our research, and the institutions in which both take place. It is remarkable that these ideas can have the ring of common sense and at the same time be revolutionary critiques of traditional practices in psychological research and education.

By style, Don is gentle and a gentleman. Beyond an impressive mastery of psychology, he is broadly literate; he reads humanistic literature, history, and philosophy as well as science. He has the ability to focus intensely, even single-mindedly. He is disciplined and meticulous as a scholar. He is just as likely to call attention to something that is silly or foolish or embarrassing as to something flattering in professional psychology. Interpersonally persuasive, he enjoys intellectual give and take. He presents his ideas forthrightly so others who may disagree have a clear target. To exchanges with critics, he brings pointed arguments and a high-minded elegance that captures the best of what academic discourse can be. To readers, he brings a style of expression that is always clear, often eloquent, laced with humor, and in all a pleasure to read.

On a personal level, I have occasionally been dismayed to find that some of my best new ideas appeared in one of Don's papers 20 years ago. Still, I am reassured to be in good company. I am personally thankful for the way he has touched my professional and personal life. Every time I read or reread one of his papers, I find something to learn, something to change my thinking. Over the years, I have been in many conversations about education and critical thinking where we have talked about the importance of getting our students to "think like a psychologist." The psychologist in my mind when I say that is Donald Peterson. Here, in his writings, we find the careful scholarship and accumulated wisdom of a person who has loved psychology and has thought deeply and incisively about the critical issues of his profession and his times.

Roger L. Peterson
Chairperson, Department of Clinical Psychology
Antioch New England Graduate School
President, 1994–1995
National Council of Schools and Programs of Professional Psychology

We, past presidents of the National Council of Schools and Programs of Professional Psychology (NCSPP), concur regarding the importance of Donald R. Peterson's work to professional psychology. We consider the issues he has raised and his treatment of those issues essential to the education of our students, important to the field of psychology at large, and of interest to others concerned with the development of professions. In the spirit of community that Donald R. Peterson has fostered, we endorse the sense of Roger L. Peterson's foreword to this book.

Patricia Bricklin, NCSPP President 1995–1996
Jules C. Abrams, NCSPP President 1993–1994
Kenneth Polite, NCSPP President 1992–1993
Elizabeth Davis-Russell, NCSPP President 1991–1992
David L. Singer, NCSPP President 1990–1991
James McHolland, NCSPP President 1989–1990
George Stricker, NCSPP President 1988–1989
Edward Bourg, NCSPP President 1987–1988
Russell Bent, NCSPP President 1986–1987
Joanne Callan, NCSPP President 1984–1986

PREFACE

For several years before I ever thought about professional schools or professional degrees, I had grown increasingly concerned about the direction clinical psychology appeared to be taking. Down. The foundations of our profession seemed to be giving way. The psychological tests on which we had based many of our hopes were not showing the strong reliabilities, validities, and practical utilities we had once expected. Psychotherapy, the single activity in which clinical psychologists spent most of their time, had come under attack as ineffective and was scorned by some critics as a waste of professional time and clients' money. Creation of knowledge through research, the main outcome foreseen by architects of the scientist–practitioner model of education in clinical psychology, was not coming through as expected either. Surveys showed that the modal number of publications by graduates of the scientist–practitioner programs, well beyond their scholarly PhDs, was not ten, not five, not two, not one, but *zero*.

Through long sessions in the richly stocked, warmly paneled library of the University of Illinois, in long, solitary walks about the tree-lined campus, through sleepless ruminations in the small hours of the night, in congenial talks and spirited arguments with respected colleagues, and finally in hard-eyed, laugh-filled seminars with graduate students, I worked out my proposals for improving clinical psychology. The profession I envisioned was directed beyond the study of individuals to the interactional study of people-in-their-environments. It was rooted in the most credible, dependable knowledge we could find about the biopsychosocial processes that constitute human behavior and experience. To examine those processes, the profession required a new paradigm for assessment that complemented test-based appraisal of states and traits with full-scale clinical use of the methods of psychological science: naturalistic observation, guided interview, and functional analysis of behavior. Professionals served the public by linking assessment with change in studying and improving the way people functioned holistically as individuals, in groups, and in organizations.

Through all my mental ambulations, the need for sustained, well-directed research to nourish the profession was obvious to me. The need for rigorous education to teach professional psychologists the best way of understanding the human condition was also clear. In 1964, however, when I first began to direct the PhD program in clinical psychology at the University of Illinois, the advantages of professional schools had not yet dawned on me, and the specific idea of the PsyD degree was not prominent in my thinking. Nowhere in *The Clinical Study of Social Behavior*, the book in which I laid out my conception of professional psychology (Peterson, 1968a), does the phrase *Doctor of Psychology* appear.

That came later, though rapidly and with strong conviction. The head of my department, Lloyd Humphreys, was a member of the American Psychological Association's (APA) committee on the scientific and professional aims of psychology (APA, 1967). At 6-week intervals, he attended meetings with Kenneth E. Clark, Paul Meehl, Carl Rogers, Kenneth Spence, and the other members of that illustrious group, probing deeply into the issues they were convened to examine. Professionally and ideologically diverse, the committee gradually reached consensus around the idea that the science and the profession of psychology, though related, were not the same, and that distinctive patterns of education for careers of scholarly research, on the one hand, and effective professional service, on the other hand, were more likely to generate productive researchers and competent practitioners than the monolithic pattern that had prevailed in the education of professional psychologists ever since the scientist–practitioner model was ratified in the Boulder conference on the training of clinical psychologists (Raimy, 1950).

Between meetings of the APA committee, Lloyd and I talked often, as did others in our department, and in time we decided to implement the resolutions of the committee in our own programs. I say more about the often tortuous process we went through in the first chapter and elsewhere in this book. Responsibility for designing a new way to educate professional psychologists required me to give more thought than ever to the public mission and nature of our profession, as well as particulars of education for the practice of psychology. Some of my thoughts were published as papers, and some of these came to be regularly assigned as readings for students in professional psychology. As near as I could tell from citations, requests for reprints, and speaking invitations, the papers were also widely read by others. The statements were spaced over a period of 30 years and broadly scattered. Some appeared in journals, others in book chapters, and some, originally given as talks to various audiences, were still unpublished. For the sake of convenience as well as coherence, there appeared to be some reason to collect the papers in a single volume. When Roger Peterson became president of the National Council of

Schools and Programs of Professional Psychology (NCSPP), he asked me to do that. This book is the result.

The first draft of the manuscript, a rather lengthy collection of papers with some autobiographical material at the beginning and some reflections at the end, has gone through two major revisions. The first was undertaken when a respected publisher, after praising the quality of the papers, decided not to publish the book for the compelling reason that collections of scholarly articles rarely enjoy brisk sales or yield acceptable financial returns. This made sense to me. I had no interest in producing an archival document that few would read and fewer buy. So I selected papers more judiciously, eliminating about half of the original set, wrote a substantial amount of new material, and reframed the book as a developmental history of professional psychology as I had experienced it. After long deliberation, the editors of APA Books agreed to publish a variant of my second draft. Along with a contract, they sent me a perspicacious review that told me my manuscript contained interesting material but was poorly organized. This too made sense to me. In putting together my "story" I had tried a half dozen ways of categorizing contents, but none of the schemes fit the materials very well or said quite what I wanted to say, so at last I had thrown up my hands and simply arranged the chapters in the order of their preparation. The reviewer suggested a more rational arrangement that, with minor modifications, forms the current structure of the book.

Except for a few technical changes and minor editorial corrections in some of the book chapters and elaboration of one paper delivered initially as an address to a training conference, I have not tampered with the original papers, though any argument supported by empirical research might be buttressed by later findings, some numerical counts will fall progressively further out of date, and the shifting flow of cultural events has altered some early interpretations. In the introductions to each part and in the final chapter, I have offered some of my own reinterpretations as retrospective comments. For the most part, however, I have trusted readers to see where I got things right and where I missed the mark, identify core propositions in each chapter, translate them from past to present, and interpret key elements in the context of their own ever accumulating knowledge and varying perspectives.

The shift from serial order to a topical organization places a special burden on readers who have been led to expect a "story" of professional psychology but then find a chapter written after my retirement in the first section of the book while others written along the way are brought in later. Notes at the beginning of each chapter show when and where the original statement first appeared. I have attempted to preserve some sense of narrative continuity through introductory comments before each part. I am unable to relieve another burden that any collection of this kind imposes on readers—that is the burden of redundancy. Certain themes are central to my argument and had to be restated in the varying contexts of the self-contained chapters. The resulting repetitions cannot be removed without violating the integrity of the independent statements. I do not know what to do about that except apologize and advise anyone whose eyes begin to glaze on sight of the seventh iteration of my definition of assessment or professional psychology to skip to the next paragraph.

The first section of the book provides a personal historical context for the rest of the volume and defines two critical issues that must be addressed by anyone concerned with preparation for the practice of psychology. General histories of clinical psychology (Reisman, 1991; Routh, 1994), psychotherapy (Freedheim, 1992), and other fields of professional psychology are available elsewhere. The history in this book is a personal account of my entry into clinical psychology in the heady early days of the scientist–practitioner movement, and the experiences, first as a student, then as a teacher, and later as an administrator, that led me to appreciate the values of scientist–practitioner education but also to propose the complementary creation of programs specifically designed to prepare psychologists for professional careers.

Then come the critical issues that all professional psychologists should consider and educators of professional psychologists must inevitably confront. Chapter 2, "Is Psychology a Profession?" is my answer to the most serious question raised by critics of professional schools and direct education for the practice of psychology. Do we, as psychologists, know enough to justify ourselves as a profession, or should we defer outright professional assertion, if we assert it at all, until we have done more research and established our discipline more firmly? I say yes to the question in the first clause and no to the question in the second. Chapter 3, on the connection and disconnection of research and practice in psychology, was written nearly 20 years after chapter 2, but my basic position is unchanged. I still maintain that psychology provides a strong foundation for professional action, as long as the relationship between science and practice is appropriately understood. In the more recent formulation, the concept of practice as applied science is disputed. Instead, the core function of the professional psychologist is conceived as disciplined inquiry, a systematic but flexible way of going about professional work, with organizations and groups as well as individuals, that brings the best of our knowledge and technique to bear in meeting the needs of our clients. From this vantage point, research-oriented programs and practice-oriented programs are seen as complementary partners rather than as competitive alternatives.

The second section of the book is concerned with direct education for practice and the Doctor of Psychology degree. In critical diatribes opposing explicit education for practice and the PsyD degree, the two ideas are often conflated, but in fact the two do not always appear together. The early programs of the California School of Professional Psychology, for example, were clearly professional in substance and intent but concluded with award of the Doctor of Philosophy (PhD) degree. In chapter 4, the first chapter of the second part, I declare a need for the PsyD degree in professional psychology. I oppose use of the PhD as a credential of professional competence in any particular field. By cultural tradition and formal educational policy, the PhD degree signifies a record of contributory scholarship in any of the arts or sciences, from medieval French literature to astrophysics. To certify doctoral-level competence in professional psychology, I propose use of a professional degree that identifies the discipline of the practitioner. This, I argue, is needed in professional psychology no less than it is needed to certify competence and differentiate practitioners in general medicine (MD), veterinary medicine (DVM), and dentistry (DDS).

Chapter 5, originally written for a volume on the history of psychotherapy (Freedheim, 1992), goes back to the first published proposal for direct professional training and the Doctor of Psychology degree (Crane, 1925), traces the theme of the proposal through the various conferences in which it was debated, and describes the rapid growth of PsyD programs following endorsement of the degree by the Vail conference on levels and patterns of training in professional psychology (Korman, 1974). Chapter 6 reviews the national record of professional training in psychology over the first 20 years that practitioner programs were in operation. By the time this article appeared (Peterson, 1985), it was clear that the psychology faculties in most research universities were either unwilling or unready to establish professional schools and that direct training for the practice of psychology was growing most rapidly in small departments and freestanding professional schools of questionable distinction. Movement of professional training outside of the research universities threatened quality. Those threats are considered, along with the characteristics of professional programs as they appeared at the time and a discussion of the distinctive but related cultures of science and practice within which the education of professional psychologists takes place.

Chapter 7 was written especially for this book. In it, I recall the ideals we were attempting to realize as we planned the first PsyD program at the University of Illinois, describe the program as it was first implemented, summarize the empirical studies we did to evaluate our own program and others that followed, discuss critical objections to practitioner programs, and examine institutional conditions that are likely to influence professional education in the years ahead.

Concerns about quality weigh heavily on many of our minds. The third part of the book is devoted to quality control. In chapter 8, I lay out seven essentials of quality, as I have come to see them, for consideration by students, faculty, administrators, and evaluators concerned with education in professional psychology. In the chapter, I go beyond the usual prescriptions for curricula, admissions, and supervision to special emphasis on the organizational structures of the institutions in which professional psychologists are educated and the differing cultural values that prevail in each of those organizations. In American psychology, important controls have been developed through training conferences in which educational issues are discussed among peers and established standards are consensually endorsed. For schools and programs in professional psychology, the agency through which many of these conferences have been organized is NCSPP. In chapter 9, I describe the origin of NCSPP, consider its evolution, and review the conferences and self-studies that have been conducted to evaluate and improve the quality of education in professional psychology.

Across all programs purporting to prepare psychologists for professional careers, in academic departments and professional schools alike, the institution most directly concerned with quality assurance in professional education is the system of program accreditation that prevails in American higher education. The history of accreditation in psychology, long opposed while psychology was identified strictly as a science—but immediately implemented when eligibility for receipt of federal money to support clinical training required a mechanism for accreditation—is reviewed in chapter 10.

The last part faces the future of professional psychology. With the advent of managed health care in the 1990s, many psychologists whose main stock in trade was psychotherapy were shocked to find themselves easily replaced by social workers, nurse practitioners, and counselors of all kinds who offered services that were not easily distinguishable from those that psychologists offer—and usually came cheaper. In chapter 11, "Making Psychology Indispensable," I suggest that none of us should have been surprised by these turns of fortune. Our discipline should never have been so narrowly defined in the first place. If professional psychology is to become uniquely useful and therefore indispensable, we will have to meet the most urgent needs of our society in demonstrably effective ways. And this, I propose, requires full extension of the professional activity that Donald Schön (1983) has described as "reflection-in-action," Stricker and Trierweiler (1995) have described as "local clinical science," and I describe throughout this book as "disciplined inquiry," along with the basic and applied research that every profession needs to grow and prosper.

Disciplined inquiry requires epistemic flexibility. Many ways of knowing are needed to understand the complexities of the human condition. The positivistic epistemologies that dominated scientific psychology until the recent past will not do. But neither will the airy, empirically groundless fictions that some radical constructionists have proposed. In chapter 12, on ways of knowing in the education of professional psychologists, Roger Peterson and I outline an epistemological formulation that retains the best of logical empiricist thought but integrates the analytic philosophies with the liberating ideas that appear in the most sensible forms of pragmatic constructionist thinking. In chapter 13, "The Reflective Educator," I review recent critiques that discredit professional psychology as scientifically groundless. I suggest that the critics have noted flaws in common practice that require our most sober attention but that a profession defined as I have defined it in this book also deserves our full respect. Education for practice is itself a profession. I urge that the full force of disciplined inquiry be turned back in on our own educational enterprise.

As this book goes to press, a century has gone by since Lightner Witmer urged his colleagues in the newly formed APA to train psychologists in clinical skills. A half century has passed since organized psychology declared officially that it was a profession as well as a science. I was a product of those times. I had just returned from a gruesome war to a homeland swelling with problems but flowing with hope, and I found a line of work that offered not only a chance for a full life but a way to come in on the side of a better world. With a speed that sometimes leaves me feeling dizzy, 50 years have passed since then. With accelerating speed, 30 years have whizzed by since Wesley Becker, Gordon Paul, Donald Shannon, and the rest of the clinical crew at the University of Illinois, helped by practitioners in the community and supported by a strong academic department, decided to see what it would be like to go all the way in educating psychologists for professional careers. Now, with residuals of the experiences that followed roaming somewhere through my consciousness, I ponder our mistakes, take heart from some promising developments, and offer some reflections on our young, still unsteady, but always exciting profession.

ACKNOWLEDGMENTS

As Roger Peterson notes in his foreword, and as we both say in our collaborative chapter in this book, all verbal constructions are inherently personal and local. Of course these are, more obviously than most. This is a story of education for professional service in psychology as I have known it. My experience, however, has been continuously and massively influenced by other people. Faculty and fellow students at the three universities with which I have been affiliated—Minnesota, Illinois, and Rutgers—have been a constant source of inspiration, challenge, and knowledge. My colleagues in NCSPP and the APA, by inviting me to join various committees, councils, conferences, and task forces, and former presidents and provosts of Rutgers University, by persuading me to stay in an administrative job far beyond my original contract, kept me focused on education in psychology when other interests might had led me elsewhere. I am grateful to them all. My debt to some of those who have affected me most will grow clear in the pages to follow.

I am especially grateful to Roger Peterson for suggesting that I prepare this book, for working with me throughout its composition, and for writing so generous a foreword. I am touched by the endorsement of the foreword by past presidents of NCSPP, and I thank them for their support. I thank Lawrence Erlbaum for his gracious treatment of my first attempt to assemble a book on education for the practice of psychology, and the sales staff of Lawrence Erlbaum Associates, Inc., for urging their employer not to publish it. That collection would have been nowhere near as interesting as I hope this book will be. I thank Gary VandenBos, Julia Frank-McNeil, and Peggy Schlegel for their courage in taking on a project as unusual and possibly controversial as this one is. I thank the thoughtful scholar who reviewed the second draft manuscript for APA Books and helped me bring a more sensible intellectual order into what would otherwise have been a serial account. I regret that editorial policy requires preservation of his or her anonymity, precludes collegial exchange, and deprives me of the chance to offer personal thanks. I am grateful to Sandra Harris, who joined Roger Peterson in the quick-response editorial team I needed to advise me through the final revision. I also thank Jules Abrams and Daniel Fishman, who provided further counsel on a near-final version of the manuscript. I thank Ted Baroody and Valerie Montenegro for herding the book through to completion. I thank the editors of APA Books for copyrighting the book on the golden anniversary of my joining the field of clinical psychology and as near as the law allows to the centennial anniversary of the field itself. Finally, I thank the late Luella Buros, whose generous gifts to the Graduate School of Applied and Professional Psychology have nurtured the environment in which this book was written and paid the author's costs of its production.

DONALD R. PETERSON
Piscataway, New Jersey

I

HISTORICAL CONTEXT AND CRITICAL ISSUES

INTRODUCTION

HISTORICAL CONTEXT AND CRITICAL ISSUES

The first chapter in this section tells its own story and needs no further introduction. Understanding the second chapter on the qualifications of psychology as a profession, however, requires some context. Following announcement that we were going ahead with a PsyD program at the University of Illinois, I gave dozens of talks to psychology faculties around the country. People wanted to know how the Illinois experiment was going and in some cases were considering establishment of practitioner programs in their own departments. I was always treated courteously, and at first my talks usually ended with enthusiastic applause. As the concept of direct practitioner training began to spread, however, and especially after professional schools and the PsyD degree were approved by the Vail conference, my speaking invitations declined and my keen clinical receptors began to pick up some hostility, especially when some members of the audience were there less out of interest in the topic than in response to external pressure. Many research-oriented psychologists were happy enough to talk about educating practitioners, but they didn't actually want to do it. At one famed research university, where the executive committee of the psychology department had clearly been dragooned into attending my colloquium by the dean of graduate studies, one of the professors left muttering, "Over my dead body." At another, students in the audience kept glancing away from me to check the scowling expressions on the faces of their department head and the director of clinical training. The students applauded politely but asked no questions after the talk.

Other educators who were advancing the cause of direct professional education met comparable resistance. Ronald Fox left the Vail conference resolved to do everything he could to establish a professional school at his home institution, Ohio State University. Among other moves, he invited Kenneth E. Clark, Nicholas Cummings, Julian Rotter, William Ryan, and me to lead a forum on education for practice in psychology. The forum turned into something of a debate, with Rotter and Ryan opposing direct professional education for different reasons, Cummings and me supporting the idea in different forms, and Clark moderating the discussion as well as offering his own views. Attendance was sparse, and attitudes toward establishment of a profession school, as I sensed them in the audience, ranged from skepticism to hostility. As I say in more detail in chapter 5, Fox later gave up on Ohio State and founded the School of Professional Psychology at Wright State University.

Chapter 2 is based on the talk I gave in Columbus, Ohio, in 1974. In developing my ideas through the preceding decade, especially in the discussion sessions that followed my colloquium talks, I had become convinced that rational objection to practitioner programs, as contrasted with emotional resistance or political opposition, was grounded primarily in legitimate questions about the scientific foundations of our profession. Did we know enough, by way of basic knowledge as well as useful technology, to justify an outright profession of psychology rather than a science–profession in which practice served primarily as an arena for research? Chapter 2 was my answer to the question. It still is.

Chapter 3 represents the fundamental position on the relationship between science and practice that I have held through most of my career, stated now in the light of 30 years of history and further thought. This version was written after I had retired from my administrative duties at Rutgers University.

1

THE EDUCATION OF A PROFESSIONAL PSYCHOLOGIST: A PERSONAL INTRODUCTION

In its occupational expression, if not in its formal definition, psychology has been both a profession and a science from the very beginning. Binet's tests, Freud's treatments, Cattell's industrial applications, and Witmer's clinic were not patiently deferred until scientific knowledge about intelligence, neuroses, performance in the workplace, and learning disabilities had been firmly established. The pioneers dug right in. They saw human problems and did their best to solve them. In the process, they developed the conceptions and encouraged the research needed to place their work on a progressively more systematic, scientifically informed foundation.

Official recognition of psychology as a profession, however, did not occur until psychology's first century was half past. The original charter of the American Psychological Association (APA) declared its purpose to be the advancement of psychology as a science—no less, no more. Not until 1946, when the American Association for Applied Psychology (AAAP) and an antiseptically scientific APA, divided since 1937, reunited as a single organization, did the term *profession* appear in the APA's constitutional statement of the purpose of the organization. The same year, 1946, saw establishment of the Veterans Administration (VA) program for graduate training in clinical psychology that brought a tidal wave of clinicians into the field, the request from the VA to the APA for a list of approved programs that led ultimately to the present system of accreditation, and continuing work by a committee, chaired by David Shakow, that defined the scientist–practitioner model of education in professional psychology.

The year 1946 also happened to be the year I got out of the U.S. Army and entered the University of Minnesota, not quite sure what I wanted to do with my life. I had studied "pre-engineering" before and during the war, but I didn't really enjoy mapping conic sections or working calculus problems, and my wartime experience, along with encouragement by teachers who thought I had some talent for writing, led me to sign up as an English major at the university. I wanted to write. Great novels if I could, otherwise journalism or a job as an English professor. To most undergraduate students in those times, psychology was seen as a course people took because it was interesting and might help them understand themselves a little better than before, but was not commonly viewed as an occupation to be considered for a lifetime career.

INTO THE FIELD

I owe my first contact with clinical psychology to Rose Boucher (boo-SHAY). Miss Boucher was the head secretary in the Psychology Department at the University of Minnesota during all my years of study there. She was the kind of person every department needs and every good department has; at once chief operations officer, first sergeant, and head nurse. She managed the staff, pacified the professors, comforted the students, and saw that everything that mattered got done, right and on time. Later I learned that her estimates of the intellectual capabilities of entering graduate students correlated around .50 with their scores on the Miller Analogies Test. Still later I came to suspect that the main reason the correlation was not higher was that the test did not sense the subtleties of intelligence as keenly as Miss Boucher's eyes and ears.

Of all the courses I was taking at the time, the only one that held an obsessive interest for me was an introductory laborabory course in experimental psychology. I enjoyed the exercises. When we lifted shot in a psychophysical experiment I wanted to find out more about critical ratios and the Weber–Fechner law. My reports were longer and more detailed than anyone else's. One of the graduate assistants who taught the course suggested that I consider psychology as a career, so one day I went into the departmental office and said to the lady behind the desk, "I'd like to talk with somebody about going into psychology." Miss Boucher looked up at me, paused a moment, and said, "Clinical?" I wasn't sure what clinical psychology was. I said "Yes." She sent me up to see Paul Meehl.

There, through an open door behind a desk clear of all materials except the paper he was writing, sat associate professor Paul E. Meehl. I had neither seen nor heard of him before. I introduced myself, he invited me in and asked what he could do for me. I told him I was an English major, though I had studied some pre-engineering before that, and was now thinking about psychology as a field of study. After that I said very little. For nearly an hour, Meehl told me, in his inimitably intelligent and entertaining way, about psychology in general and clinical psychology in particular; what it was, what kinds of careers might lie beyond the doctorate, how long it took to get a PhD, how I might support myself through graduate study. The field seemed to be exactly what I was looking for. It appeared to be intellectually challenging, morally satisfying, scientific yet humane, suited to all my inclinations so far as I knew them. Besides, it offered a sure way to pay the costs of graduate education. The new Veterans Administration (VA) training program in clinical psychology seemed especially attractive to me. By the time the meeting was over, I had decided to become a clinical psychologist.

My undergraduate advisor was Kenneth E. Clark. Before my first meeting with him, I spent hours laying out a program that included a lot of fringe material in psychology and some leftover courses from my time as a student of English literature. Clark looked at my program and said, "You've got this all wrong." He changed my minor from English to a 15-credit sequence in biostatistics. Then he wrote out a program that started with his own notoriously difficult course in statistics and proceeded over the following year through Donald G. Paterson's equally rigorous course in individual differences and the other basic courses in history and systems of psychology, personality, social, and abnormal psychology that constituted a psychology major at the University of Minnesota.

I ate it up. Midway through my senior year, I decided to try for highest honors. Besides grades and scores on a general culture test, the summa cum laude badge required defense of a dissertation before an interdisciplinary committee of top scholars. I wrote a paper on psychoanalysis. Late in the spring, I was ushered into a room and seated in a chair facing a world-reknowned economist, a distinguished mathematician, one of my professors in the English Department, and representatives of two other disciplines. The only psychologist on my committee was William T. Heron, well known at the time for his studies of genetic determinants of maze-learning abilities in rats.

Professor Heron began the inquisition. "Mr. Peterson, you have written a paper on psychoanalytic theory. In science, what is a theory?" I mumbled. I rambled. I had only the vaguest layman's notions about scientific theory. The questioning went on through two more sweaty hours. I suppose I got a few things right. I don't remember. I do remember the last question. I had concluded my paper with the argument that the definitive test of any theory with implications for psychological treatment was pragmatic. Whatever the critics might say on other grounds, psychoanalysis was okay "because it works." Professor Heron nailed my coffin. "What evidence can you adduce to support that claim?"

The chair of the committee asked me to step outside. A very long time went by. I was asked back in to hear the verdict. The chair noted the glaring weaknesses in my responses to their questions. Others made clear that I had much to learn before I could pretend to be a scholar. But they had decided to award me highest honors anyway on the basis of my grades, test scores, and the limited success I had shown in responding to some of their questions. They added that they had made a compensatory adjustment in evaluating my performance because they believed I had lost my composure after the first question and never regained it. This was merciful and accurate as far as it went, but the effect of the examination went deeper than transient anxiety. I had entered the room quite secure, perhaps a bit smug, about the scope and depth of my knowledge. I left with a desolate awareness of my ignorance and a fierce determination to learn.

When the time came to apply for graduate school, I did not consider applying anywhere besides the University of Minnesota. I had been told that admission standards were high and competition stiff, but I had only missed four items on the Miller Analogies Test and had become fairly well acquainted with some of the faculty. Besides knowing Clark and Meehl, I had worked as an unpaid assistant to Harrison Gough in constructing the questionnaire that later became the Socialization Scale of the California Psychological Inventory. That was the first time I learned how much fun research could be. Gough generously listed me as second author of the published report (Gough & Peterson, 1952). I knew about Yale and Columbia, but I couldn't imagine that their programs were any better than the one at my doorstep, and for many years I had felt an affectionate respect for my state university, even a certain mindless loyalty. During my youth in the 1930s, when my attitudes toward women, religion, and universities were forming, the Ivy League football teams were no match for the Golden Gophers. I didn't want to go anywhere else.

GRADUATE STUDENT DAYS

I remember my first year of graduate study as a time of hard work and great joy. For my half-time clerkship in the VA program, I was assigned to the Mental Health Clinic at Fort Snelling. There, under the baleful eye of Mildred Bessie Mitchell, some seven or eight of us trainees began to learn the tests that would form the core of our diagnostic armamentarium. At the same time we were taking a course in intelligence testing in the Institute of Child Welfare (later Human Development) and a program of study in the Psychology Department that included Starke Hathaway's course in physiological psychology and Paul Meehl's introduction to clinical psychology. The University of Minnesota was one of the first to relax foreign language requirements in graduate education. We were allowed to substitute a "collateral field of knowledge" for one of the required languages. Meehl, who was by then my advisor, suggested that I consider philosophy of science. I signed up for Herbert Feigl's senior-level introduction to the subject and was delighted by Feigl's warm, witty way of posing the questions we addressed, as well as the knowing but always provisional way he framed his answers.

Early in my first term of graduate study I stopped by Meehl's office for some kind of registrational business, and he asked me what I was grinning about in his class. I told him I didn't know I was grinning, but I might have been smiling. Well, said he, what were you smiling about? I said my courses with Hathaway and Feigl came on the same day as his, and I had noted some similarities in style. He said, "Oh, that's it." Actually, that wasn't what mattered. What mattered was that I was overjoyed to be in the presence of fine minds and caring people. At last I had found where I belonged.

The remaining years of graduate study rolled by in the rhythm of stressful demand, intellectual excitement, intermittent panic, and occasional triumph that every graduate student experiences in a strong program. Standards were high. I do not remember taking any easy courses. One I remember as most difficult was a course in learning theory in which we examined the major theories of the time and constructed a theory of our own to correct the deficiencies we perceived in all the others. Other courses I remember as especially difficult were neuroanatomy and clinical neurology, which we took alongside second- and third-year medical students. The courses in the medical school were taught by distinguished researchers. In the classroom and on rounds, however, teaching doctors to practice medicine, they didn't waste time talking about their own research. In neuroanatomy we learned the structure of the central nervous system through books, lectures, and slides and by dissection of a human brain. In clinical neurology we learned how to conduct a neurological examination and diagnose neurological diseases. Instructors in psychology as well as medicine were not reluctant to give failing grades when failure was deserved. They felt a strong responsibility to weed out poor students. At the end of the first year, several of my classmates were dismissed.

Besides Meehl's introduction to clinical psychology and Feigl's courses in the philosophy of science, a course I remember as giving me the greatest knowledge and pleasure was a course in biographical psychology taught by the benign chair of the department, Richard M. Elliott. Elliott was a gentleman scholar in the finest tradition, and he led us through many ways of thinking about the psychologies of human lives. Our textbook was Henry Murray's *Explorations in Personality*. Many other readings were required. For a term paper, we were to write a psychobiography of some person whose psychological development and adult makeup struck us as interesting. I chose the poet Percy Shelley as my subject. Now, in my later years, examining the moral dilemmas and cultural blindspots of Thomas Jefferson, Andrew Jackson,

Woodrow Wilson, and other people who have shaped the course of bigotry in America, I can still hear Elliott's gentle voice describing the turning points that set directions in every human life and remember his ways of bringing order out of the complexities of the human journey.

Of all the intellectual experiences I had in graduate school, the ones that have served me most faithfully were those concerned with the philosophical foundations of inquiry in psychology. I have described some of these experiences in a statement that followed a postmodern critique of positivism (Fishman, 1993).

> When I was a graduate student at the University of Minnesota some 40 years ago, I had the privilege of studying philosophy of science in classes taught by Herbert Feigl, a core member of the Vienna Circle, inventor of the term "logical positivism," and author of the first paper on the Vienna Circle's views ever published in the English language. I had the further privilege of attending seminars on the philosophy of psychology taught jointly by Herbert Feigl and Paul Meehl. The meetings were affectionately known as the "Feegle-Meegle seminars" by those of us fortunate enough to take part in them; Alex Buchwald, Jim Jenkins, David Lykken, David Premack, and Norman Sundberg, among others. In our discussions, we considered the issues that continually preoccupy metatheoreticians of all varieties. How can one tell the difference between a good construction and a bad one? What kinds of language shall we use to describe the events that we observe? What are the guiding principles that lead to powerful theoretical conceptions? How can we test the theories that guide our inquiries and order our knowledge of the phenomena we are trying to understand?
>
> Our discussions took place in the assumptive framework of critical realism. We believed in the existence of a material world that was there before we started to think about it and would continue after we were gone. We understood that scientific theories were human inventions, that observations required interpretation, and that our conclusions were probablistic rather than absolute. Despite our awareness of the human role in theory development, however, I do not remember ever hearing anybody suggest that our constructions *were* the basic reality we were there to consider. If anybody had seriously proposed a radical fictionist premise, I suspect our response would have resembled David Hume's dismissal of George Berkeley's idealism as both irrefutable and incredible.
>
> We spent a lot of time talking about the characteristics of sound scientific method. Feigl had laid out a simple list of criteria in 1949; intersubjective testability, definiteness or precision, sufficiency of corroboration, coherence or systematic structure, and comprehensiveness or scope of knowledge. We did our best to examine the subtleties of those criteria, but did not dispute them as reasonable standards for systematic inquiry.
>
> We escaped the trap of restrictive operationism early. MacCorquodale

and Meehl's (1948) definition of hypothetical constructs gave us a way to consider phenomena that were inaccessible to direct observation, and flowed smoothly into later formulations (e.g., open concepts, Pap, 1953; nomological networks, Cronbach & Meehl, 1955) that offered freedom to explore new domains but at the same time imposed demands for all possible precision and coherence in our investigations.

> We talked the language of operant behaviorism, Murray's personology, and Freudian psychoanalysis with equal comfort. It is true that we did not recognize some inherent contradictions among those conceptions, and we made no pretense of articulating them in detail, but we held a tacit faith that any logical inconsistencies that might turn up could be resolved through reason, and any substantive differences that might appear could be settled through empirical test.
>
> Nobody in our circle of empirical realists ever said that objective knowledge was free of social context. Nobody ever said that the scientific enterprise was devoid of human value. Nobody ever said that every concept in our lexicon had to be quantified. Nobody ever said that biographical narratives were unscientific and therefore useless. What we did say was that our task as scientists was to expose regularities in nature that would not be seen except through systematic investigation, and that the verisimilitude of any scientific proposition resided ultimately in its relation to empirical fact.
>
> We psychologists have made many mistakes in our first 100 years, both in our profession and in our science. The decision to state our ideas in factually testable form, however, to seek in our conceptions as much precision, coherence and comprehensiveness as the subject matter allows, and to expose our formulations relentlessly to the light of natural observation, was not one of them. (Peterson, 1993b, pp. 13–14)

Our jobs as clinical trainees in the VA were equally stimulating and demanding. Mitchell was tough. When trainees gave a test we were expected to do it correctly. Most of our other supervisors were hard on us too, though not all of them were equally competent. We started doing psychotherapy in the second year. The prevailing mode seemed to be a blend of Rogerian listening, psychosocial theory drawn mainly from Horney and Adler, and the kind of no-nonsense counseling that E. G. Williamson and other Minnesotans had espoused. I made a deliberate effort to learn as many tests as I could, including some, like the Szondi, that I would not dream of imposing on a graduate student today, and others, like Harriet Babcock's tests of neuropsychological functioning, that have long since been superseded by more refined procedures. I also arranged my training assignments to cover as broad a range of patient populations as possible. To the outpatient clientele at the mental health clinic I added the wards of the VA Hospital in St. Cloud and "Station 60," the inpatient psychiatry service in the medical school. The last year, I accepted a National Institute of Mental Health (NIMH) fellowship and spent most of my time working on my dissertation, but I had reached that stage short of any clinical experience with children, so I volunteered to work a day a week at the Washburn Child Guidance Clinic in Minneapolis.

My dissertation topic grew out of clinical experience at the St. Cloud VA Hospital. One day I was assigned to test a young man who had suffered an acute schizophrenic break in which he suddenly "knew" that he was Jesus Christ. Among other actions inspired by this realization, he tried to walk across the Mississippi River. He was fished out by the police, who found no identifying papers on him but guessed that he might be a veteran and took him to the VA Hospital for necessary care and appropriate disposition.

I studied the young man as he was led into my office. Gaunt, bearded, confused, he said his name was Jesus Son of the Blessed Virgin Mary. I thought he looked familiar. I asked him if he had ever been known by any other names. When he told me his earthly name I recognized him. A year or so before, I had tested him at the Fort Snelling Clinic. He lived in St. Cloud but had been staying with relatives in St. Paul at the time. I sent for his file.

When it came I read all the reports in it. Among other discoveries I saw a profile on the Minnesota Multiphasic Personality Inventory (MMPI) that offered a near-perfect match with the "psychotic signs" that Meehl (1946) had defined. To my relief, I also found that I had diagnosed the patient as a "latent schizophrenic" and warned anyone who treated him that he might decompensate into psychosis at any time.

One of the psychiatric residents had taken the young man into treatment. The psychiatrist overrode my recommendation in favor of formal designation as an "anxiety reaction." He saw the patient once a week for a few sessions in a psychodynamically guided search for the origins of his fears, but the patient soon dropped out and the resident closed the case with an acknowledgment that his psychotherapeutic efforts had not done much good.

Later I began to wonder if there were similar cases in the outpatient clinic files—cases in which the opportunity for accurate diagnosis was available but ignored and that collectively might offer some guidelines for predicting psychotic breakdown and subsequent hospitalization of psychiatric outpatients. There were more than 100 such cases. With appropriate controls and data analyses, they formed the basis of my dissertation and a follow-up study on the diagnosis of subclinical schizophrenia (Peterson, 1954a, 1954b).

LIFE AND TIMES OF A YOUNG PROFESSOR

When the time came to start thinking about a job, I felt fairly confident about my academic preparation but less than well seasoned as a clinician. I had not completed an internship in a form that would be required today. I had ranged over a wide variety of problems and populations during my four years of graduate study, but I had not seen many patients of any particular kind. I had never worked on a neurological service and wanted to. I recognized that the short time I had spent working with hospitalized psychiatric patients had only begun to teach me about them. Except for one depressed woman on Station 60 and two timid little girls I saw at the Washburn clinic, all my clinical experience had been with males.

As with most of my other concerns, I talked this over with Paul Meehl. I wondered if it might not be a good idea to devote several years, perhaps five, to postdoctoral clinical work. Meehl asked me what kind of career I wanted over the long haul. I said I wanted a teaching, research, and clinical job in a university. Meehl told me it was a lot easier to move from an academic position to a clinical one than the other way around and that if a job turned up at a good university he would be glad to recommend me for it. I asked him to keep me in mind.

Shortly thereafter, I was told that two academic jobs were available, one at Stanford and the other at the University of Illinois. Stanford paid $4,000 for the nine-month academic year; Illinois paid $4,500. A classmate of mine had taken a job as a consulting psychologist with the firm of Rohrer, Hibler, and Replogle at a salary of $10,000 per year. He urged me to join him, but I had already settled for the more modest financial returns of academia, so for a time I was torn between Stanford and Illinois.

Only a few years earlier, Lyle Lanier had become head of the psychology department at the University of Illinois. He was brought there by George Stoddard, president of the university and a psychologist by training, to build the department. Lanier had recruited a senior faculty that included Raymond Cattell, Joseph McVicker Hunt, O. Hobart Mowrer, and Charles Osgood. Along with such well-known scholars as P. T. Young, Ross Stagner, and Lee Cronbach, who were already on the faculty at Illinois, this formed a distinguished cast.

I was already leaning toward Illinois when Lanier called and engaged me in a long telephone conversation. He asked me about my thesis and I described it for him. He asked me what I would like to teach and I told him. He asked me how I would feel about working a day a week in the department's newly founded psychological clinic, and I said I wanted very much to do that. Lanier offered me the job and I accepted then and there. For him there was no vita, no colloquium, no interviews with faculty and students to guide his decision. All he had was a phone conversation and recommendations from Meehl and others at Minnesota. For me, there was no visit to the campus, no talk with faculty and students, certainly no discussion of living conditions or fringe benefits. I based my acceptance on the reputation of the Illinois faculty and the warmth and intelligence in Lanier's voice. Soon after that I received a letter from Stanford saying they had offered the job to somebody else. It didn't matter to me. As my interests developed later, toward education for practice, and as Stanford's program evolved, away from practice and toward experimental psychopathology, we would have become a poor match.

Among the clinical psychologists who came out of the Minnesota program around the time I did, several went into academic positions in good state universities; Indiana, Iowa, and Oregon among them. About an equal number went into clinical jobs in the VA and elsewhere. One I have already mentioned joined a consulting firm. Another rented an office and started a private practice. I think it is fair to say that recommendations for the top academic jobs were reserved for the students who had done best all around in the graduate program. But no shame was attached to acceptance of a clinical job. The fellow who went into private practice was a close friend of mine who, like me, had worked out his career plan in long discussions with Meehl. He was an able student and was known among us as a fine clinician. Neither Meehl nor I nor anyone else I knew thought less of him nor wished him anything but well in his decision to make his living as a practicing clinical psychologist.

When I got to Illinois, I was assigned to teach two sections of an undergraduate course in personality and an undergraduate course in child development. I was reasonably well prepared to teach personality, but my knowledge about human development was spotty so I had to work hard to stay ahead of the students in that course. Often I would spend a day or more preparing a single lecture. Teaching was very important to me. I saw it as my main job. Lanier and most of my faculty colleagues seemed to see my job the same way, though the research I had done was valued and more research was clearly expected in my future.

I went to work right away at the clinic, taking my share of the more difficult cases and supervising students on the cases assigned to them. In those days the concept of the psychiatric team was very much in force. Intake was handled by our social worker. Psychologists gave tests and did psychotherapy. Because the University of Illinois medical school was in Chicago, we had to import medical coverage and psychiatric supervision by way of a psychoanalyst who commuted to Urbana by train once a week. Our father figure was a dapper man, handsome and expensively dressed. Intelligent and compassionate too. His interviews showed a penetrating skill, and the effects were sometimes dramatically revealing. I learned a great deal from the demonstrations he offered from time to time. However, he was given to interpretations that I sometimes considered far-fetched, and whenever I challenged one of those in a case conference he grew visibly irritated. On two or three occasions he raised questions before the group about the dynamic origins of my hostility. I didn't think I was hostile. I thought I was seeking clarity and truth. But he may have read me better than I knew. I began to get headaches during the conferences and avoided them as often as I could.

At the same time I developed a poorly earned reputation of my own for clinical skill. My reputation was based mainly on hearsay surrounding some of the cases I treated. One of those was a senior faculty member in the chemistry department who happened to be on the board of trustees of the Unitarian Church in Urbana. Joe Hunt, then director of clinical training, was on the same board, and my patient told Hunt that I had been very helpful to him. So

Hunt, who had never seen me work as a clinician, got the idea that I was a good psychotherapist and probably shared his opinion with Lanier and other faculty members.

I also gained a reputation, earned or unearned, as a good teacher. I was a bit surprised but too innocent to be suspicious when Lanier's secretary asked to audit my early classes. I learned later that Lanier routinely assigned her to check out new faculty and trusted her opinion more than student ratings. She must have given a good report, because shortly afterward Lanier asked me to teach the large introductory course, an assignment we all considered as important as any in the department, and put me on his advisory committee to help manage the entire undergraduate curriculum.

When I finished publishing my thesis and the study that followed, I considered several directions for further research. Because most of the clients who came to our clinic were children, I thought I might try to find out more about children's behavior disorders. Because parental influences were obviously important in the origin of the problems as well as their treatment, studying parent–child relationships seemed worthwhile. I was still interested in the psychology of schizophrenia and sketched out several ideas that followed my dissertation research.

The actual work I started to do, however, was directed less by rational choice than by serendipitous personal contact. Besides case conferences, research seminars were held weekly at the clinic. PhD candidates tried out their thesis plans there, and faculty took turns talking about their work. Following a presentation by Ray Cattell, he and I fell into a conversation about extending his factor analytic studies of personality to children. All of his previous work had been done with adults. I had never done any factor analyses, but I had long believed that the most urgent need for basic knowledge in psychology was for sound descriptive information, and I was eager to learn factor analytic technique, so Cattell and I got a grant to hire two assistants and set about converting all his tests and rating scales into forms suitable for children. When we were done with that, we ran the whole Cattellian number, complete with objective tests, life records, and oral questionnaires, over the full range of personality traits as Cattell conceived them, on primary-school- and kindergarten-age children. I thought it good fun. Our team met one evening each week at a local bar to discuss strategy over beer, and we often left trying to outdo one another reciting Shakespeare. I was better with the sonnets than the plays. Cattell usually won.

Illinois had built one of the early digital computers, ILLIAC, so our capacity for multivariate analyses was vastly expanded over all previous capabilities. We were not satisfied with the analytic programs for rotating factors that were available at the time, however. In our efforts to improve the structures that came through Quartimax and Oblimax, Ray and I spent hours together gazing at swarms of dots in unlabeled 2×2 frames over 16-plus dimensional space and adjusting axes visually to line up with any clusters that appeared. I was never very confident about my rotations. To me, the operation was all too reminiscent of the Rorschach. But Cattell usually seemed sure enough as we handed our matrices in for each adjustment. When we published our reports a few years later, we both wrote as if the psychic architecture had been convincingly revealed to us.

My doubts about Cattell's approach to factor analytic research did not reach troublesome proportions until considerably later, and then they were augmented by another line of inquiry that began, like my collaboration with Cattell, in a happy personal contact. We admitted a student named Herbert Quay. I was in on Quay's admission, as a matter of fact. Joe Hunt had asked a few of us junior faculty people to help him with admissions, and here came the application of this older fellow, with a Master's degree from a small southern college, who had worked for a time in a boys' reformatory and was currently on the staff of the Milledgeville State Hospital in Georgia. He had good grades and high test scores, but he didn't look like the hot young graduates of Yale and Brown who were starting to come our way. In the meeting of our admissions committee, somebody said he wasn't so sure about Quay, with apparent intent to reject. I said, "I think he looks interesting." Hunt said, "Let's give him a chance."

Not long after he entered the program, Quay came to my office and introduced himself. During his time working in the correctional institution, he had designed a brief questionnaire the items of which discriminated statistically between adjudicated juvenile delinquents and high school students with no history of legal offense. He knew the study Gough and I had done along similar lines (Gough & Peterson, 1952) and thought we might consider some extensions of the work. The idea of combining empirical methods of item selection in the Minnesota tradition with factor analytic refinement of dimensional structure was especially appealing. There began a collaboration and a friendship that continues to this day. We got another grant and began our work on personality factors in juvenile delinquency.

While my work with Cattell and Quay was still in process, I came up for tenure review. At the time, 5 years beyond the doctorate, I had only published three articles. They had all been anthologized in books and were fairly widely cited, but my publication record looked puny by contemporary standards. Not that I hadn't tried. I had not gone far into factor analytic research before I recognized three points at which the mathematically elegant procedure could go astray. One, as I have already mentioned, lay in the rotation of vectors. This problem was soon to be solved to my satisfaction by the Varimax routine (Kaiser, 1958). Another lay in the number of factors retained for rotation. Given the typically low level of intercorrelations among items that I saw in the matrices I examined, I had a hunch that some of the weak little factors that Cattell extracted toward the end of the process were either random or grossly unstable. Later studies (Peterson, 1960, 1965) showed that I was right, so this problem was solved simply by retaining a smaller set of more dependable dimensions. The most serious problem, however, lay in setting out the list of variables that went into the analysis in the first place.

On this point, I had no quarrel with Cattell. In his grand attempt to map the entire field of personality, he had begun with the 17,256 descriptive terms Allport and Odbert (1936) had gleaned from the dictionary. This seemed a reasonable way to start. When I began to study the factor analytic research of other investigators, however, I found few studies that matched Cattell's in rationality. Different investigators examining the "same" domain came up with completely different structures. The studies collectively seemed to be producing more chaos than order, mainly because their authors were examining different sets of variables, often chosen, it seemed to me, with only the flimsiest kind of justification. Garbage in, garbage out.

I wrote an essay on the topic in which I reviewed relevant literature, defined the problem, and proposed two solutions: a deductive procedure whereby variable sets were derived from theory and an inductive procedure whereby descriptor sets were developed through a series of steps much like those that Glaser and Strauss (1967) later described as the discovery of grounded theory. I sent the manuscript to the *Psychological Bulletin*. The editor rejected it on the recommendation of an anonymous reviewer. Ray Cattell had offered helpful and favorable comment on an earlier draft, and I was pretty sure that I was on the right track, so I thought, "OK, if you birds want to keep on confusing yourselves, go ahead. At least I've figured out how to run my own research."

This left me with a short publication record, but at the time I was too naive to care. In one of our many conversations, Lanier said to me, "Tenure is not in the position. It's in the man." I knew he was right. I never had any doubt that I would be promoted when the time came, as indeed I was, presumably on the strength of my reputation as a teacher, my alleged skill as a clinician, and my promise as a researcher. Today, I doubt that an assistant professor with my record would be promoted to tenure rank at Illinois, Rutgers, or any other major research university I know.

It took me a long time to catch on to a basic difference between the cultural values that prevailed in the Minnesota clinical program at the time I left it and the Illinois program at the time I entered. Joe Hunt was fond of saying, "Clinical practice is a good source of hypotheses for research." Of course I agreed. That was where most of my own research had started. What Joe did not say was that he did not consider psychotherapy and other forms of clinical work of much value in their own right. He wanted people like me, who had done some psychotherapy and seemed to be good at it, on the faculty, but he had never done any psychotherapy himself. He had written about it. During his time as chief administrator of a clinic in New York, he had designed and published a therapeutic movement scale as a criterion measure for outcome research in psychotherapy. Hunt was mainly known, however, as the author of a much-cited study of the long-term effects of infantile food deprivation in rats (given unlimited access to food as adults, the previously starved little fellows hoarded food far in excess of their physical needs) and as editor of the two-volume work, *Personality and the Behavior Disorders*, which in those years was a basic textbook in nearly every graduate clinical program in the country. Joe was a creative, good-natured, caring man who inspired and nurtured generations of students. He was kind to me personally, and he was an intellectual delight. He asked large questions, offered thoughtful, well-documented answers, and contributed gigantically to knowledge in psychology. But he never saw much value in direct professional work.

With few exceptions, neither did anyone else in the Illinois department. Clinical work was done in the psychological clinic and in the student counseling center, the staff of which did not hold tenure-track positions and were not necessarily expected to do any research, although they gained some status if they did. William Gilbert was director of the counseling center. Bill had published some work on interview procedures and was sometimes brought in on promotion decisions. I was a member of the departmental advisory committee in which those decisions were made, so I was also a part of these decisions. During deliberations about a man who had joined our faculty a few years after I had, I noted his heavy engagement in clinical supervision and said, "I think this counts as much as his research." Bill said, "Think again."

The balance of values, weighted toward research and away from practice from the beginning, shifted still further in the late 1950s and early 1960s. Throughout this period, we continued to hire new faculty. With one exception, people were brought in mainly for the sake of the research they were expected to do. One result was the creation of a first-class research department. The place was flooded with grant money and buzzing with excitement. Hunt's work on cognitive development; Osgood's work on the measurement of meaning; Mowrer's work on the moral basis of psychopathology; Fiedler's work on leadership; Eriksen's work on visual perception; Humphreys' work on the structure of intelligence; work on small-group process by Steiner, Triandis, and McGrath; Hirsch's work in behavior genetics; Paul's work on clinical treatment; all these research programs and more were going on all at once. We were strong across the board and in some areas the strongest in the land. When Ray Cattell, Lee Cronbach, Nate Gage, Ledyard Tucker, and Lloyd Humphreys were all on the Illinois faculty at the same time, nobody topped us in the field of psychological measurement. Sidney Bijou, Wesley Becker, Carl Bereiter, Gordon Paul, and Leonard Ullmann led the pioneers in behavioral approaches to education and clinical treatment. Nobody did it better.

The department was a busy hive, and I was a happy worker in it. Besides continuing my other studies in the late 1950s, I helped organize a team at the clinic to study parent–child relationships. Ours were the first controlled studies to include the roles of fathers as well as mothers in the development of children's behavior disorders. Wesley Becker's circumplex model of parental behavior came out of that research. So did the Behavior Problem Checklist that I developed for use with young children, and Herbert Quay extended into the adolescent years. A revised form of the checklist is still widely used to screen behavior problems in the schools. Later, I extended the research on parent–child relationships to a cross-cultural comparison of families in Sicily and Illinois. Then, as now, I believed wholeheartedly in the value of sound research and did everything I could to advance it.

DIRECTING THE CLINICAL PROGRAM: CHANGING IDEAS ABOUT CLINICAL PSYCHOLOGY

Around 1960, Lyle Lanier became dean of the College of Liberal Arts and Sciences and shortly after that executive vice president of the university. Lloyd Humphreys came in as head of the psychology department. In 1963, the director of the psychological clinic died, and Lloyd asked me to take over the job. That same year, Joe Hunt resigned as director of clinical training to accept a senior research fellowship from NIMH. Lloyd asked Wesley Becker to take over Hunt's administrative job. Wes did not enjoy the administrative work, however, and asked to be relieved of it. Lloyd then asked me to direct the clinical program and continue to direct the clinic as well.

I did that and kept on teaching, but at the same time I began to develop serious misgivings about the main lines of research I had been following. The work Quay and I had done on personality factors in juvenile delinquency hit a dead end, or so it seemed to me. Herb and I developed several tests and rating schedules that seemed promising at the time. Our tests were composed entirely of items that distinguished statistically between delinquents and nondelinquents, and conceptually comparable factor structures emerged across the various measures we had devised. Some rather important theoretical and practical implications seemed to follow from our findings. When we looked at empirical correspondence across measures, however, between self-reports and teacher ratings of "psychopathic delinquency," for example, the correlations were next to negligible. The same pattern of findings came out of our studies of children's behavior problems. I reanalyzed data from the studies Cattell and I had done with equally disturbing results. Questionnaire responses, teacher ratings, parent ratings, and objective tests, each analyzed independently, yielded conceptually similar dimensional structures. But for any given trait, say *extraversion* or *surgency*, the scores obtained by objective testing correlated at best in the .20s or .30s with those derived from observer ratings or self-reports. With access to less than 10% of the variance in any of the characteristics we were trying to measure, strong theoretical statements were clearly unjustified. Basing practical decisions on so shaky a foundation seemed to me professionally irresponsible.

I published the results of my findings and expressed my concerns

(Peterson, 1965), but that did not solve the problem. Something was seriously wrong with the whole approach to personality research as commonly practiced in those times. I began to believe that radical changes in conception and method were required. For the next few years, I did no further empirical research. I read, I walked about the campus, and I thought a lot.

I did not stop teaching, though in those years my contacts with students were limited mainly to clinical supervision and management of the general proseminar in psychology required of all entering graduate students. Our students were top of the line: intelligent, energetic, critical, and sufficiently assertive to keep the faculty on our toes. Many of them gained considerable fame later on. The contributions of Gordon Paul in treating severely mentally ill people, of Don Meichenbaum in helping to invent cognitive behavior therapy, of Dan and Susan O'Leary in classroom management, of Tom Borkovec in treating sleep disorders, of Janet Wollersheim in eating disorders, of Don Kiesler in interpersonal behavior, of Richard Price in environmental and community psychology, and of Carl Haywood in cognitive development come quickly to mind, and there were many others who did outstanding work in applied psychology. Gordon Paul must have had a dozen job offers when he got his PhD, but he elected to stay at Illinois.

Neither did I stop practicing, though in my long walks on campus I realized that my practice had changed fundamentally over the years. In my Minnesota days, I had thought of clinical practice mainly as individual psychodiagnotics and psychotherapy. In my work with children at Illinois, however, I routinely involved parents, teachers, probation officers, or any others who could be seen as "significant others," in Sullivan's terms, and who might provide useful diagnostic perspectives or help with treatment. At first, we commonly assigned two therapists in cases in which, say, changes in the behavior of the mother were at least as important as changes in the behavior of the child. One clinician would see the mother and another would see the child. Weekly meetings of the two therapists were interpolated between sessions with the clients. Where one clinician was on the faculty and the other was a student, the extra sessions served both planning and supervisory functions.

We were frequently shorthanded, however, and in those cases I would see parents and children or husbands and wives together. From the vantagepoint of the clients this was a less confusing procedure than to have each person seeing a different psychologist. They didn't have to work out the inevitably different experiences they had had with their separate therapists. As a direct service operation, seeing the people most centrally involved with the problem together as a group was obviously more efficient than assigning multiple therapists who had to arrange extra meetings between sessions. It also seemed more effective. Of the problems we saw 90% were interpersonal, and working directly on the interaction patterns of the people in the group got to the heart of the matter and stimulated change more quickly than working with people individually. At first I didn't have a name for it, but I was doing family therapy. I realized that this required a different way of thinking about people; an interpersonal, transactional way of thinking at a different level from any form of individual psychology, behavioral or psychodynamic.

All the while I was consulting at the Kankakee State Hospital. When I first came there, I ran across children on the adult wards. They seemed lost. Maybe a psychologist or social worker was seeing some of them, but in most cases nobody was, except for the aides and activity therapists. Ayllon and Azrin (1968) were beginning their work in behavior modification on the wards of Anna State Hospital in southern Illinois. I proposed that we develop a program along similar lines for the children at Kankakee. One of the staff psychologists agreed to help organize the program and manage it after we got it going. In the process of reassigning children to a separate unit and planning the program, I realized that I was engaged in still another form of practice. On the wards at Kankakee, I was planning to initiate and evaluate structural change in an organization. This required conceptualization and methodology of still another kind.

The main fruit of all this labor was my manifesto for a comprehensive clinical psychology to guide assessment and change at individual, group, and organizational levels. I sought a psychology that would at once foster effective practice and encourage the kinds of research through which professional efforts might be progressively improved. I recently looked back on some of the thoughts that were on my mind at the time.

> More than 25 years have passed since I began the inquiries that led to the publication of *The Clinical Study of Social Behavior* (Peterson, 1968a). Drawing on the research and previous considerations of Endler, Hunt, and Rosenstein (1961), Fiedler (1965), Raush and his collaborators (Raush, Dittman, & Taylor, 1959), Sells (1963), Vernon (1965), and others, along with my own research and reflections (Peterson, 1965), I reached several conclusions that were uncongenial with the prevailing theories and practices of the time. The first and most fundamental conclusion was that the environment as well as the person *had* to be brought into any useful account of human behavior. A strong body of evidence showed that situational influences on human activity were grossly underemphasized in the psychodynamic and trait theories that dominated the field of personality in the 1960s and before. Neither the person alone nor the environment alone, but people in their environments, were the proper objects of useful inquiries.
>
> As a clinician, I was also convinced that the main aim of psychological assessment was to gain information related to change. Whatever else one might want to know about people and their environments, any practically useful information had to be employable in designing interventions for the benefit of the people under study. This meant that human interactions had to be studied as interruptible processes over time, rather than as static traits or states. The motion picture rather than the still

photograph or the X-ray became an appropriate metaphor for the portrayal of human action.

A third proposal was that any assessment strategy for the study of social behavior be guided by a reasonably well-defined conception of the phenomena we intended to examine. I hesitated then, and still do, to use the word "theory." A fully articulated, generally accepted theory is nowhere to be found in this sector of our field. Yet all assessment is guided by some conception that tells investigators where to look even if it is silent about what they will find. Presenting the conception in a reasonably clear way should help examiners establish the empirical relations and infer the causal influences governing social behavior as the work of assessment proceeds.

A fourth proposal was that assessment strategies be based procedurally on a full range of the methods of behavioral science. These are systematic observation in natural settings, verbal inquiry especially by way of interviews, records of behavior and experience, the planned elicitation of behavior by experimental analogues, and above all the functional analysis of behavior, in which all available information is combined to design a plan for change, influences are exerted to produce the change, and further inquiries are conducted to see whether or not the desired changes have come about. If they have, the process of inquiry and intervention may stop. If not, further inquiry, reformulation, and a new design for change may be required.

Finally, I suggested that the same general strategy for assessment and intervention could be applied to groups and organizations as well as individuals, and concluded the book with case studies of a phobic young man, a disturbed family, and a state hospital that appeared at the time of my initial inquiries to be harming its inmates at least as much as it was helping them.

Walter Mischel's book, *Personality and Assessment* (Mischel, 1968), was written during the same period and appeared at the same time as mine. Although Mischel and I had worked independently, our conclusions showed an almost eerie correspondence. Mischel's book was addressed primarily to researchers, with secondary implications for practice. Mine was aimed mainly toward practitioners, with secondary implications for research. The principal substantive difference between the books was that Mischel examined the issue of situational influence and the resulting consequences for theory and research so exhaustively that his statement could not be ignored by reputable scholars. I disposed of that topic in a single chapter, and then went on to sketch a radical plan for the redesign of clinical psychology that my professional colleagues were not entirely ready to accept. I take comfort in the fact that contemporary professional psychology embodies most of the principles I proposed in 1968, however much or little my work had to do with the change. (Peterson, 1992b, pp. 127–128)

None of the conceptual struggles I had undergone diminished my respect for solid research. They merely pointed in new directions, along which leading psychologists in many sections of the country were already proceeding. Albert Bandura's approach to aggressive behavior was clearly more powerful than any trait-based studies of juvenile delinquency could ever be. Gerald Patterson's work on family process tied theory, measurement, and treatment together in ways no correlational study of parental attitudes could ever do. Soon after *The Clinical Study of Social Behavior* (Peterson, 1968a) came out, my own research on interpersonal process was due to begin.

The emphasis on research in the Illinois Psychology Department, salutary as it was in most of its effects, also carried less fortunate consequences. At least I thought so. We had come to be governed by the unwritten rule that every single faculty member had to be a successful, highly visible research scholar whose work would bring grant money into the university and advance the fame of the department. Any assistant professor who failed to do that was not there for long. Any student honest enough to confess an intention to practice psychology following graduation was denied admission. More and more often, contemptuous remarks were heard about "hand-holders" among our students and some of our faculty. Research, in its nature no more than a means to the end of knowledge, had become an end in itself. It seemed to me we had lost the balanced view of the scientist–practitioner envisioned at the Boulder conference (Raimy, 1950) and embodied in the program I had known at Minnesota.

THE CLARK COMMITTEE AND THE CHICAGO CONFERENCE: PROPOSALS FOR A NEW APPROACH TO CLINICAL TRAINING

The year I began to direct the clinical program, 1964, was the same year in which the deliberations of the APA Committee on Scientific and Professional Aims of Psychology—the so-called Clark Committee—concluded its deliberations (APA, 1967). The chair was the same Kenneth E. Clark who had rewritten my plan for an undergraduate major nearly 20 years before. One of its most influential members was my mentor, Paul Meehl. Another influential participant was the head of my department, Lloyd Humphreys. Lloyd and I began to talk seriously about acting on the central recommendation of the committee—the development of a graduate program expressly designed to prepare people for the practice of psychology. With his long history of distinguished work in applied psychology, Humphreys held an appreciation of effective professional service that went beyond that of many of his colleagues. We both valued research, but neither Lloyd nor I thought research was the only useful thing a psychologist could do. If psychologists were going to enter careers of professional service, we thought they should be trained directly for the work they were going to do and that completion of graduate studies should be certified by award of a professional degree.

Humphreys brought the issue of training for practice before the department with a specific proposal for creation of a program leading to the Doctor of Psychology (PsyD) degree. Arguments hummed in the halls. White papers flew through the mail. The discussions were indecisive, however, and no action was taken until after the Chicago conference on the training of clinical psychologists (Hoch, Ross, & Winder, 1966), in which our proposal for a PsyD program was the most hotly debated item on the agenda.

When university classes began the next autumn, Humphreys and I offered to meet with any person or group who wished to discuss the Chicago conference or any other matter involved in the training of professional psychologists. I talked with small groups of people in our clinical, personality, and social psychology programs. Lloyd talked with groups of colleagues in experimental psychology and measurement, and both of us met with individuals on request. I remember the conversations as open and stimulating but not very certain about outcome. Morton Weir, who was later to become head of the department and still later chancellor for academic affairs, sighed deeply at the end of one of our meetings and said something like, "I've talked with you and I've talked with Lloyd. I've talked with Bill Gilbert and I've talked with Wes Becker, and I still don't know which way to go."

By the end of October, however, further discussion seemed unlikely to be helpful, so a department meeting was called, the proposal to develop a professional program was again formally stated and discussed, and ballots were distributed for return by mail. This time results were decisive. Full-time faculty voted 3.5 to 1 to go ahead with the program.

We went to work immediately to formulate the detailed proposals required for administrative action. Bill Gilbert, among all our faculty the strongest opponent of the PsyD concept, agreed to chair the curriculum committee. Other faculty members came together too, regardless of their original positions, and offered to work as needed to get the program going. We also asked for help from professional psychologists outside the academic department. Mortimer Brown, then assistant to the director of the Illinois Department of Mental Health, and Robert Jones, then chief psychologist at the Danville VA Hospital where many of our clinical students received part of their training, offered professional experience as well as extensive knowledge of mental health organizations to our discussions. By the time we were finished with the proposals, we felt reasonably well satisfied that we had designed a better program than any other then available as preparation for effective psychological service to the public. The concept of the program as an educational experiment was prominent in our thinking. Not only would we do our best to design the program rationally, we would test it continually by the best empirical means we could contrive. With our plans well formed and with the strong support of a highly regarded department, the remaining university sanctions were fairly easy to obtain.

The proposal for a professional degree submitted to the graduate college had to be reviewed for recommendations by an area subcommittee concerned with new programs in the social and behavioral sciences and eventually approved by the executive committee of the college before the program could go into effect. By the time these groups had completed their work, two amendments had been added to the proposal I had written for the Chicago conference. The earlier statement made no mention of a dissertation. The proposal finally approved by the graduate college, however, included a demand for a "report on some aspect of the internship experience" and provision for both preliminary and final examinations by committees made up exclusively of members of the graduate college, election to which depended primarily on a strong record in research. Both requirements were to have repercussions later on, though I did not fully foresee the implications of those innocent statements—"internship report" and "graduate college committee"—at the time the proposals were approved. The formal approval, which came in March 1966, seemed victory enough.

Both Humphreys and I expected some opposition from the university senate. For most of the preceding year, the senate had been engaged in long discussions about the aims of higher education. Many senate members thought the university was moving toward some kind of vocational-school status in its emphasis on practicality and immediate relevance of education. They deplored abandonment of traditional scholarly aims. Several professors of this sentiment were well known for the force of their rhetoric, and Lloyd and I feared that some of them would see our proposal as another threat to truth and beauty.

The meeting at which our proposal was considered, however, was almost totally consumed by an argument over elimination of the undergraduate language requirement. Discussion was heated and prolonged, for the issue was of more than scholarly interest to many a professor at the meeting. By the time the proposal for a professional program in clinical psychology was presented, everyone was exhausted. When the question was called, a fairly large number of softly voiced "ayes" could be heard. I waited for a shout of "noes," but not a single opposing vote was cast.

Approval by the board of trustees that governed our university and the board of higher education that governed all university programs in the state came in due course, in May and December of 1966. I have always believed that Lanier's support had much to do with university approval at those levels.

Putting the program into effect required more than approval. We needed money. The university immediately provided three new faculty lines that we used to hire some promising young clinical and community psychologists. We also needed help from outside, however, and submitted requests for additional training support to NIMH and the Illinois Psychiatric Training and Research Authority. Like most university clinical training programs in those times, the one at Illinois had been receiving funds from NIMH for two decades, at first in small amounts for a few trainee stipends and then in larger amounts not only for student support but to help pay faculty salaries. In 1966, our clinical training grant was in its 20th year and provided more than $39,000 in faculty personnel costs as well as $37,000 for student traineeships.

Our proposal requested an increase in the amount of support. The gist of our argument was that we planned to provide two options to students in clinical training, one emphasizing scientific work and leading to the PhD degree, the other emphasizing professional training and leading to the PsyD degree. Students who wished to become full-scale scientist–professionals could obtain both degrees in either order. We planned to admit more students, and this required additional stipendiary support. We planned to expand our clinical training resources both by hiring additional full-time faculty and by providing pay for adjunct faculty among professional psychologists in the local community.

Receipt of our proposal was acknowledged by NIMH, and not long after a site visit was arranged. Charles Spielberger was in charge of psychology training programs in NIMH at the time. He told me later that he put together the toughest team he could assemble. We expected nothing less. The site visitors conducted their inquiry in the usual way, by examining facilities, by questioning the head of the department and the director of clinical training about details of the program, and by talking with faculty, administrators, and students to gain information and evaluate attitudes toward the program. All the reviewers seemed to be working hard to maintain a balanced view of our proposal, but some of them had publicly opposed the idea of practitioner programs in psychology, and their efforts seemed strained. One of our clinical faculty members said later, "He [the site visitor] asked me to talk about the advantages and disadvantages of the program as I saw them. So I started to do that. First I would mention an advantage, then I'd mention a disadvantage, then another advantage, then another disadvantage, and so on. I kept this up for quite awhile until I noticed that every time I talked about a disadvantage he wrote it down, but when I talked about an advantage he stopped taking notes. So I stopped saying anything about disadvantages and talked only on the good side."

On balance, however, the review seemed thorough and fair. The visitors were seasoned reviewers. Among other benefits of their appraisal was some wise advice to reduce the size of our entering classes. I had overestimated our capacity. "Bad planning," said our critic. Otherwise we seemed to look good to them. Much later, Spielberger reported that the chair of the site-visit team had described our program as "the best scientist–practitioner program in the country." However accurate or inaccurate that characterization may have been, our request for funds from NIMH was approved, as was a comparable request to the Illinois Psychiatric Training and Research Authority. Ours was the first training grant awarded by the latter agency to a program in psychology.

MOVING INTO ACTION

With the program planned, administrative sanctions in place, faculty hired, and financial support assured for the next 5 years, we were ready to move ahead. I prepared a brochure announcing "Programs in Clinical Psychology." A section headed "Training for Research: The Doctor of Philosophy Degree" described the research-oriented program that we continued to offer. A section headed "Training for Service: The Doctor of Psychology Degree" described our newly formed practitioner program. Copies were sent to practically all the colleges and universities in North America. At the same time, I wrote an article (D. R. Peterson, 1968b) for the *American Psychologist* that declared our intention and described the program in more detail.

As everyone who lived through those years will remember, the late 1960s were turbulent times in America. The year we first admitted students to the PsyD program, 1968, also saw the assassination of Martin Luther King, Jr., and the riots that followed; the assassination of Robert Kennedy and the despair brought on by seeing another of our hopes cut down too soon; the agony of the Vietnam War; and the clash of the establishment and the counterculture, of police and the antiwar dissidents, at the Democratic National Convention in Chicago. Our society seemed to be cut and bleeding. At the same time, however, hopes in psychology were never stronger, nor were our supports from outside. Along with key faculty from several other universities, I spent the summer of 1968 in and out of Boulder, Colorado, where Bernard Bloom had organized a program designed to bring social and clinical psychology forward into a new age of community engagement. With funds from NIMH, the program allowed us to fly all over the country visiting programs in which psychologists were doing something systematic and useful about the conditions that plagued our society and encouraged us to build a strong community force in our professional and research programs. Far from producing despair, the troubles of the time spurred us on in our efforts to create a more effective profession.

2

IS PSYCHOLOGY A PROFESSION?

Psychology has had more trouble than most disciplines in defining itself as a profession. By the lofty ideals of its academic tradition, professional work has often seemed more of an embarrassment than an achievement. Psychology began as philosophy, established its independence as a natural science, and developed its first significant applications as a science–profession. These evolutionary shifts have demanded basic redefinitions of identity not required, say, of medicine, which has always been directly concerned with improving human health, or law, which has always focused on the immediate human application of legal codes.

Now psychology appears to be entering another evolutionary stage. While continuing to develop as a scholarly discipline, it is also becoming an outright profession. The Vail conference of 1973 endorsed the principle of training professional psychologists as well as scientists and scientist–professionals. If the principle is fully understood and generally accepted, it will have far-reaching influence on our field and ultimately on the public we are supposed to be serving. It will affect the kinds of work we do and the settings in which work is done, the kinds of training we offer and the forms of the institutions in which training is conducted, the kinds of organizations we establish and the functions these organizations will perform. As this article appears, five American universities will be training psychologists directly for professional work and granting a professional degree upon completion of doctoral training. Several other institutions are considering the development of professional schools or programs. For better or for worse, the transformation of psychology into an explicit profession is already well advanced.

The decisional and administrative process involved in establishing schools of professional psychology exposes assumptions about the characteristics of the discipline with a harsh and disquieting clarity. Questions about the qualifications of psychology as a profession could be comfortably evaded by a "science" or a "science–profession." Now they must be directly confronted. If a university proposes to initiate a professional program in psychology, the answer to the question "Is psychology a profession?" has to be "Yes," not "Maybe" or "No, but I think it will be in a few more years." Right now the question is very much in doubt in the minds of many psychologists.

THE CHARACTERISITICS OF PROFESSIONS

Before considering the qualifications of psychology as a profession, it is necessary to agree on some conventions about the nature of professions. Several scholars have attempted to set these out. The most inclusive statement is that of Hickson and Thomas (1969), who found 20 definitions of *profession* in the literature and from those abstracted 14 criteria that various writers had proposed as defining characteristics of professional occupations. Some of the criteria were substantive in nature (e.g., skill based on theoretical knowledge, requirements for education and training). Others were normative (e.g., expectation of altruistic service, adherence to a code of conduct). Some had to do with role relationships (fiduciary client relationship, loyalty to colleagues). Still others were concerned with organizational matters (e.g., establishment of a professional society, licensure). Among all the definitions I have read, one proposed by Abraham Flexner, who played such an important part in framing guidelines for medical education in the early part of the twentieth century, seems best to capture the qualities professions ought to have if they are to serve the needs of society as well as the occupational group itself.

According to Flexner (1915), any "profession" will meet the following conditions: (a) The objectives of professional work are definite and immediately practical. (b) Educationally communicable techniques for the attainment of those objectives are available. (c) Applications of techniques involve essentially intellectual operations, and practitioners exercise responsible discretion in matching techniques to individual problems. (d) The techniques are related to a systematic discipline, such as science, theology, or law, whose substance is large and complex, and hence ordinarily inaccessible to laymen. (e) Members of the profession are organized in some kind of society, with rules for membership and exclusion based in part on professional competence. (f) The aims of the professional organization are at least in part altruistic rather than merely self-serving, and entail a code of ethics whose sanctions are also invoked, along with those of competence, in determining membership in the society and therefore legitimate practice of the profession.

Please note that a profession, in Flexner's definition, is not an art, and it is not a trade. It is not based on the creative intuitions and expressions of the practitioner, and it is not made up of the mechanical application of unvarying techniques to human objects. Professional work requires the intelligent, disciplined design of complex services to serve a clientele whose needs and resources differ from one case to another and for whom the most helpful services may change from one occasion to another. For the most part, the fundamental attitude of the professional practitioner, though not the product of his work, resembles that of the scientist. Flexner (1925) was considering medicine, but he might just as well have been writing about psychology when he said,

> The investigator obviously observes, experiments and judges; so do the physician and surgeon who practice . . . in the modern spirit. At bottom the intellectual attitude of the two are—or should be—identical: neither investigator nor practitioner should be blinded by prejudices or jump at conclusions; both should observe, reflect, conclude, try, and watching results, continuously reapply the same method until the problem in hand has been solved or abandoned. To what extent scientific results have already been obtained, to what extent the spirit and methods of science already prevail in practice—these are questions that are for the moment beside the mark. . . . The spirit and the method of the endeavor, rather than the measure of success won in a brief period, are, for education, the significant criteria. (p. 4)

Later in the same statement, Flexner identifies the non sequitur that has since confused so many psychologists, that is, that since science and practice require a common attitude, all practitioners should be scientists. In Flexner's words,

> the assertion that the intellectual attitude of investigator and practitioner should be identical does not mean that practically investigation and treatment coincide; it does not mean that practitioners should all be experimenters or that investigators must all be practitioners. (p. 12)

While we are identifying non sequiturs, let us consider another common misconception about the nature of professions. Some adherents of scientist–professional role conceptions fear that if our discipline becomes an outright profession, then evaluation and improvement of services will cease. That is a prediction. It might come true, but it need not if the profession is organized to evaluate services as well as to deliver them. A responsible professional must be concerned with the quality of the work performed for clients. Ethical demands require evaluation of those services. The techniques will never be as effective as they might be, and anyone who is creative enough to improve them owes the profession and the general public a description of the procedure that will allow its use by others. There is nothing in the nature of a profession that requires technological stagnation. In fact, the concept of a profession, as presented here, decidedly includes responsibility for the evaluation of services and, if possible, for their creative improvement.

THE QUALIFICATIONS OF PSYCHOLOGY AS A PROFESSION

Let us return to the criteria by which professions may be identified, and then proceed with an examination of psychology in regard to those criteria. There is relatively little argument among psychologists about the first and last of Flexner's standards, which have to do with the practical objectives of professional work and with the need to organize professional societies that impose both technical and ethical controls upon professional practice. The main differences concern the central criteria of professional identity, that is, those criteria that require a demonstrably useful, educationally communicable technology, based in a complex, reasonably well-established intellectual discipline, before a profession can be established. Here is where we part ways, with Rotter (1971a), Maher (1965), and others of their persuasion saying we are not far enough along yet, whereas Meehl (1971), Holt (1971), and others keep saying that we are. I focus here on clinical psychology, a field I know well and for which I believe strong claims of professional legitimacy can be made. It is quite possible that equally strong claims could be made for industrial and school psychology, but I am not well enough acquainted with those fields to evaluate them.

To the general public, and I fear to many psychologists, clinical psychology is still thought to be made up almost entirely of evocative psychotherapy and test-based psychodiagnosis. As the field has evolved over the past 20 years, however, it has become much more comprehensive than that. The definition I offer my students these days has clinical psychology concerned with the development and application of principles and methods for the assessment and modification of human problems in individuals, groups, and societal organizations. In its scientific aspect, clinical psychology is dominantly concerned with technological development. In its professional aspect, clinical psychology is dominantly concerned with the application of available techniques to serve public needs. The disciplinary base, the supportive and heuristic paradigm for a clinical psychology of this scope, is not personality theory, which in any distinctively useful definition has to be limited to the molar behavior of individuals. It is certainly not medicine. We are not dealing with mental diseases but with psychological dysfunctions. The appropriate disciplinary base for clinical psychology as it is practiced today is general psychology. The range of the necessary discipline extends from biological psychology, through the individual psychology of covert as well as overt behavior, over the social psychology of interpersonal relationships, to the psychology of organizational process.

Definitions are always somewhat arbitrary. There is nothing in the nature of clinical psychology that requires broad definition. In principle, the early statements, which focused on study of the individual and emphasized psychodiagnosis and psychotherapy, could be preserved today. But such restriction seems unwise. As the review to follow will show, knowledge about the complex cognitive–affective processes involved in traditional individual psychotherapy is not very secure. If that is all there is to clinical psychology, it is difficult to defend as an independent profession. If professional work with individuals includes a wider array of change procedures, however, and if skill in the study and modification of individual behavior is complemented by knowledge of interpersonal process and organizational function, professional psychology is standing on a tolerably firm basis now. Perhaps more important, a comprehensively defined professional discipline should be more flexible in responding to changing public needs and applying new technical developments than a narrower definition would allow. At its most powerful, professional psychology is applied general psychology. Nothing less will allow us to deal with the range of human problems we are attempting to understand and resolve.

But such an ambitious definition of the field also brings doubt about our accomplishments and uncertainty about our prospects for useful professional service. Where is the general behavior theory on which psychological technology is supposedly based? Where are the proven techniques for examining and aiding people, groups, and organized agencies to function more effectively? To many thoughtful critics, the theory we need appears to be hopelessly indefinite and the methods we employ either untested or demonstrably inadequate. One of the most eloquent spokesmen of the skeptical view is Julian Rotter (1971a), who has said,

> Diagnostic testing is waning in clinical practice and less and less time is being spent on it in university training programs. Traditional individual psychotherapy is under attack for its inefficiency from a social point of view, as well as for its record of lack of successful outcome. . . . On the other hand . . . new techniques of therapy are developing almost as fast as projective tests did in the early 'fifties when every clinician had his own . . . magic road into the core of personality. . . . [But] the new methods of treatment are not flourishing because of new knowledge or because basic psychology has recently developed to the point that . . . new applications are possible. The methods are often widely embraced in the absence of

> hard data as to their efficacy. . . . [We need] a scientific, communicable body of knowledge on which to base our practice. The knowledge which we have now is woefully deficient. . . .

I think there is a systematic bias in that view. Psychologists of my generation were trained as scientists, to collect data representatively, to analyze data systematically, and to formulate conclusions conservatively. But in avoiding the errors of incautious assertion as we evaluate our own discipline, many of us have made an error of the second kind and have failed to credit accomplishments and to acknowledge the effective services we are able to provide. What we need is a realistic appraisal of modern psychological technology. With that, we may be able to forecast our prospects for further technical development and arrive at rational decisions on such issues as the creation of professional degree programs and the establishment of professional schools of psychology.

Professional Knowledge in Biological Psychology

Let me start the appraisal with some comments on the state of clinically useful knowledge in biological psychology. This is not the place I would begin if I were merely trying to win a political debate, because I do not believe psychologically applicable knowledge about the biological functioning of the human organism is very impressive at this time. We are much stronger in other areas. I am beginning at the biological level partly because discussions of this kind conventionally begin there, but also because the need to note limitations as well as accomplishments may force me to a more realistic view of the state of clinical psychology than my sentiments and previous political commitments might otherwise encourage.

We know enough about biological psychology to apply it professionally now. We are not ignorant about the way the human brain works. From the work of Luria (1966), Penfield and Rasmussen (1950), Hebb (1949), and literally thousands of others, we have accumulated an enormous mass of knowledge about the structure and function of the central nervous system and of the relations between that system and such psychological functions as sensation, perception, emotion, cognition, and motor behavior. Furthermore, this knowledge has been put to use by such people as Halstead (1947), Wepman (see Halstead & Wepman, 1949), and Reitan (1966, 1967) in the development of clinically useful tests of brain dysfunction. This is not the place to attempt a critical review of the literature on psychological techniques for the assessment of central nervous system disorder. If I were to attempt such a review, I would comment on the limitations as well as the merits of the procedures available to us at this time. Two recent studies (Lacks, Colberg, Harrow, & Levine, 1970; Watson, Thomas, Anderson, & Felling, 1968), for example, have seriously qualified some earlier claims about the discriminatory power of the Halstead–Reitan battery in the diagnoses of neurological lesions. The weight of the evidence for the utility of those procedures, however, is strongly positive (Russell, Neuringer, & Goldstein, 1970), and in the clinical study of people with brain damage I believe it would be a more serious error not to use methods with this degree of established usefulness than to use the methods in fear that they might introduce some diagnostic error.

No critical review of the still larger and more fundamental literature on human neuropsychology could possibly come to the conclusion that we now know everything we need to know about brain–behavior relationships. Of course we do not. Of course we need further research. But the work we have done already provides us with a reasonably sturdy foundation of knowledge about the processes with which we are concerned, and with a communicable set of procedures, which we can put to use in the clinical study of human beings with neuropsychological dysfunctions. That is all we need for professional work in dealing with those problems.

Besides neuropsychology, we know a good deal about the psychophysiology of emotion and can put that knowledge to use in professionally important ways. From the work of Funkenstein (1955), Lacey (1967), Ax (1953), and again literally thousands of others, we have built a very substantial base of information about psychophysiological arousal systems and about the measurement of psychophysiological functions. As Lykken (1974) recently pointed out, the use of those techniques in such fields as polygraphic interrogation should be regarded as forms of applied psychology. The lie detector is a psychological test. The fact that we have failed to take initiative in this field is seen by Lykken as a kind of scandal. The tests are given anyway by people who haven't the slightest idea what a term like *base rate* or *false positive* might mean, and the evidence is used in ways that affect human lives vitally. Our failure to enter the field of clinical psychophysiological measurement does not come entirely from lack of knowledge. It comes in part from a weakness of professional assertion.

There are other areas in which present knowledge of biological psychology could be employed in clinically useful ways. Biofeedback regulation is one such field. Genetic counseling is another. Again, I do not propose that we have a full and secure knowledge of all important psychobiological functions or that the utility of our clinical methods is documented by an impregnable body of evidence. All I have claimed is that present knowledge of human biological psychology offers a reasonably substantial base for important clinical applications. I have also suggested that if we do not put publicly useful knowledge into responsible, professional application, others are likely to put parts of that knowledge into irresponsible, nonprofessional application. We should weigh the costs of inappropriate use of inadequate knowledge in any choices we make about scientific and professional emphases in psychology.

Professional Knowledge in Individual Psychology

Now let us consider the state of knowledge and the clinical use of knowledge about individual human behavior. Here the ground is stronger. The behavior of organisms has been the dominant focus of psychological theory and research for the past half-century, and more is known about the clinical analysis and modification of individual behavior than is known at either more molecular or more molar levels of organization. In this discussion I do not refer only to operant conditioning and systematic desensitization, which some people mistakenly conceive of as covering the full extent of "behavior therapy." Anyone who comprehends the basic paradigm shift that has occurred in clinical psychology over the past 20 years must appreciate immediately that there is no such thing as an individual "therapy" in clinical psychology that is anything other than "behavior therapy." Clinicians always aim to modify some kind of behavior, covert or overt, simple or complex, and their individual treatment efforts are most consistently viewed as forms of behavior modification in exactly the same sense that psychology is conceived as the science of behavior. This leads to the following claim: We know a great deal about the principles governing individual behavior and about the application of those principles in a technology of behavior change. As documentation, I cite the mass of research that is summarized and conceptually organized in such works as Bandura's (1969) *Principles of Behavior Modification*, Kanfer and Phillips' (1970) *Learning Foundations of Behavior Therapy*, Franks' (1969) *Behavior Therapy: Appraisal and Status*, and Bergin and Garfield's (1971) *Handbook of Psychotherapy and Behavior Change*.

By now, many different conditioning procedures have been employed over a wide range of clinical problems. People documenting this argument usually begin by mentioning systematic desensitization. I will too. Even at the time of Gordon Paul's (1969) review for Cyril Franks' *Behavior Therapy: Appraisal and Status*, 75 investigations by more than 90 different therapists with nearly 1,000 different clients had been done on systematic desensitization, and Paul's conclusion, "the findings were overwhelmingly positive," was justified. By now, much more research has been done, and evidence for the efficacy of the method has only become stronger over the passing years, though, like any other method, it has limitations too. Some research has raised legitimate and important questions about the processes involved in the "conditioning" of affective states. Marcia, Rubin, and Efran (1969), for example, have done some work suggesting that the processes are not as simple and direct as a simple Pavlovian or Sherringtonian model might lead one to presume. But then few responsible theorists ever thought they were. Basic research on the more complex processes needs to be done; there is no question about it. That has nothing to do with the efficacy of clinical desensitization. There is a specifiable procedure, which has a predictable effect on clients whose behavior conforms to a definable pattern. That is all we need to know to justify the professional use of the method.

What else do we have besides desensitization? Operant conditioning, of course. Anyone who has read Lovaas (1968) on the clinical modification of bizarre behavior and the development of adaptive behavior in schizophrenic children or the work of Bijou (e.g., 1966) in teaching skills and eliminating dysfunctional behavior patterns with retarded children can come to no rational conclusion but that the methods those people employ have dramatic effects in dealing with problems that seemed clinically unmanageable only a few short years ago. Never mind that we still do not know much about the development of schizophrenic disorders. We need to continue studying that. Never mind even that behavior patterns revert to previous topographies when people return to the original contingencies that generated and maintained the behavior in the first place. That is exactly what anybody who understands operant conditioning would expect. Never mind that behavior modification programs are politically and administratively difficult to manage (Reppucci & Saunders, 1974). Of course, any psychologist who tries to organize an effective institutional behavior modification program has to know a great deal more than operant tricks. To my mind, operant conditioning is sorely insufficient as general psychological theory (cf. Peterson, 1968a) and downright ridiculous as a basis for modern political philosophy. That is beside the point. The methods of operant conditioning have been defined with enough clarity so that they can be taught to practitioners for use in the public benefit. Properly applied, they have shown clearly documented utility in modifying a wide range of clinically significant behavior patterns. That is all we need to know for professional use.

Within recent years, the application of principles and methods of human learning to individual clinical problems has moved substantially beyond the desensitization of small animal phobias and monotonous reconfirmation of the law of effect in operant-conditioning research. The use of modeling procedures (Bandura, 1969) and other fairly direct educative methods such as assertion training (e.g., McFall & Twentyman, 1973) have shown very respectable utility in dealing with various skill-deficiency problems. Not only imaginal desensitization but various other methods, such as Stampfl's implosive procedures (Stampfl & Levis, 1967), and various in vivo desensitization methods (e.g., Sherman, 1972) have proved useful in modifying emotional reactions and many patterns of maladaptive instrumental behavior related to those emotional reactions. Aversive conditioning methods are risky, but skillfully employed, within an appropriate contract between practitioner and client, aversive methods have been helpful in dealing with several kinds of problems that are very difficult to manage in other ways. Davison's (1968) work with sexual disorders and Lovaas's (see Lovaas, Schaeffer, & Simmons, 1965) procedures for the control of self-destructive behavior offer quite convincing examples.

We have not done so well yet with the complex cognitive–affective, personal–interpersonal phenomena that usually go under the heading of psychotherapy. Recent outcome surveys (e.g., Meltzoff & Kornreich, 1970) are more encouraging than early reviews by people like Eysenck (1952), but this does not help much. We are not going to learn about the effectiveness of psychotherapy, let alone the process, so long as we persist in approaching the problem as if we were dealing with a single method for use with all forms of "mental illness." We need to approach the many issues involved in a much more refined and analytic way, as one facet of the general heuristic in behavior modification—that is, "What treatment, by whom, is most effective for this individual, with that specific problem, under what set of circumstances, and how does it come about?" (Paul, 1969, p. 62). That question, of course, is never "answered." Our technology is developed, progressively and infinitely, within the general framework provided by the question. We always have some more or less definite knowledge about some issues in the larger set, and we never know as much as we might.

If we agree that the operations which have traditionally been subsumed under the general heading of "psychotherapy" are those dominantly verbal clinical procedures designed mainly to produce complex cognitive–affective changes related interactively to equally complex behavioral and interbehavioral processes, then I maintain we are beginning to make some progress. Trexler and Karst (1972), for example, have shown that systematic modification of the "things people say to themselves" as proposed by Albert Ellis can change not only the target anxiety which treatment efforts were planned to reduce but also the irrational beliefs that presumably mediated that anxiety. In an extended series of investigations, Meichenbaum (1973) has shown that reasonably well defined cognitive change procedures can dependably affect impulsive behavior in children and the "psychotic" behavior of adults, as well as the covert verbal processes that apparently mediate those kinds of behavior. Work of this kind is only beginning, but some accomplishments in the clinical management of cognitive–affective behavior are already fairly impressive.

In offering the "realistic" appraisal I promised you, I must accompany every claim of technical knowledge with a qualification. Broad-spectrum behavior modification procedures, in their most intelligent forms of clinical application, are ordinarily used in complex combinations and sequences, which have not been thoroughly tested with the particular classes of clients and problems under treatment. People like Arnold Lazarus (1971) may use a blow-up procedure, modeling, verbal reinforcement, and some very "dynamic" verbal–interpersonal exchanges in a single session with a client whose exact pattern of problems will never be represented in any study our literature contains. That is all right. Some of the methods have produced some of the changes he is trying to accomplish. It is a professional problem, not a problem for science, to use those methods for the greatest possible benefit of the client, to assess the effects of the methods critically, and to continue to work until changes have occurred or a contractual decision to define new goals or to terminate treatment has been reached.

All of us would like to know more about individual psychology. I presume we will know more in the future. But the science of the past 50 years and the technology of the past 15 years have given us a start. The knowledge we have will be used in any case. And I do not believe that any other discipline offers better knowledge about the analysis and change of individual behavior than psychology does.

Professional Knowledge in Social Psychology

We are beginning, just barely, to develop a social psychology that is professionally useful in the analysis and modification of interpersonal relationships. We are not nearly as far advanced in this area as we are in dealing with individual problems. The methods we have been using to study interpersonal process were borrowed mainly from individual psychology. They are not only untested in the interpersonal context, but they are also fundamentally inappropriate to the task. The amount of systematic research on process and outcome in encounter groups, for example, is negligible. Yet workshops are conducted, personal growth and effective interpersonal relationships are promised, and the services are sold to the gullible public at a rate that seems disgraceful to any responsible professional psychologist.

We are not completely lacking in the coherent conceptions and the documentably useful methods required for a clinical psychology of interpersonal behavior. The theoretical formulations that seem most powerful to me are those that have moved beyond the sensitively conceived but ambiguously defined formulations of Sullivanian theory to the more systematic social psychology of interpersonal perception and exchange. The basic social psychology involved is represented by the work of Thibaut and Kelley (1959) and Homans (1961). A clinically pertinent extension of those ideas can be found in Carson's (1969) *Interaction Concepts of Personality*. The necessarily subtle conceptions of transactional exchange theory have not yet been translated into communicable methods for the assessment of interpersonal process, nor into systematic strategies for changing dysfunctional interpersonal perceptions or communications. Some progress has been made, however, in the modification of overt interpersonal behavior. The studies of people like Patterson (1971), in the analysis and management of parent–child relationships, and Stuart (1969), in modifying relationships between marital partners, offer clear examples. Work on the improvement of sexual relationships, as pioneered by Masters and Johnson (1970), also meets the conditions of theoretical rationality, educational communicability, and demonstrated effectiveness required for general professional use. We should move rapidly in the development of better methods for studying and changing interpersonal behavior, but at least we have made a start.

Professional Knowledge in Community Psychology

The next proposition is double-barreled: We know enough about the organization of mental health systems to improve enormously on the services offered by traditional institutions, but we know very little about the systematic analysis and planned change of social systems in the general sense required for a professional community psychology.

Sooner or later, any thoughtful professional dealing with severe, long-standing human problems is bound to recognize that treating those problems one by one is a losing game. The "whole system" has to be changed if general and lasting effects are to be brought about. Community psycholgy began in the traditional fields of mental health, and it is still in those fields that the strongest evidence of beneficial change can be found. One of the most commonly cited examples is the work of Fairweather. Over 15 years of frustrating but cumulative enterprise, Fairweather, Sanders, Maynard, Cressler, and Black (1969) created new settings for chronic mental patients, the well-known "lodges," which are more humane, far more effective in keeping people at productive work in the community, and far less costly than traditional mental hospitals have been. Another frequently mentioned body of research, which pertains to the organization of mental health services, is the work on token economies (Ayllon & Azrin, 1968). By arranging staff behavior and resources to reinforce adaptive behavior rather than psychotic behavior, clearly significant though transitory changes can be brought about. A more impressive approach to the organization of behavior modification programs has recently been employed by Gordon Paul and his colleagues (see Paul & Lentz, 1976). They compared a sophisticated, very carefully monitored social learning program with a milieu program and with the usual state hospital regime of drugs, "activity therapy," and the like as to their effects on the behavior of severely psychotic, chronically hospitalized mental patients. The social learning program was clearly superior to the milieu program, and both were clearly better than the usual state hospital regime as measured by such indices as time in the community and a highly reliable measure of behavioral improvement. The program is based on a reasonably coherent body of psychological theory, the techniques are well-defined and can be taught to others, and the methods work. Professional application requires no more.

Less has been accomplished in the field of primary social change. After early work in traditional mental health systems, many psychologists began to seek still more fundamental changes in the social systems that modulate all human behavior and from which all human problems can be seen to arise. The discipline of community psychology arose, with a grand mission of reorganizing all those social systems perceived as detrimental to the quality of human existence and the creation of new settings in which more fulfilling lives could develop.

The enormous literature that has since evolved on planned social change has been thoroughly reviewed by others (e.g., Cowen, 1973). I think it is fair to summarize the literature by saying that the field of community psychology is very vigorous, as gauged by the amount of content produced in a short span of time, exceedingly diverse as to the variety of systems involved and the means employed in attempting to change them, and—unless I have missed something—of absolutely *no* documented utility so far in changing the primary systems of our society.

The last proposition is a strong one, and I hope someone can show me I am wrong about it. My own reading of the literature on "primary prevention" of psychological disorders has led me to the conclusion that none of the programs tried so far has worked, including some of the most highly touted programs in the country. Morton Bard's (1970) famous police training program, which I mention not as a bad example but as one of the best community programs I know, did not reduce the incidence of assaults or family homicides in the precinct where the program was in effect. Bard speaks enthusiastically of the effects of the program in reducing injuries to police officers, but the differences he reports are based on such small samples that no legitimate statistical tests can be employed. If a test is run anyway, under conditions that would inflate the likelihood of apparent significance, the difference still turns out to be statistically unreliable.

"Outreach" programs have become all the rage on college campuses lately (Bloom, 1970, 1971). A University of Illinois PsyD student did a critical analysis of the literature on those programs for his doctoral field project and was forced to conclude that selective factors determining participation in the programs were so badly confounded with prospect of benefit that the effects of the programs could not be clearly appraised. Another student analyzed the literature on suicide prevention programs (Schneidman, Farberow, & Litman, 1970). He could find no evidence that those programs did anything to prevent suicide, though of course they may have had other desirable effects such as improving public awareness of a serious psychological problem.

Where does this leave us in the field of community change? Short of a profession, I think. A century and a half has passed since Auguste Comte called for the creation of a science of societies, but we still do not have the applied experimental sociology we need for legitimate professional action. Some promising theoretical formulations (e.g., March, 1965; Sarason, 1974) are beginning to appear, and some very interesting projects are under way in community psychology programs all across the country, but I doubt Flexner would be satisfied that these are enough to justify a distinct profession of community psychology, as apart from the more general base that a professional psychology comprehending biological functions, individual psychology, and the social psychology of interpersonal relationships would offer.

IN CLOSING

How can we move from the selective descriptions of accomplishment I have just offered to a more general evaluation of technological development in psychology? How far along are we? How far is far enough to justify professionalization? Questions of that kind must be approached cautiously, and any quick answers must be regarded skeptically. After Flexner had defined the characteristics of professions in 1915, he applied his own criteria in an appraisal of social work and decided the field did not yet qualify as a profession. Ten years later, William Hodson became president of the newly formed American Association of Social Workers and reexamined the same topic: Is social work a profession? He decided that it was. Looking back on both appraisals from outside the field and after 50 years of further history, I cannot see that much real change took place in the basic paradigm or the technical utility of social work from 1915 to 1925, and I doubt that social work would qualify even today as a profession by Flexner's original standards.

But I think psychology does qualify as a profession, for all the reasons I have just discussed. A good operational test of the integrity of that opinion can be made by asking various forms of the question, Do you have enough confidence in professional psychology to allow it to affect your own life? Thus, Would you hire a doctor of psychology? Would you go yourself, or refer someone you love, to a professional psychologist for help with a serious psychological problem? In one way or another, we have to ask, Would you want your sister to marry one?

My answer to appropriate versions of the question, across all levels of professional psychology is, "You bet I would." If I develop a cerebral thrombosis that leaves me aphasic and partially paralyzed, I will want a well-trained neurologist to study my damaged brain and to prescribe anticoagulants to lessen the likelihood of another stroke. But I would also appreciate the service of a competent neuropsychologist who could evaluate my sensory, perceptual, cognitive, and motor capabilities as well as dysfunctions and help me in the psychoeducational task of making the most of whatever functional competence might be attainable for me. If I become phobic, I will seek desensitization, and I will want somebody who knows what he is doing to perform the operation. If I develop further interpersonal problems, as I recently did in my marriage, I will go again to the same skillful, understanding professional psychologist who helped me before. If I ever show obvious signs of psychosis and am committed to a mental hospital, I hope that one of our doctors of psychology is on staff, instead of the psychologically ignorant, professionally untrained incompetents of all disciplines I would likely find in control of my life today.

3

CONNECTION AND DISCONNECTION OF RESEARCH AND PRACTICE IN THE EDUCATION OF PROFESSIONAL PSYCHOLOGISTS

Among all the misunderstandings that contaminate rational discussion about the education of professional psychologists, none is more fundamental nor more difficult to dislodge than the idea that the direct education of professionals entails a rejection of research. No one I respect has ever suggested that. I never have. My central claim is that scientific research and professional service are different in important ways, and that different forms of education are required to prepare people for careers of research, in the one case, or careers of professional service, in the other case. Combinations are possible, but rarely fit the dispositions of students or the demands of employment following graduate education.

Because I have been writing and speaking on this topic for more than 25 years and still hear otherwise sane and literate people ask me why I am opposed

---

This chapter was originally presented as a Distinguished Education and Training award address at the 98th Annual Convention of the American Psychological Association in Boston in August 1990. From *American Psychologist*, 46, 422–429.

to science, I hold no illusion that my remarks will put the confusion to its final rest. All I intend in the following statement is to approach the issue of relations between research and practice from a somewhat different direction than I have taken before and hope that my comments will be constructive.

First I will offer a brief review of the history of education for the practice of psychology, within which three clear phases can be marked. Then I will examine assumptions about relations between the science and the profession that have predominated in each phase, and conclude with the recommendation that basic scientists, applied researchers, and professional psychologists pursue their distinct but related missions in complementary and cooperative ways.

HISTORY OF EDUCATION FOR THE PRACTICE OF PSYCHOLOGY

Preprofessional Phase

From the beginning, the American expression of psychology has contained a strong utilitarian component. More than our European counterparts, we have asked what uses can be made of knowledge about human function. The first psychological clinics were formed in the United States. Psychological tests were originally devised in Britain and France, but the testing movement and assessment more generally have been predominantly American inventions. The first time-and-motion studies in industry were done by American psychologists. The first studies of worker morale were done here. Psychoanalysis as a profession took root more firmly and grew more profusely in America than in Europe. Throughout our history, in the schools, in mental health settings, in the military, in the workplace, American psychologists have pressed the applications of psychology as far as they will go.

As intrepid as American psychologists have been in forging ahead with applications, however, they have avoided the issues of education for practice with a phobic caution. For the first 65 years of our history, psychologists entered careers of practice with no systematic preparation for professional work. They were educated as scientists. The people who created psychology, of course, came from other fields. Freud was a physician. Pavlov was an experimental physiologist. William James was educated as a physician, and his heart was in philosophy. As professorships and then departments of psychology were established, people who entered the field learned whatever their teachers had to tell them. Students who went to Cornell and studied with E. B. Titchener learned structural psychology and the introspective method. Students who went to Harvard and studied with William James learned a dynamic functionalism. Whatever the content, however, and no matter who taught them, what they learned was scientific psychology as their professors defined it. Aside from demonstrations in the clinics of the day, such clerkships and practica as their advisors might arrange, and the limited internships that were sometimes tacked onto the academic courses and dissertation required for the PhD degree, no systematic preparation for practice was available. When psychologists entered professional careers, as they did in increasing numbers after World War I, they had to figure out what to do by trial and error, or if they were fortunate, as apprentices to a mentor who had walked the path before them. In the development of education for the practice of psychology, it is fair to call the first two thirds of our 100-year history a preprofessional phase.

Scientist–Practitioner Phase

All this changed after World War II. As Americans faced the return of 16 million veterans and perhaps 100,000 psychiatric casualties, the need for psychiatrists, social workers, and clinical psychologists to help our military heroes return to civilian life was widely recognized, and use of public funds to train them found immediate political sympathy. Through the Veterans Administration (VA) and the National Institute of Mental Health (NIMH), the federal government supported the devlopment of programs in clinical and counseling psychology. Like all federal grants, those from the VA and NIMH imposed conditions of accountability. The institutional setting of every funded program had to be stable and supportive. Curricular content had to be specified. A system for program accreditation had to be established. With large financial incentives in sight, academicians somehow overcame the ambivalence that had impeded previous efforts to define the education of professional psychologists. In the report of the Shakow Committee (American Psychological Association [APA], 1947) and then at the Boulder conference (Raimy, 1950), the basic conditions for educating professional psychologists were set. The institutions in charge were academic departments. The model of training was that of the scientist–practitioner. The APA would assume responsibility for accrediting programs. With clear definition of an educational philosophy and a bounding growth of clinical programs all across the country, we entered the scientist–practitioner phase of development in education for practice in our field.

Before I say another word, I need to make clear that I am not unsympathetic to the Boulder model of education in psychology. In its modesty, the scientist–practitioner concept has enormous power. It acknowledges that the conceptual, methodological, and substantive bases for the practice of psychology forever need improving, and that an unending flow of sound research is required to bring that improvement about. I believe our research universities should continue to nuture strong research-oriented scientist–practitioner programs. I believe we should exploit every opportunity to link practice and research as Barlow, Hayes, and Nelson (1984), Stricker and Keisner (1985), and many others have proposed. I applaud the work of the recent Gainesville conference in reaffirming the values of the scientist–practitioner concept and in reexamining the educational process through which scientist–practitioners are prepared for their careers. As the only way to prepare people for the practice of psychology, however, the Boulder model has serious limitations, and these began to show in the 1960s.

Professional Phase

Situated as they were in academic departments, controlled as they were by researchers, the Boulder-style programs all too often neglected training for practice. Worse than neglect, practice was often demeaned. I remember sitting in a room at the University of Illinois while a student defended his dissertation before the six members of his committee, all researchers of some note and all very stern about the rigors of scientific methodology. The student had attempted a group factorial study of treatment outcome. Troubles mounted as the experiment ran its course. Clinical subjects dropped out; uncontrollable influences crept in. During the exam, the members of the committee, one after the other, tore the study into bloody ribbons. The student was devastated. He did not know what to say except to promise never to do any research again. After he left the room at the end of the session, the committee members clucked solemnly about the faults in the investigation. I did not dispute their objections to the study as a scientific experiment, but I tried to defend the student on two grounds. One was that clinical research was more difficult than running rats in T mazes. This remark did not endear me to the people on the committee who were running rats in T mazes. I also tried to defend the student by saying that I had supervised some of his practicum work and found him to be a very competent clinician. I said that he knew what he was doing—that he was dedicated, responsible, and effective. I said that if any of my loved ones got into psychological trouble, I would feel very comfortable sending them to this person for help. I met a stony silence. Nobody else in the room thought it mattered much for any of our graduates to be a good clinician. Certainly none of the others considered professional expertise sufficient qualification for a PhD. At the end of the session, one of the committee members said, "We've wasted our time on another hand-holder."

From my experience in the Illinois Psychology Department and as a consultant to the Illinois Department of Mental Health (see the description of Elba State Hospital in my 1968[a] book, *The Clinical Study of Social Behavior*), I became convinced that we could do much better than we were doing to educate practitioners, and I felt that it was my responsibility as director of clinical training to do so. By then, Thorndike (1955) had shown that the interests of psychologists in the kinds of activities that occupy clinicians were bimodally distributed. Levy (1962), along with Kelly and Goldberg (1959), had shown that the modal number of publications by clinical psychologists was zero, for all the training in research and all the preaching about science students received in graduate school. From several quarters, but mainly from those who were developing behavioral approaches to clinical problems, a reasonably coherent conception of human functioning and some demonstrably effective procedures for assessment and change had come into view (Peterson, 1968a). Technically, I thought we were ready to form an outright profession. Morally, I felt we were obliged to do so.

Every year I signed a contract with NIMH for our training grant. I had done some fairly careful evaluations of our own program, and it bothered me to report that we were graduating fewer than seven students per year and that 85% of those were going into academic positions. An impressive number of the people who came through the Illinois clinical program in those times are now distinguished leaders in the scientist–practitioner community. I am proud to have been part of their education. But I could not believe that the taxpayers of the state of Illinois and the United States of America were paying me to educate college professors.

I would never have had the courage to act on my convictions, however, without the support of others. At a national level, this support came from the APA Committee on the Scientific and Professional Aims of Psychology (1967), usually called the Clark Committee, after its chairman, Kenneth E. Clark. Locally, inspiration and active leadership, as well as support, came from my friend and colleague, Lloyd Humphreys, who was then head of the Psychology Department at Illinois and was also a member of the Clark Committee. The Clark Committee embodied an uncommon concentration of talent and experience. Jerome Bruner, Kenneth Spence, Paul Meehl, Carl Rogers, and others of their stature were in the group. When people of this distinction, following deliberation every six weeks for a year and a half, proposed a two-track, practice-research, PsyD–PhD educational system, I did not see how others in our field could ignore their recommendation, and I did not feel that my own sentiments were entirely misplaced.

On a national scale, however, the ideas proposed by the Clark Committee did not get far. The concept of outright professional education was considered but voted down in Minnesota, debated but defeated in Tennessee, and noted but ridiculed in Michigan. Lloyd Humphreys carried the idea forward nationally, and he and I brought the idea before our colleagues at the University of Illinois as a specific program proposal. For several weeks the halls were noisy with discussion. The Chicago conference on the Professional Preparation of Clinical Psychologists (Hoch, Ross, & Winder, 1966) took place soon afterward. Humphreys and I presented our version of the Clark Committee proposal there. The idea was basically repudiated by the conference at large, but the participants gave us tacit approval to attempt our experiment at Illinois, so we went back and did it.

All through this time, another kind of ferment was bubbling away in California. The need for competent practitioners there was pressing, and all of the California universities combined were producing fewer than 20 clinical psychologists per year. Catalogue descriptions and admission policies made clear that the programs were designed to educate researchers rather than practitioners. Appeals by representatives of the California Psychological Association asking universities to expand their clinical programs went unheeded. In my view, it was this failure of the universities to respond to the challenge of education for practice that set the stage for creation of the freestanding California School of Professional Psychology and led ultimately to the professional school movement.

The public need for competent practitioners was urgent. The pressure exerted by well-qualified students to enter careers in professional psychology was intense, but the flow of admissions was choked to a trickle by the universities. In the community of practitioners, would-be educators lay waiting to form their own schools if the universities failed to meet the demand. Although there were scattered antecedents, establishment of the PsyD program at the University of Illinois and of the California School of Professional Psychology marked the beginning of the third phase, the professional phase, in the devlopment of education for the practice of psychology.

After nearly 25 years, the institution of direct professional education in psychology is firmly established. The National Council of Schools of Professional Psychology (NCSPP) now includes 35 member organizations: 16 are in universities and 19 are in freestanding professional schools. A total of 7, all but 1 in freestanding schools and all but 1 in California, award the PhD degree; 28 award the PsyD degree. The "professional school movement," as it is sometimes called, will not stop, although it appears to be slowing down. The schools were formed to meet community needs that were not met by traditional programs. The leaders are devoted to their mission, well organized, politically influential, and legally empowered to continue their operations. The professional schools will not go away, however wistfully academicians may pine for the good old days of scientific purity. The challenge before us now is to educate people for the practice of psychology in the best possible way.

RELATION OF SCIENCE AND PRACTICE IN THE EDUCATION OF PROFESSIONAL PSYCHOLOGISTS

Suppose we abandon the illusion that most graduates of doctoral programs in psychology will become productive researchers. Suppose we accept the fact that the interests of many people entering the field lie in practice rather than research and that many will enter jobs that impose high demands for competent professional service but offer little opportunity for research. How can we educate those people in the most effective way?

Detailed answers to that question are forthcomimg through the continuing conferences and reports of NCSPP (Bourg et al., 1987; Callan, Peterson, & Stricker, 1986; Peterson et al., 1992) as well as the activities of the Joint Council on Professional Education in Psychology (JCPEP, 1990). Fundamental to all of these statements is the premise that "education and training for practice is grounded in the evolving knowledge base derived from the scientific discipline of psychology" (JCPEP, 1990, p. 3). Views of the relations between research and practice, however, have themselves changed as our discipline has evolved.

During the preprofessional phase of our development, the linkage of science and practice was assumed to be fairly direct. As shown in Figure 3.1, the first task was the establishment of basic psychological science. Once the laws of psychological nature were known, applied research could produce the technology required for effective professional service. In this scheme, temporal priority, generality, and social value are all ordered from left to right. Attempting professional application before the necessary research was done and the laws of nature were understood was considered dangerous. The value of universal scientific principles, as soon as anybody came up with them, would clearly exceed that of applied research, and the contributions of applied researchers in providing techniques for solving classes of problems would outweigh those of professionals, who would merely apply the techniques to individual cases—although some credit might be given to professionals for artistic skill in using the procedures that science had provided.

Movement into the scientist–practitioner phase required bolder assumptions. Armed with our tests, assured by evidently successful records in treating stress casualties and selecting airplane pilots and spies in World War II, and committed to work and do no harm within the medical culture, we were prepared to offer our professional services, such as they were, to an otherwise underserved public, as long as we also devoted our special energies to the pursuits of systematic research. A reciprocal relationship between science and practice, as represented in Figure 3.2 was assumed. It was never assumed that research and professional service were of equal importance. Our science–profession was still dedicated fundamentally to advancing knowledge and improving technology. Once the right research was done, professional applications would follow more or less routinely.

Even in the applications, however, it was considered important to "think scientifically." Even if practitioners rarely produced research, the argument went, they needed to "know how to think" in their approach to professional problems. So students were trained to do theory-driven, verifica-

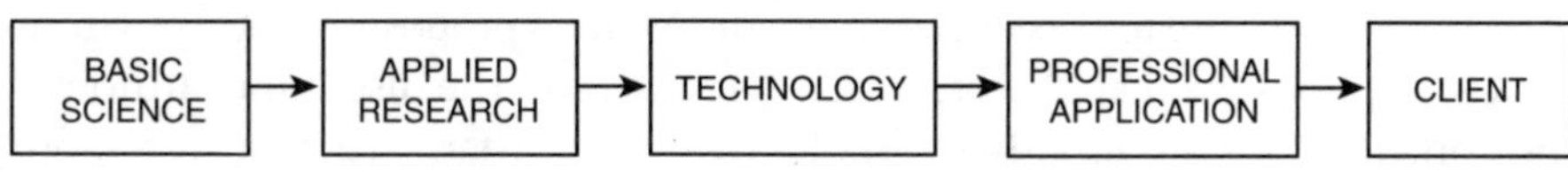

Figure 3.1. Professional activity as appled science.

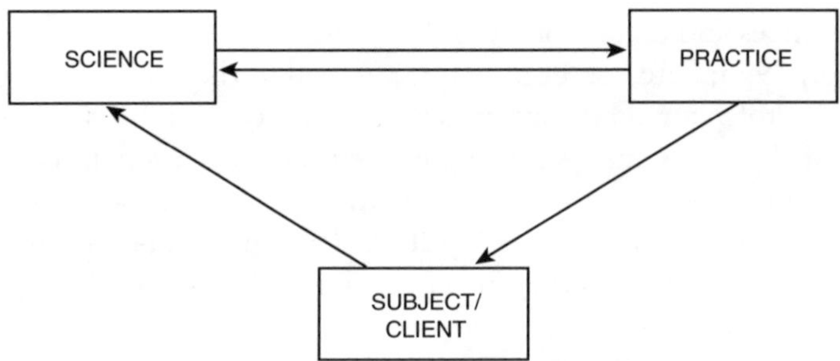

Figure 3.2. Science and practice as reciprocally related.

tional research within a positivist philosophy of science carried over from the preprofessional phase of our development. All of the emphasis on experimental design and quantitative methods, all of the insistence on involvement in research throughout graduate study, and all of the importance assigned to the dissertation in traditional research programs were presumably essential not only in preparing students for careers of productive scholarship, but in teaching them to "think like psychologists" in professional practice.

Since the early days, important changes have come about in the more liberal scientist–practitioner programs. Training for practice is not neglected to the degree it was before the professional schools came along. Neopositivist philosophies are being replaced by less restrictive epistemologies. A gradual broadening of the scope of defensible inquiry has been underway at least since the time of the Chicago conference. The elaboration of single case and time-series methodologies and of quasi-experimental designs has allowed scientist–practitioners to examine issues of greater practical importance than they could consider when the demands for close experimental control of confounding influences forced them into laboratories. Yet a recent survey of the statistical and methodological curricula in American and Canadian PhD programs still shows a heavy emphasis on training for traditional laboratory research, a neglect of newer, often more useful procedures, and no evidence that the methodological curricula have advanced much in the past 20 years (Aiken et al., 1990).

This condition is unfortunate in the education of scientists and scientist–practitioners. In the education of practitioners, it is pernicious, for it offers the illusion of training in rigorous thought but not the genuinely useful training in strategies of inquiry that effective practice demands. Science and practice differ in fundamental ways. Science begins and ends in a body of systematic knowledge. Basic research begins with a conception, which guides investigation, whose results either refute or sustain a proposition derived from the conception. Even applied research is focused on the discipline, although the contributions are usually technological rather than theoretical; a more accurate test, a more effective method of treatment. Scientists are free to choose the issues they examine. In the interest of precision they limit the scope of inquiry and control extraneous influences. Type 1 errors, in which natural effects are falsely claimed, are scrupulously avoided to keep from misleading other investigators and the lay public, and to avoid damaging the credibility of the scientific enterprise and the individual scientist when the falsity of the claim is revealed in later investigations. Type 2 errors, in which effects that actually occur in nature are denied or neglected, do not matter so much. Science moves at its own deliberate pace. Each new finding is integrated with those that have come before, and each body of research is consolidated before entry into the next area is attempted. Between rare discontinuities, the scientific view of nature is gradually illuminated as the process of discovery unfolds.

Professional activity begins and ends in the condition of the client. Whether the client is an individual, a group, or an organization, the responsibility of the practitioner is to help improve the client's functional effectiveness. The practitioner does not choose the issue to examine; the client does. The simplifications and controls that are essential to science cannot be imposed in practice. Each problem must be addressed as it occurs in nature, as an open, living process in all its complexity, often in a political context that requires certain forms of action and prohibits others. All functionally important influences on the process under study must be considered. A scientist examining cognitive activity in psychotherapy may control biological and social influences by subject selection or other means. A clinician attempting rational–emotive psychotherapy with a patient who is drinking 16 ounces of hard liquor every night must include the physiological and interpersonal effects of alcohol abuse in any useful formulation of the problem and in any useful program for its treatment. At its best, practice runs ahead of research. Each case is unique. The pattern of conditions the client presents has never occurred in exactly this form before, and the most beneficial pattern of professional action cannot rest only on scientifically established procedures, although any contingencies established in prior research must not be ignored. The measure of effect goes beyond statistical significance to functional importance. It is not enough to determine whether a difference is random or replicable. The difference has to matter to the client. Insofar as the logic of statistical analysis applies to professional action, errors of the second kind are just as damaging as errors of the first kind. To ignore a condition that truly affects the process under study can literally be fatal.

The process of inquiry in disciplined practice is represented in Figure 3.3. The needs of the client, not the need for general knowledge, drive the study. Instead of starting with science and applying what we know for sure, we start with the client and apply all the useful knowledge we can find. If some of the knowledge is qualitative or "humanistic," we work within it not because we are muddle-headed or tender-minded, but because that is the form of knowledge that provides the best understanding of the client. The first step in

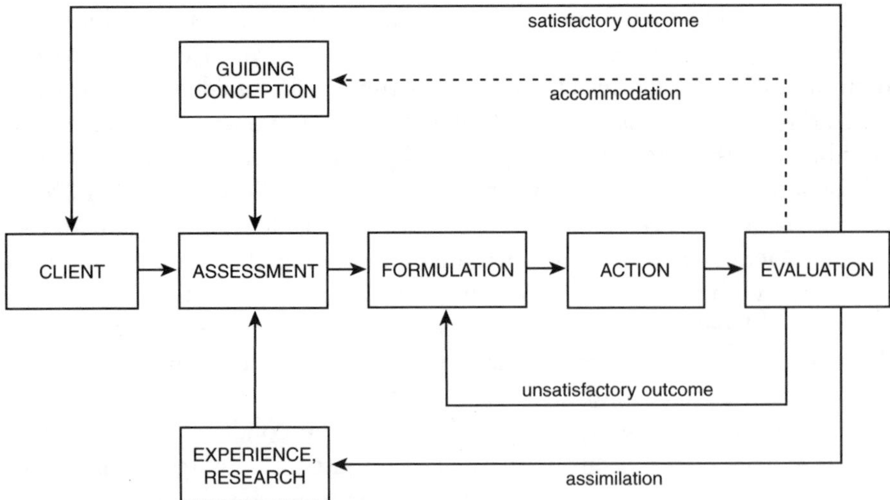

Figure 3.3. Professional activity as disciplined inquiry.

disciplined inquiry is assessment, whose intricacies I cannot even summarize here but whose most useful form consists essentially of a close study of the functional processes involved in the case at hand by multiple methods, in natural settings, over time (cf. Peterson, 1968a; Peterson & Fishman, 1987). The assessment is guided by a conception of the process under study, which includes a theoretical identification of the aspects of functional process that need to be examined, as well as the epistemological assumptions and axiological values that underlie the theory. The assessment is also influenced by the prior experience and knowledge of the examiner. This includes any empirical research that pertains to the class of conditions represented by the client, but also includes remembered examples of similar cases in the previous experience of the practitioner. From the assessment, a formulation of the particular case is developed—that is, the best understanding that the examiner can construct.

The issue that the client initially presented is typically reframed at this stage. The formulation implies some form of action, either an intervention that offers the best available prospect of benefit to the client or a decision that will be useful to the client. The effects of action are then evaluated. If client and examiner agree that the decisions they have reached or the changes they have accomplished suffice for the client, the inquiry is concluded. If either client or examiner consider the outcomes insufficient, further cycles of reformulation, action, and evaluation may continue until an acceptable outcome is reached. Acceptable outcomes may include the decision by either or both parties that the attentions of the practitioner are of no use to the client.

Each case the practitioner studies adds to the store of knowledge he or she can bring to the next case. Usually the experience is assimilated within the body of comparable experiences the practitioner has accumulated previously. Occasionally, however, the outcomes or other characteristics of a case are so sharply inconsistent with the guiding conception the practitioner has followed until that time that an accommodating change in the conception is required.

If the inquiry, or a run of inquiries, has been conducted in a sufficiently systematic way to allow generalization of findings, contributions to research or theory may result. In professional situations, however, the interests of the client prevail over all other interests, and this usually means that data cannot be collected in a way that satisfies the demand for rigorous scientific analysis. Decisions are informed by sufficient approximation. Interventions are delivered in confounded packages for maximum immediate effect. The idea that every client can be a subject and every practitioner a scientist is a noble aspiration, but for the most part it is also a romantic fantasy.

Question: How can we teach students to conduct inquiries of the kinds that are needed in practice? Answer: By requiring them to conduct inquiries over the range of settings and client conditions that they are likely to encounter in practice, under close supervision in which the support required for confident professional action is provided but in which the formulations and actions of the trainee are systematically subjected to critical review. The educational policy that governs the curriculum in practitioner programs is that students need to learn to do what they will be doing throughout their professional careers, not what their professors are doing nor what the professors think the students ought to be doing. The belief that training in traditional experimental design and quantitative method will transfer to the world of practice violates one of the few principles of learning that psychologists have established, namely that generalization of performance skills from one situation to another depends on the similarity of stimulus conditions across situations. Students need to learn the skills of practice by practicing in the settings they will encounter as professionals.

Nearly all practitioner programs include a dissertation requirement. Conduct of dissertation-type research is not conceived as the primary aim of training, but as a natural product of the kind of critical analysis in which the student is engaged throughout graduate study and will continue throughout his or her professional career. Instead of defining "scientific method" beforehand and requiring students to select a problem that suits the method, problems are chosen because they are found to be important in practice, and methods are molded to suit the problem. The only constraints are that the issue has to be professionally significant and the inquiry has to meet stringent standards of scholarship. The topics that are studied under these conditions and the methods that are used in examining them are quite different from those that are seen in scientist–practitioner programs.

Ducker (1980) surveyed dissertation policies and practices in the 144

APA-approved programs in clinical counseling and school psychology listed in the *American Psychologist* for 1979. At that time, only 6 of the programs were designed to educate practitioners, so the sample is made up almost entirely of scientist–practitioner programs. Among the 74 respondents who returned surveys, 66% claimed that they had no specific policies limiting the types of designs appropriate for dissertations. When asked what designs were actually used in dissertation research, however, 41% mentioned laboratory experiments and 22% mentioned field experiments. Descriptive studies, phenomenological analyses, and case studies were mentioned by 1.3%, that is, only 1 of the 74 respondents.

No comparable study of dissertations in practitioner programs has been done, but a description of PsyD dissertations by Rutgers students offers a demonstration of the kinds of investigations that are undertaken when practical significance drives the project and methods of inquiry are chosen to suit each problem. Over the three academic years ending in 1987, 1988, and 1989, 73 dissertations were completed by students in the Rutgers practitioner programs. Of these, the most common studies, 41%, were needs analyses and descriptions of available professional services. When students asked what they needed to know most in order to practice effectively, the questions that arose most often were, "What are the needs in the community, and what kinds of services are offered to meet these needs?" Studies included a nationwide survey of programs for gifted children, a nationwide survey of mental health services for black students in predominantly white colleges, and several investigations in which experienced professionals were interviewed to find out how they handled situations that the students had encountered but about which no useful information, scientific or otherwise, could be found in the literature. A study of clinicians who had extensive experience working with lower income urban Hispanic clients and a study of clinicians who became pregnant while they were doing psychoanalytic therapy (to see how they handled transference and related issues) offer examples. Several follow-up studies of participants in established service programs were also undertaken.

Next most common were projects in which the student–practitioner designed, implemented, and evaluated a service project of some kind, or tried to. Twenty-seven percent of the studies were of this kind. The range of programs and settings was extensive: educational programs of many kinds, prerelease and probational programs in corrections, training programs in corporate settings, data management systems in public agencies, and a wide range of clinical programs with various clinical populations. Many of the investigations were carried through to a successful conclusion, but a considerable number bogged down because key administrators moved, political climates changed, or some other condition prevented completion of the project. In those cases, reports of the initial plan and subsequent experience were merely added to the lore on which practice so often is based.

Seven dissertations were concerned with the psychometric properties of assessment procedures, five were diagnostic studies of specified clinical populations, five were replicated case studies, and five were conceptual analyses, nonempirical "think pieces" in which the student examined the literature on an issue of professional importance and developed his or her own conception of the topic. In the years from 1987 to 1989, only one student elected to do a laboratory experiment.

Data-gathering procedures included survey questionnaires (most common), interviews (next most common), performance records and direct observations, standardized tests, new unstandardized tests, and narrative accounts, both written and oral. Students typically had to design their own survey procedures and then develop inductive coding systems to aid in interpreting the data. The context of discovery prevailed much more often than the context of verification. Such strategies as grounded theory (Glaser & Strauss, 1967) were often used to make sense of narrative information in new areas of investigation.

Data were typically examined both qualitatively and quantitatively. Sophisticated statistical analyses were only occasionally justified or required. The most common statistical procedures were frequency comparisons and other nonparametric methods, simple correlation, *t* tests, and simple analyses of variance. In some cases more complex methods, such as factor analysis and multiple regression analyses, were useful. The rudimentary course in quantitative methods that is required of all students in the Rutgers PsyD programs provided both necessary and sufficient preparation for most of the studies. Where more sophisticated procedures were needed, the students had no trouble learning them or finding expert assistance.

Scholarship was appraised not by applying inappropriate standards of scientific research but by raising the questions appropriate to competent professional inquiry. Does the method suit the problem? Is a thorough understanding of pertinent literature shown in the report? Is the account conceptually coherent? Is it free of internal contradiction? Is it accurate, that is, consistent with known empirical facts? Are the limits of the study appreciated and clearly stated? Is the presentation articulate and rhetorically persuasive?

A few of the dissertations are of general interest in their own right. A model program for developmentally disabled children and a descriptive study of the life histories of elderly black women, for example, carry a significance beyond the local needs that inspired them. Others may be useful as exploratory studies. They raised as many questions as they answered and fairly cried out for more thorough, controlled research on the issues they brought to light. Most of them, however, are useful only in reference to the particular problems they were designed to address. They do not replace PhD dissertations. They certainly are no substitute for long-term programmatic research on topics of general importance. In requiring PsyD dissertations, we ask students to demonstrate mastery of systematic strategies of inquiry appropriate to the problems that they encounter in professional work. That is what they do, and that is all most of them do.

Any practitioner who expects to serve the needs of a human community has to realize that those needs are wide ranging. Biological, psychological, interpersonal, and organizational processes are all involved in human functioning. None can be neglected in the education of professional psychologists. The curriculum must be comprehensive. Just what to teach over the wide biopsychosocial range allows some variation. Stuffing students' heads with a complete encyclopedia of empirical facts is impossible and would be useless anyway because most of the issues that preoccupy researchers are irrelevant to practice. Trying to teach all currently available techniques is equally impossible and would be unwise in any case because today's techniques are bound to be replaced by better ones if researchers do their work effectively. What doctoral professionals need on entry into the world of practice is (a) a guiding conception of human function that incorporates all of the aforementioned levels within a life-span developmental perspective, (b) those substantive facts that are decisively important in understanding the functional processes involved, (c) disciplined strategies of inquiry and change that provide a systematic approach not only to familiar problems but novel situations as well, (d) a repertoire of techniques for assessment and change at the individual, group, and organizational levels, (e) an eagerness to learn new conceptions and methods as these become available, and (f) the analytical skills, more philosophical than scientific, that are required to identify useful conceptions and sound practices.

EPILOGUE

A science-based profession can be formed in either of two ways. Practice can be restricted to fit the science, or the science can be developed to fit the practice. The former course is implicit in the concept of professional activity as applied science that was commonly assumed in the early history of psychology and is sometimes proposed by leaders in our field today. In all of human civilization, however, no profession has ever grown that way. Road builders did not wait for highway engineering to produce a developed technology before they cleared trails, packed down dirt, and added cobblestones, then gravel, and finally asphalt and concrete to provide efficient surfaces for wheeled vehicles. When they needed to go from one place to another, they got there the best way they could. Medical practice has been closely linked with scientific knowledge for less than 200 years, but physicians were doing their best to heal the sick for thousands of years before. The best thing scientists in psychology can do to improve practice is not to deride their professional colleagues for going beyond tested knowledge but to extend the base of disciplined knowedge and improve the procedures that professionals need to meet the demands of public service.

Basic research, applied research, and professional work are all required, although it is absurd to expect the same people to do them all. We are likely to serve the public most effectively and to advance most rapidly as a discipline if basic scientists, applied scientists, and professionals work toward their separate goals in cooperative and complementary ways. When I reviewed the history of professional education in psychology at the beginning of this article, I spoke of preprofessional, scientist–professional, and professional "phases" of development, not "stages" in which each period replaces the one before. Direct education for the practice of psychology has not replaced the education of scientist–practitioners, any more than the education of scientist–practitioners replaced the education of basic scientists. The metaphor of an increasingly complex tonal wave and the image of a string quartet come to mind. When the viola and the cello join the violins, the violins do not stop playing. All blend together in a rich harmony. If dissonance is heard, it is not useful for the performers to smash the instruments of their fellow artists. If the cellist hears the viola going flat, a gentle comment to the partner is in order. But the best thing all of them can do is tune their own instruments.

II

PRACTITIONER PROGRAMS AND THE DOCTOR OF PSYCHOLOGY DEGREE

INTRODUCTION

PRACTITIONER PROGRAMS AND THE DOCTOR OF PSYCHOLOGY DEGREE

When I give talks on professional psychology I am often introduced as the "father of the PsyD degree." Although I am entirely willing to acknowledge my responsibilities in the birth of the first PsyD program, I was biologically incapable of fatherhood when the Doctor of Psychology concept first appeared in print. At that time, I was only 2 years old. Following conceptual justification of the PsyD degree in chapter 4 of this section, I go back, in chapter 5, to the first published proposal for direct professional education and a professional degree in psychology (Crane, 1925). There I note the collective yawns and "referrals to committee" that greeted early proposals; describe the affirmative recommendations of the Clark Committee (APA, 1967); the debate and general repudiation of the idea that came through the Chicago conference (Hoch, Ross, & Winder, 1966); implementation, despite those reservations, in the Illinois program (Peterson, 1968b); institutional legitimation in the Vail conference (Korman, 1974); and the rapid growth of PsyD programs after that.

In the 20 years following establishment of the first program, some clear patterns had emerged. Although psychologists with PsyD degrees were readily employed in a wide range of settings, appeared to perform effectively, and were more satisfied with their training than were PhD graduates of scientist–

practitioner programs, psychology faculties in major research universities did not rush to create practitioner programs in their own academic departments. With a few exceptions, the new programs were developed in small psychology departments and freestanding professional schools. This entailed a threat to quality. The dangers are discussed in chapter 6, along with descriptions of the curricular and cultural stabilities that had evolved through "twenty years of practitioner training in psychology" (Peterson, 1985). Distinctive features of the culture of practice and the culture of science are described in that chapter, along with conditions that would encourage complementary blending of the cultures.

Serious concerns over the quality of education for practice in psychology continue to haunt many psychologists, and they are deeply felt by educators responsible for preparing psychologists for lifetime careers of professional service. In chapter 7, I recall the ideals we hoped to realize in the first PsyD program at Illinois and show how our program was designed to fulfill our aspirations. From the outset, the Illinois program was conceived as an educational experiment, subject to systematic empirical evaluation. In chapter 7, I summarize the studies we did to examine professional training in psychology. Then I consider critical concerns about PsyD programs and the PsyD degree, especially fears that we are overproducing poorly educated practitioners and threatening the scientific foundations of our discipline. In closing the chapter, I distinguish rational from irrational concerns and describe the institutional realities of professional training in psychology today.

The following section of this book begins, however, with an analytic justification of the need for the PsyD degree. Until the Illinois program went into effect, the PhD degree was awarded to graduates of clinical programs, and many educators have maintained that that usage is both honorable and wise. The argument for continued use of the PhD degree to signify completion of doctoral education in professional psychology was most thoughtfully articulated by George Stricker (1975). Stricker noted accurately that the Vail conference, which recommended award of the PsyD degree in practitioner programs and the PhD degree in research programs, did not offer a clear rationale for the recommendation. He cited his own program at Adelphi University and the programs in the California School of Professional Psychology as examples of use of the PhD degree to certify completion of programs clearly designed to prepare psychologists for professional careers. (At the time, the regional accrediting agency that monitors higher education in California still allowed award of the PhD to graduates of doctoral professional programs.) Stricker then noted that nearly all PsyD programs required dissertations or other scholarly projects and argued that if the scholarly work in those projects was of doctoral quality, those who completed the projects deserved the PhD degree. If not, no doctoral degree of any kind should be awarded.

I had not thought of the professional degree as a prize to be won by hardworking scholars. From my view, the question at issue was not one of just desserts but of public certification of professional competence in psychology. The PhD degree, by tradition and official policy a credential that signifies contributory scholarship over all the arts and sciences, could not be used over the long run to certify doctoral-level professional competence in any particular discipline. Professional psychology, I argued, needs its own professional degree (Peterson, 1976a). (The article now appears as chap. 4.)

4

NEED FOR THE DOCTOR OF PSYCHOLOGY DEGREE IN PROFESSIONAL PSYCHOLOGY

Questions about the degree to be employed in certifying doctoral-level competence in professional psychology, and related questions about the nature of professional psychology, have been the subject of many discussions since professional psychology began. From Boulder on, all of the major training conferences have been preoccupied with these issues. Through the Chicago conference (Hoch, Ross, & Winder, 1966), the prevailing definitions were clear and uniform. Professional psychologists were truly scientist–professionals, and the PhD degree was appropriate to certify attainment of the knowledge a scientist–professional ought to have. The most recent conference, at Vail, Colorado, in 1973, endorsed different principles, namely that psychological knowledge was mature enough to warrant creation of explicitly professional programs in addition to programs for training scientists and scientist–professionals and that different degrees be used to designate the professional and scholarly roles. Specifically, the Vail conference resolutions recommended that completion of doctoral-level training in professional programs be designated by award of the Doctor of Psychology (PsyD) degree and that completion of doctoral-level training in programs designed to train scientists or scientist–professionals be designated by award of the Doctor of Philosophy (PhD) degree (Korman, 1974).

In a recent article in this Journal, George Stricker (1975) correctly notes that propositions concerning the maturity of disciplines and the identity of psychologists are distinct from those related to degrees and the certification of professional competence. He also notes correctly that the Vail conference report does not thoroughly justify its recommendation for use of the PsyD degree in professional psychology. For that justification, Stricker refers principally to an early statement of mine (Peterson, 1968b). He then presents a set of counterarguments which lead to the position that professional psychologists are most appropriately viewed as scholar–professionals and that the PhD degree should be employed as a mark of competence in our profession.

In attempting to resolve this controversy, two complexly related issues must be distinguished. The first concerns the definition of professional psychology. Are practicing psychologists most appropriately regarded as scientist–professionals, scholar–professionals, or directly as professional psychologists? The second issue concerns the doctoral credential of professional competence. How shall we certify professional knowledge, privilege, and responsibility in our field? Is the Doctor of Philosophy or the Doctor of Psychology a more fitting degree?

DEFINITION OF PROFESSIONAL PSYCHOLOGY

I have argued elsewhere (Peterson, 1976b) that psychology cannot deliver maximum public benefit and probably cannot survive as a profession unless it is comprehensive in scope. A fully useful professional psychology is that discipline concerned with the assessment and improvement of the psychological functioning of human beings as individuals, in groups, and in social organizations. The theoretical, methodological, and substantive base for professional psychology thus goes far beyond psychoanalysis, operant conditioning, or any other formulation that emphasizes only special aspects of human behavior. The disciplinary basis for modern professional psychology is comprehensive systematic psychology, from biological psychology, through the overt and covert processes of individual psychology, through the interpersonal psychology of small groups, to the structures and processes of social organizations. The parallel range of professional skills includes the assessment and regulation of psychobiological processes, the analysis and change of individual psychological process, the analysis and change of interpersonal relationships in dyads and larger groups, and the appraisal and planned change of social organizations.

Specialization can and will occur in the postdoctoral careers of professional psychologists. Some will become most thoroughly expert in individual behavior modification or psychotherapy. Others will concentrate on the study and improvement of interpersonal behavior in families or work groups. Still others will become specialists in program evaluation and the related tasks of organizational change. But in predoctoral education, comprehensiveness is required. A psychologist who knows only evocative psychotherapy, however eclectic the orientation, or only individual behavior modification, however broad the spectrum of effect, does not qualify as a professional psychologist.

When the term *professional* is joined by a dash to another term, such as *scientist* or *scholar*, further qualifications are implied. Parsimony rules, in diction as in science, and complex designations such as *scientist–professional* or *scholar–professional* must entail some properties beyond those of the simpler term *professional,* or there is no point in using them.

People who insist on calling professional psychologists scientist–professionals or scholar–professionals are not always clear about the surplus meanings of the terms. However, only three major meanings make any sense: (a) The scientific–professional or scholar–professional is an active producer of scholarly knowledge; (b) the scientist–professional or scholar–professional employs a scientific, scholarly approach in dealing with professional problems; (c) the scientist–professional or scholar–professional bases professional applications on disciplined scientific and scholarly knowledge. In arguments supporting scientist–scholar–professional concepts, any or all of these meanings may be intended. For the sake of clarity, they need to be considered one by one.

The Scholar–Professional as Producer of Knowledge

In the original objectives of scientist–professional programs, graduates were clearly expected to be producers as well as appliers of knowledge. As experience showed, however, that objective was not impressively realized. Levy's (1962) general survey as well as the follow-up study of VA clinical psychology trainees by Kelly and Goldberg (1959) both showed the modal number of publications by PhD-bearing "scientist–practitioners" to be zero.

Upon consideration of some other data, the findings are not difficult to understand. The interests of psychologists are not positively correlated, as the scientist–practitioner model requires, but are independent (Thorndike, 1955) or may even be negatively correlated (Peterson & Baron, 1975). The situational demands of most professional settings are not conducive to research. When practitioners who are not really interested in scientific investigation anyway are placed in settings that do not encourage scholarly inquiry, low production should be expected.

When the term *scholar* replaces *scientist*, as suggested by Stricker (1975) and Derner (1975), changes are implied in the nature of the inquiry involved and in the products of inquiry. At least within the historical traditions of psychology, "scientists" are most likely to be doing empirical investigations, ordinarily experimental in design, and the products are most likely to consist of substantive research reports. "Scholarly" inquiry is more liberally conceived. It may include theoretical analyses, methodological innovations, or any other intellectually disciplined enterprise.

In the development of dependable, professionally useful knowledge in psychology, broadly defined scholarly inquiry offers a strong advantage over narrowly defined research. This is so because many issues of vital concern to practitioners do not lend themselves to experimentation but still require the most systematic possible investigation by other means. The resolutions of the Chicago conference emphasized this advantage. Stricker (1975), Derner (1975), and others who urge us to speak of "scholarship" rather than only of "research" echo the same emphasis.

But when the same writers promote the scholar–professional model for the education of professional psychologists, they do not appear to be thinking mainly of professionals as producers of new knowledge. When Derner (1975) argues that "the university should accept professional practice as an appropriate primary training goal and therefore training [*sic*] *scholar–professionals*" (p. 3), he is not promising new theories, techniques, or facts as the main outcome of professional education. Anyone who makes such a promise must be prepared to show that the graduates of scholar–professional programs contribute to scholarly knowledge in significant ways.

Science and Scholarship as Approaches to Professional Problems

The second sensible meaning of the *scientist–scholar–professional* term is that professional psychologists employ the same methods and modes of thought in approaching professional problems as scientists and scholars do in approaching the general issues of the discipline. The pertinence of a scientific approach to professional problems has been appreciated for many years. Fifty years ago, Abraham Flexner (1925) emphasized that both scientific investigators and responsible practitioners had to base their conclusions on careful observation, experimental trial, and intelligent analysis. Both had to "observe, reflect, conclude, try, and watching results, continuously reapply the same method until the problem in hand has been solved or abandoned" (p. 4).

In psychology, the scientific approach to professional problems probably found its most thorough expression in the writings of George Kelly (1955), who made not only every practitioner but every successfully treated client a scientist in spirit. Many others have respected the value of approaching professional tasks in a disciplined, that is to say, "scholarly," way and in using the methods of natural science to the limits of professional benefit. The author of this article, for one, has written a book proposing that the clinical study of social behavior be approached through full exploitation of the observational, elicitative, and experimental methods which psychological science provides (Peterson, 1968a).

Neither the need to deal with professional problems in a scholarly way nor the power of scientific method in dealing with professional problems, however, means that science, scholarship, and practice are all the same. This too has been realized for many years by thoughtful scholars. After insisting that scientific investigator and practitioner alike must approach problems with a firmly disciplined attitude, Flexner (1925) quickly added, this "does not mean that practitioners should all be experimenters or that investigators must all be practitioners" (p. 12). In fact, the attitudes required for scholarly inquiry and professional practice are different in many ways. Some of the most important differences have been discussed by Albee and Loeffler (1971). Basically, say these writers, scientists are "framers of falsifiable sentences." They are free to examine any phenomena that interest them. They state propositions in ways that will allow clear refutation. They must scrupulously avoid Type I errors, which assert relationships falsely, at the expense of relatively frequent Type II errors, which deny relationships actually present in nature. They must maintain attitudes of openness about the methods of inquiry and a guarded skepticism about the correctness of any proposition that appears in the substance of the discipline.

In contrast, professionals are mainly "appliers of knowledge to the solution or relief of human problems." They must focus on matters of importance to their clients. They are not allowed the luxury of attacking only clearly definable questions. They must frequently act on the basis of weakly supported propositions and thus risk Type I errors, because ignoring significant relationships may be as damaging to clients as presuming relationships that do not exist. Sometimes maximum benefit can be obtained by withholding methodological details from clients and from asserting professional action with a confidence that available scientific knowledge does not justify. Open method and cautious conclusion, the foundations of science, can destroy effective professional service.

Disciplined scholarship and some aspects of scientific method are pertinent to professional practice. This pertinence has been thoroughly understood by philosophers of professional education at least since the time of Flexner. But scholarly, scientific, and professional pursuits are not all the same. The differences need to be acknowledged along with the similarities.

Profession as Application of Disciplined Knowledge

The third reasonable meaning of "scholar" or "scientist" in the qualified terms *scholar–professional* or *scientist–professional* is that professional practice must be founded upon scholarly knowledge. This is the distinguishing feature of a profession as against a trade or other vocation. A true professional is not a mechanical purveyor of techniques. Professionals must be skilled in techniques, but the techniques must also be related to a systematic discipline that the professional thoroughly understands. The application of techniques requires responsible intellectual judgment in matching complex methods to the complex needs of the client public. In this sense, a "professional" must be a "scholar" in order to be a professional at all.

Complete definitions of professional function also include some emphasis on the responsibility of professionals for evaluating and improving the quality of professional service. Thus Parsons (1959) conceived a profession to be "a category of occupational role which is organized about the mastery and fiduciary responsibility for any important segment of a society's cultural tradition, including responsibility for its perpetuation *and* for its future development" (p. 547). This is the justification for the projects and reports required in most professional psychology programs. The projects are pertinent to the improvement of professional service. They are not regarded as the dominant form of activity of professional psychologists. They are simply a part of responsible professional work.

Any defensible concept of "profession" already implies the foundation of practice in scholarly knowledge and responsibility for the evaluation and development of professional service. That is true of all professions, not just of psychology. Further qualification, as in the scientist–professional and scholar–professional concepts, is unnecessary.

If the term *scholar–professional* is taken to imply production of new knowledge, it is false. If the term implies an approach to professional problems, it is misleading. If it suggests merely that any profession is based in a scholarly discipline, the term is redundant. There is no need to call professional psychologists anything other than—professional psychologists.

NEED FOR THE DOCTOR OF PSYCHOLOGY DEGREE

If professional psychology is defined comprehensively so that the knowledge base and the range of skill extend from biological psychology through organizational psychology, and if the term of graduate education is limited to 4 or even 5 years, there is no way to train professional psychologists thoroughly except through explicitly professional programs. Prevailing PhD programs do not accomplish the task adequately. They cannot if they are restricted to 4 or 5 years in length and if enough emphasis is placed on training in scholarly inquiry so that graduates are well prepared to contribute valuable knowledge to the discipline. A PhD program can train specialists in one form or another of professional application. Psychotherapists, or experts in individual behavior modification, or neuropsychologists, or community psychologists may emerge from well-designed PhD programs, but the range of professional skill cannot be as broad as a doctoral professional program demands. As professionals, PhD psychologists can attain only a breadth of knowledge and a level of proficiency more appropriately designated by a master's degree. To certify attainment of the more thorough knowledge that can be provided in a doctoral-level professional program, the highest credential of professional competence, the Doctor of Psychology degree, should be employed.

ACCREDITING POLICIES IN HIGHER EDUCATION

For a time in the history of American higher education, responsibility for the development of programs and the granting of degrees was invested almost entirely in the degree-granting agencies themselves. Practically any agency could offer any degree its perpetrators chose. Over the past 20 years, however, state and regional accrediting organizations have developed strong controls over the formation of legally legitimate educational programs and the degrees that can be awarded upon completion of those programs. Most states now have a supra-institutional regulatory agency of some kind, such as a commission or board of higher education, which sanctions the creation of programs and the granting of degrees. At the national level, various councils have been created to define policy, and regional accrediting organizations have been established to perform the evaluations required for adequate quality control in higher education.

Effective regulation, however, still resides mainly at the university and state levels. A legitimate program in professional psychology must ordinarily be approved by the following executive bodies: (a) the unit in which training is conducted, such as a department or a school of psychology; (b) an institution-wide council concerned with graduate programs, such as the executive committee of a graduate school; (c) an institution-wide representative organization of faculty and usually of students, such as a university senate; (d) an agency concerned with the public accountability of the institution, such as a board of governors, regents, or trustees; and (e) a supra-institutional agency concerned with financial distribution and fiduciary control, and hence of general educational policy, such as a board of higher education. In some states, the actual evaluation is delegated to one of the regional accrediting organizations, so the sanction of that agency is also required.

Within such a complex system, standards and practices inevitably vary from one agency to another, but in regard to doctoral-level education in the professions and sciences, a relatively uniform policy prevails. The PhD degreee is employed to credit scholarly accomplishment in all disciplines. Professional competence in any given discipline is certified by a doctoral degree employing the name of the discipline involved, for example, Doctor of Business Administration, Doctor of Medicine, Doctor of Psychology. The following policy statement, issued by the Council of Graduate Schools in the United States (Council of Graduate Schools in the United States, 1969) and endorsed by the Association of Graduate Schools in the Association of American Universities, clearly expresses the principle that governing boards in higher education are enjoined to follow.

> *The Doctor of Philosophy* (PhD) degree, first awarded in the United States in 1861, has become the mark of highest achievement in preparation for creative scholarship and research, often in association with a career in teaching at a university or college. The Doctor of Philosophy shall be open as a research degree in all fields of learning, pure and applied.
>
> *The professional Doctor's* degree should be the highest university award given in a particular field in recognition of completion of academic preparation for professional practice, e.g., the Doctor of Medicine (MD), Doctor of Dental Surgery (DDS), Doctor of Veterinary Medicine (DVM). (p. 2)

Members of regulatory agencies who are not themselves psychologists have difficulty understanding why psychology should be treated differently from any other discipline in this regard. It seems reasonable to believe that professional psychology bears the same relation to the general discipline of psychology as medicine does to the life sciences or engineering does to the physical sciences. In fact, no special case can be made for psychology, and the general rule that distinguishes careers devoted to the development of scholarly knowledge and careers devoted to professional applications of knowledge will not be violated for psychology or any other discipline by most academic executive groups.

There are good reasons for maintaining the distinction. In fact, the public contribution of a creative scholar who formulates a more powerful theory, articulates a more lucid principle, develops a more revealing method, or discovers previously unknown facts of nature is more durable and general, and therefore more valuable, than the contribution of any one professional. The value is set by the calculus of public benefit, not by attitudes of academic chauvinism. It is the element of creative, extended, lasting contribution that is central to the concept of true scholarship, and the public valuation of scholarship needs to be preserved. An attempt to gain that credit by seizing the PhD degree as a label of creative scholarship without making the basic contributions of creative scholarship is accurately regarded by most members of academic governing councils as fraudulent.

Insistence on use of the name of the pertinent discipline in professional doctorates is necessary to reduce public confusion about the meanings of professional degrees. This idea will be extended in the following section, but it must be mentioned here from the viewpoint of those responsible for academic accreditation. It is important for people using professional services to know the difference between doctors who deal with animal diseases and those who deal with human diseases. The DVM amd MD degrees help to clarify this distinction. If the PhD could be employed as a mark of professional competence in any discipline, there would be no way to tell which professions knew what. Different professional degrees must be related to different bodies of knowledge and skill. Academic regulatory agencies entrusted with the power to approve degree programs and degree labels must respect those differences and in fact assume responsible leadership for enforcing the distinctions.

PUBLIC CERTIFICATION OF PROFESSIONAL COMPETENCE

Many forms of professional service are available to the public in today's complex society. Members of each profession must employ a credential that certifies mastery of the knowledge and skill required for effective professional service in the discipline upon which practice is based. Users should be provided with a clear, immediately identifiable label that enables them to tell one professional from another and offers a guarantee of professional competence in the services they choose.

The PhD degree cannot meet any of these purposes, because of its generality as a credential of scholarly accomplishments over all the arts and sciences. A PhD degree, standing alone, may mean that the bearer knows a lot about experimental psychology, or botany, or physics, or medieval French history, or anything else. Most PhD degrees held by practicing professional psychologists today were not awarded in professional psychology. They were awarded in psychology, and hence do not distinguish professionally competent people from psychologists who possess no professional skills whatsoever. Perhaps a quarter century of effort could change the academic credentialing system so that professional competence, say, in clinical psychology was identified by a PhD degree "in clinical psychology." But for reasons given above, a general effort of this kind is not only likely to fail but cannot be justified. If the same doctoral degree were used to designate both professional competence and contributory scholarship over all disciplines, the resulting public confusion would be hopeless.

How much simplier it is to follow the semantics of professional designation already established in our culture and employ the name of the pertinent discipline in certifying professional competence within each field. A Doctor of Medicine is professionally competent in medicine. A Doctor of Psychology is professionally competent in psychology.

Professional degrees are employed not only affirmatively to assure competence but restrictively to prohibit unqualified people from the use of influential, hence potentially dangerous, practices. In due course, a well-established profession of psychology must rid its ranks of all except comprehensively educated, thoroughly trained practitioners. Experimentalists whose professional training is limited to a couple of courses in psychodiagnostics and an internship will have to go. So will the MDs who now infest our mental health systems, offering as psychologically useful knowledge little more than psychoanalytic jargon and psychotropic drugs. These people are literally "practicing psychology without a license." The profession of psychology must be limited to those who comprehend the basic discipline and are skilled in its application.

The PhD degree cannot be employed restrictively by psychologists. Psychology does not own the PhD degree. Psychology does own the Doctor of Psychology degree and can therefore control its use. In principle and in time, we must limit the highest professional responsibilities to those who have earned a certificate of comprehensive professional knowledge in psychology. The responsible use of our own degree will eventually allow us to do so.

Opposition to the Doctor of Psychology degree is based mainly on the premise that it is a second-rate credential. Those who oppose the degree are characteristically vague about the nature of the presumed inferiority, but only a few meanings are plausible. "Ratings" of degrees, first, second, or farther down, are not inherent properties of the degree themselves. They are products of social attribution. One must then ask who is making the evaluation, what qualities the evaluation is based on, and what the consequences of evaluation might be before deciding whether one credential is superior to another.

One important set of evaluations is made by employers, who review the qualifications of prospective employees in appointing people to professional positions. I did not proceed very far in organizing the first PsyD program until I had surveyed the attitudes of employers toward the degree (Peterson, 1969). In that study, I found that employers expressed far greater concern about the knowledge and skills of professional psychologists than they did about degrees. The overwhelming majority of respondents to the initial survey said they would be delighted to hire psychologists with the qualifications our Doctors of Psychology were to gain. Later, the actual job-seeking experience of the first PsyD graduates showed that the degree offered no general handicaps in the professional job market. With some employers, it offered an apparent advantage (Peterson & Baron, 1975).

Other evaluations are made by "the public." Here the characteristics of the evaluators vary enormously, and postulations about the nature and the consequences of the appraisals are based more on presumption than on fact. My main presumptions are that most people employing the services of psychologists want to be sure the psychologists are qualified to do professional work, that they are comforted when they hear they are dealing with "doctors," but that further discriminatory refinements are rarely made. A few known facts (Nunnally & Kittros, 1958) support these views. Certainly, the clients of most public institutions do not know or care much about degrees. They want competent, caring professional service and accept effective help gratefully whenever it appears. Some clients are concerned about the differences between medical doctors and other doctors. Many are confused about the differences between psychiatrists and psychologists. In dealing with those confusions, I have not found it helpful to explain that psychologists hold

Doctor of Philosophy degrees, though most clients are willing to accept the idea of a PhD in clinical psychology as pertinent to professional work with problems in living. Lately, out of curiosity, I have told a few well-educated clients that I have a "doctorate in psychology," in establishing the contractual agreements for our work together. No one yet has questioned the title. Except for the minuscule PhD culture itself, public discriminations among doctoral degrees are very poorly refined. I see no evidence of any general prejudice against the concept or the credential, Doctor of Psychology. If and when the PsyD degree attains general currency as a certificate of professional competence in dealing with psychological problems, appropriate discriminations will be much easier for all concerned.

A third important set of evaluators is made up of psychologists themselves. Here again, facts are few and presumption guides belief. My presumptions are that most academic psychologists value competent professional service but they distinguish between active scholarship and professional application and see the use of a scholarly degree by professional psychologists as dishonest. Many practicing professionals gain security from the PhD degree. But if the security is based on the pretense of contributory scholarship, it is a false security and cannot sustain us. Our security must come substantively from thorough knowledge of professional psychology and symbolically from a title that guarantees essential knowledge.

If professional psychology is defined comprehensively, if it is based in the disciplined knowledge of psychology, if useful skills are taught and the highest standards of excellence maintained in the training of professional psychologists, there is nothing inferior about it. The Doctor of Psychology degree is the one credential that can certify attainment of that knowledge and skill with the force and clarity needed to establish psychology as a profession. We are a profession. We need our own degree to say so.

5

THE DOCTOR OF PSYCHOLOGY DEGREE

The first formal proposal for a professional program leading to the Doctor of Psychology degree was made by Loyal Crane in 1925.[1] In an article titled "A Plea for the Training of Psychologists" (Crane, 1925) Crane expressed his concern about confusions in the training of clinical psychologists. Scientific education and the PhD credential were inappropriate for practicing clinicians. People receiving professional services were not clear about the differ-

From D. K. Freedheim (Ed.), *History of Psychotherapy: A Century of Change*, pp. 829–849. Washington, DC: American Psychological Association.

Some of the material in this chapter appeared originally under the title "Origins and Development of the Doctor of Psychology Concept" in *Educating Professional Psychologists* (pp. 19–38), edited by G. R. Caddy, D. C. Rimm, N. Watson, & J. H. Johnson, 1982, New Brunswick, NJ: Transaction Books.

[1]Despite my own efforts and those of the historians and archivists whose help I have sought, I have been unable to find out where Crane was working when he wrote the article, where he received his doctoral education, or anything else about him. He is identified in the heading of the article only as "Loyal Crane, PhD." Authors affiliated with universities who submitted manuscripts to the *Journal of Abnormal and Social Psychology* in those days seemed always to identify the institutions that employed them, and in his article, Crane discusses requirements in the New York Mental Deficiency Law for recognition as a "qualified examiner of mental defect." It seems safe to assume that he was working in one of the "insane asylums" or institutions for the "feeble-minded" in New York state at the time.

ences between psychiatrists and psychologists. They were either unsure or incorrect in guessing what psychologists were supposed to do. Relations with the medical profession were ill-defined, and when definitions became established, they were usually detrimental to psychologists. According to Crane however, the main problems arose not from public misperception but from the profession of psychology itself. The designation *psychologist* lacked social and legal specificity. Anyone who chose to use the title could do so. The PhD was no guarantee of professional competence "for the simple reason that the degree may be obtained as well by the student of chemistry, mathematics or history as by the student of psychology" (Crane, 1925, p. 228). Because psychology had failed to come to grips with the responsibilities of professional training, the limited prestige psychologists gained from members of related professions and the general public was sadly justified.

Why not, said Dr. Crane, put truly "relevant" substance into the training of professional psychologists and use a professional degree to certify completion of that training? He proposed a 4-year graduate curriculum with heavy emphasis on psychology and those aspects of medicine most clearly pertinent to the study and treatment of psychological problems. He suggested that the Doctor of Psychology degree be awarded upon completion of the program. Would not this help bring professional psychology the recognition it deserved? Would not this help clarify the relationship between professional psychology and medicine? Would not the public, ill-used by psychology in the past, but now treated by fully competent professional psychologists, benefit gratefully from the improved services Doctors of Psychology would bring them?

Crane's plea scarcely brought a ripple to the stream of professional activity as it was flowing at the time. Soon after Crane made his statement, A. E. Davies (1926) published a comment on the uncertain state of knowledge in early twentieth-century psychology and stressed the difficulties such limitations entailed for professional applications of psychology. Inevitably, he suggested that a committee be formed to study the various issues involved, and in due time a committee was appointed. The group was made up of Andrew Brown, Robert Brotemarkle, Clara Town, and Maud Merrill, with Brown as chairman. Their efforts constituted the first systematic consideration of the issues involved in education for the practice of psychology by an officially designated organization (Reisman, 1966).

A survey of self-defined "clinical psychologists" working in various professional settings at the time showed that there was little agreement either about the nature of the field or the kinds of preparation that psychologists should have for professional work. In their recommendations, the Brown Committee suggested that clinical psychology be conceived as "that art and technology which deals with the adjustment problems of human beings" and that training be based on a comprehensive knowledge of psychological science extending on the one side to the biophysical bases of human disorder and on the other to the knowledge of sociology and social psychology required for a grasp of family and community life. At least 1 year of supervised practical experience was to be required, and completion of formal training was to be certified by award of the PhD "or equivalent degree in psychology from an accredited university" (APA, 1935).

However contemporary and reasonable these recommendations may seem today, nothing much came of them at the time they were made. Clinical psychology had not yet established the knowledge or developed the technology to qualify as an independent profession. In most of its applications, it was functionally ancillary and administratively subordinate to medicine. In the politics of professional power, clinical psychology did not have the force to be regarded even as a significant upstart by well established medical professionals. Fernberger's analysis of American Psychological Association (APA) composition in 1928 showed that only 104 doctorally accredited members were engaged in primarily clinical work. The medical authorities in control of mental health services were careful to see that the professional activities of psychologists were restricted to diagnostic testing, under medical supervision. "With occasional noteworthy exceptions," Crane had written, "the attitude of the medical profession toward the practicing psychologist is one of tolerant condescension, courteous withal yet ever watchful lest, during an unguarded moment, some remunerative executive post, which should 'properly be filled by an M.D.', pass into the control of a psychologist" (Crane, 1925, p. 228).

Even at that early time, a few ideological leaders recognized that medicine was not a suitable base for a profession dealing with human psychological problems. Sigmund Freud (1927) had argued at length that psychology, not medicine, was the basic discipline on which the practice of psychoanalysis should rest. Even earlier, in 1923, Karl Menninger had expressed his belief that medicine was an insufficiently comprehensive foundation for dealing with the full range of human problems. He realized that preventive efforts as well as remedies were needed, and that the intellectual discipline at the base of professional work would have to include psychological and social substance as well as biological content. He proposed the term *orthopsychics* to designate the field (Reisman, 1966).

Neither Freud's argument nor Menninger's was heeded by the politically dominant medical practitioners of the day. Most psychoanalysts came into the profession by way of medicine and managed to define all practitioners who did not possess medical credentials as "laymen." Even Freud failed to grasp the significance of this semantic condition. He presented his arguments concerning the psychological basis for psychoanalytic practice under the self-defeating title, "The Problem of Lay Analysis." Medical men in charge of the rapidly forming psychoanalytic societies were firmly opposed to Freud's views, and medical training soon became established as a requirement for the fully qualified practice of psychoanalysis. Karl Menninger's proposals were molded to fit medical definitions by the society he organized to deal with human problems. The first group became known as the American Orthopsychiatric Association, rather than an orthopsychic or orthopsychological association. Active membership was required to hold office, and although members of all human service disciplines were invited to participate in the organization, active membership was restricted to Doctors of Medicine.

At the time Crane, Freud, and Menninger presented their proposals, professional psychology was small in size, indefinite in function, uncertain as to usefulness, and unclear about its own identity. Then and for the two decades to follow, the discipline was too weak to be taken seriously as a profession.

THE BOULDER CONFERENCE: SCIENCE ABOVE ALL

The first strong definition of clinical psychology came with statement of the scientist–practitioner concept by the Shakow Committee (APA, 1947). Clinical psychologists were to be trained for research *and* practice. They were to be psychologists (read "scientists") first, and pratitioners second. The concept was ratified and elaborated in the Boulder conference (Raimy, 1950), whose impact is considered thoroughly in previous histories (e.g., Reisman, 1966; Watson, 1953) and does not need a detailed discussion here. For this account, it is enough to note that the Boulder conference accomplished most of the aims it was designed to meet. The profession of clinical psychology was more securely established than it had been before, and the research needed for improving professional service was encouraged. During a period when the technical stock of clinical psychology consisted almost entirely of test-based diagnoses and evocative psychotherapies whose weaknesses were even then beginning to show, emphasis on research and development was sorely needed. Even more clearly, identification with science carried an important political advantage. In moments of candor, both psychiatrist and psychologist might admit their doubts about the benefits they could offer their clients. But now, when the psychiatrist said, "At least I know medicine," the psychologist could reply, "Well, I know science" and feel as secure as the physician. Psychologists might lose power skirmishes now and then, but their identity was established, and assurance as scientists, if not as professionals, could not easily be shaken.

The Boulder model served its purpose, but it also had its limitations as the only pattern for training clinical psychologists. Within a decade, flaws in the concept of a science–profession began to show. One problem with the scientist–practitioner programs was that they offered a poor match with student interests. Contary to the assumptions of the Shakow Committee and the Boulder conference, few students entered clinical training with strong interests in both research and service. As Thorndike (1955) suggested and later research (Peterson & Knudson, 1979) confirmed, clinical psychologists tended to be interested *either* in research *or* in practice (more commonly in the latter). A single hybrid program, requiring devotion to productive scholarship as well as human service, was ill-suited to their needs. Students interested in practice had to conceal their intentions to gain admission to research-oriented graduate programs. Once admitted, they either had to maintain the pretense, reveal their aims and incur the disfavor of their professors, or withdraw from training altogether.

An even more fundamental problem was that clinical programs in academic psychology departments came to emphasize research much more strongly than practice and offered poor preparation for the careers of professional service toward which many graduates were headed. In 1962, a turning point was reached in American psychology. For the first time, psychologists in academia were outnumbered by those in nonacademic positions (Tryon, 1963). At the APA convention in Los Angeles in 1964, impassioned practitioners seized microphones to shout that they had been betrayed by their professors. They had not been given the training they needed to meet the demands of professional life. For all the praise of science students heard in graduate school, relatively few did any research once they became immersed in practice. In two surveys (Kelly & Goldberg, 1959; Levy, 1962), the modal number of publications of clinical psychologists was shown to be zero. The scientist–practitioner model was designed to meet the dual purposes of scientific inquiry and professional service. In trying to reach both aims, it evidently accomplished neither. As scientists, the Boulder-style PhDs were unproductive. As professionals, they were incompetent.

THE CHICAGO CONFERENCE: TIMID EXPERIMENTATION

These conditions did not go unnoticed in organized psychology. In 1963, the APA formed a committee on the scientific and professional aims of psychology with Kenneth E. Clark as chair and a distinguished membership that included Jerome Bruner, Lloyd Humphreys, Paul Meehl, Carl Rogers, and Kenneth Spence, among others. The committee met every 6 weeks over the academic year 1963–1964 and examined the issues of scientific and professional education in a searching way. With near unanimity, the committee concluded that the PhD programs then in effect for educating scientist–practitioners were neither preparing scientists for contributory research nor professionals for effective practice. They recommended creation of a two-track educational system. Students interested predominately in research would be prepared to do research and receive the PhD degree. Students interested in combining careers of research and practice would complete both courses of study and receive both degrees (APA, 1967).

The Clark Committee report was widely discussed in psychology departments and at state-level training conferences around the country, but the recommendation to develop professional doctoral programs was not generally well received. Psychologists in the state of Washington considered the issues of professional training at some length, but all they finally proposed were some master's-level programs in applied psychology, and even these failed to materialize in the years to follow. A training conference in Ann Arbor, Michigan, denounced the Doctor of Psychology concept and reaffirmed the scientist–professional model. Only two departments appeared to give the Clark Committee proposal the kind of consideration that might lead to the actual formation of professional doctoral programs. In Stillwater, Minnesota, Paul Meehl presented the main arguments for explicit professional training before a conference of psychologists working in academic and professional positions in that state. Meehl later said the conference participants seemed to agree with most of his proposals, but when a vote was called on the actual development of a Doctor of Psychology program in Minnesota, the proposal failed.

At the University of Illinois, Lloyd Humphreys brought the preliminary report of the Clark Committee before the psychology department faculty and proposed that Illinois undertake the formation of a Doctor of Psychology program. A formal debate was conducted on the issue, and at the end of the debate, a standing vote was taken among the 40 faculty members who attended the meeting. A more precise split of opinion could not have occurred. Ten people voted for the proposal, 10 voted against it, and 20 were undecided. This took place in June 1965, a summer away from the Chicago conference, where the issues of direct professional training were to receive more thorough examination than they had in previous national conferences.

The general outcomes of the Chicago conference are on record (e.g., Hoch et al., 1966) and are discussed elsewhere in this volume. On the issue of outright professional training, ambivalence prevailed. As a majority opinion, the concept of the PhD-bearing scientist–professional stood supreme. A need to experiment with other patterns of training, however, was also generally appreciated, and the members of the conference were willing to wait and see what experimental efforts like the proposed Doctor of Psychology program at Illinois would come to. At the final vote, 12% gave "full endorsement" to the training alternative offered by a professional degree program. A larger group, 31%, offered "active encouragement" to such a development. The majority, however, 57%, were merely willing to extend "recognition" to the idea that explicit professional training programs might be attempted in some university departments, and that the results of those efforts should provide a basis for evaluating the programs at a later time.

I was seated next to Israel Goldiamond at the final plenary session. As the debate wore on into the early morning hours, Goldiamond became more and more amused at the blend of presumption and timidity our colleagues were showing, and he began to write his own resolutions. On the proposal for separate schools of psychology, rather than mere departments, he wrote, "We urge APA to consider a series of universities of psychology, within which the various specialties will be separate colleges, the subspecialties divisions, and the faculty members departments. Thus we would have a Department of Matarazzo in the Division of Interview Analysis in the College of Clinical Psychology in the University of Psychology." On the issue of levels of training, Goldiamond wrote, "We firmly resolve to look at a Bachelor of Psychology program. We observe a Master of Psychology program, provided it is not called a Master of Clinical Psychology program. We note a Doctor of Psychology program."

However pusillanimous the resolutions of the Chicage conference seemed to some of us at the time, they at least allowed experimentation with the educational process and offered a willingness to let the results of responsibly conducted training experiments speak for themselves. After further debate in the autumn of 1965, another vote was taken at the University of Illinois to determine whether or not to establish a practitioner program there. This time, results were decisive. Full-time faculty voted 3.5 to 1 to go ahead with the program. Three more years were required to plan the curriculum, develop the admission procedures, gain the approvals, secure the supports, and recruit the faculty needed to operate the program. In September 1968, the first class of students began graduate study (Peterson, 1968b). Although other doctoral practitioner programs had been attempted before—at the University of Ottawa in the 1940s and at McGill University in the 1950s—and although the PsyD program at the University of Illinois has since been discontinued, the Illinois program carried the force of a respected faculty in a prestigious university, a rigorous curriculum, and an appearance of solidity that paved the way for other programs to follow.

In efforts to gain APA accreditation, early classes were disadvantaged by the policy that denies eligibility to programs that have not yet produced graduates. On grounds of institutional strength and stability, we proposed that a new category, " provisional approval," be created to accommodate programs that met the structural conditions for accreditation but were too new to offer performance records of graduates. The category was established in 1971. In 1972, the Illinois program became the first to be approved under the new designation we had helped create. Related problems were encountered with the U.S. Civil Service Commission, where requirements for clinical psychologists in the highest grades specified attainment of the PhD degree. With support from top-level administrators in the Veterans Administration (VA), the Civil Service requirements were rewritten in ways that accommodated our graduates. Because most state licensure and certification laws already allowed acceptance of other doctoral degrees than the PhD, such as the EdD, they did not appear to present problems of discriminatory exclusion, though they clearly presented problems of permissive overinclusion. Most of the laws permitted people with very questionable training in professional psychology to obtain the legal credentials needed to keep their jobs. For the time being, few changes were needed to assure the employability of our graduates, but we earnestly hoped that the movement we were starting would encourage more stringent licensure legislation in the future.

During the next few years, discussions about practitioner programs took place in many universities. Serious proposals were advanced in several, including New York University, the University of Minnesota, and Harvard, where the EdD rather than the PsyD degree would have certified completion of a program in clinical psychology and public practice, had the program gone into lasting effect. For various local reasons, proposals for practitioner programs failed in all of the major research universities. During the 5 years following establishment of the Illinois program, only the Hahnemann Medical School and Baylor University developed PsyD programs.

THE VAIL CONFERENCE: OPENING THE DOOR

Dissatisfaction with professional training as conducted in traditional PhD programs continued to deepen, however, and insistence on change was expressed in many ways. At the time, the PsyD program at Illinois appeared vigorous and successful. The California School of Professional Psychology (CSPP) had grown in size and significance. Actions to develop professional schools in other states were well advanced. Important changes had occurred within and beyond psychology. Clinical psychology was a different discipline from that conceived at the Boulder conference. School psychology was assuming a more definite form and higher stature than before. Early methods of assessment, treatment, and reeducation had been found wanting, and the assumptions underlying those methods had been questioned. A more mature professional psychology, yielding a few demonstrably effective methods and promising others, had taken shape. In the world beyond graduate school, the job market had changed. Psychologists with PhDs could no longer be sure of university positions and research opportunities upon graduation. At the same time, the public need for psychological services continued to grow. Mental hospitals were still being staffed by psychiatrically unschooled physicians and inadequately trained psychologists. The need for competent professional psychologists was as great as ever, and forecasts of our social future acknowledged a continuing need for effective applications of psychology. Programs that offered clear and obvious public benefits received more support than at any time since the early days of the land grant agricultural and technical schools. Psychology, higher education, and the general public all seemed ready for the development of expressly professional training programs.

These conditions culminated in another national training conference, at Vail, Colorado, in 1973. Again, the complete report of the conference is on record (Korman, 1976). For professional training in general and the Doctor of

Psychology concept in particular, two resolutions were particularly important. First, "The development of psychological science has sufficiently matured to justify creation of explicit professional programs, in addition to programs for training scientists and scientist–professionals." Second, "We recommend that completion of doctoral level training in explicitly professional programs be designated by award of the Doctor of Psychology degree and that completion of doctoral level training in programs designed to train scientists or scientist–professionals be designated by award of the Doctor of Philosophy degree. . . . Where primary emphasis in training and function is upon direct delivery of professional services and the evaluation and improvement of those services, the Doctor of Psychology degree is appropriate. Where primary emphasis is upon the development of new knowledge in psychology, the PhD degree is appropriate" (Korman, 1974, p. 443).

In the year following the Vail conference, activities leading to establishment of the Graduate School of Applied and Professional Psychology at Rutgers University took place in rapid order. For years, an organizing council had been working to develop a school of professional psychology in New Jersey. The group consisted mainly of private practitioners in the state, with help from private citizens who possessed both personal interests in the education of professional psychologists and financial means to help the school get under way. Supportive relationships with legislators in the state were also formed. The original hope of the organizing council was to establish a freestanding school in the California pattern. The New Jersey Commission of Higher Education, however, had different rules from those in California. The leaders of the council were told that a degree-granting charter would be awarded only if enough capital were amassed to qualify the school as a private college, an amount far in excess of any sum the council seemed able to realize. From the council's side, the search began for a receptive university host. From the side of higher education, proposals to develop a school of professional psychology were put forward by the College of Medicine and Dentistry and by Rutgers, the State University of New Jersey. After a round of reviews and hearings, responsibility for establishing the school was assigned to Rutgers.

When the Graduate School of Applied and Professional Psychology admitted its first class of students in September 1974, it became the first university-based school of professional psychology to grant the Doctor of Psychology degree. Two PsyD programs were created, one in school psychology and the other in clinical psychology. The PhD program in clinical psychology already in operation at Rutgers was continued. However, its purpose, to educate people for research in applied psychology, was more clearly defined than before.

The Vail conference also recognized "the variety of new organizational settings within which professional training programs have begun to develop: e.g., medical schools; departments, schools and colleges of education; freestanding schools of professional psychology; autonomous professional schools in academic settings—in addition to departments of psychology in universities" (Korman, 1974, p. 443). This endorsement encouraged the establishment of professional schools, both inside and outside of universities, as well as Doctor of Psychology programs. The two developments were closely related, but not isomorphic. The founders of the California School of Professional Psychology (CSPP) thought they had enough resistance to overcome in establishing the first freestanding professional school of psychology without taking on the additional challenge of a new, controversial degree. They invoked the precedent and rationale of the Adelphi program in persuading educational authorities in California that the PhD degree was the appropriate credential for "scholar–professionals" in psychology. Other professional schools in California followed suit. In states other than California, however, and especially in university-based programs wherever they were located, the joint policy of the Association of American Universities and the Council of Graduate Schools in the United States held sway. This policy is firm in stipulating that the professional doctor's degree be awarded in recognition of academic preparation for professional practice, whereas the Doctor of Philosophy degree be awarded in recognition of preparation for research, whether pure or applied. The MD, DDS, DVM, EdD, and DBA are cited as examples of professional degrees in the policy document.

The years following the Vail conference saw rapid development of Doctor of Psychology programs, as shown in Table 5.1. The growth curve based on data in the table accelerates around 1974–1976 and shows an approximately linear increase from then on. Most of the recent additions, however, are not entirely new programs or professional schools. Rather, they are satellite campuses of previously established freestanding schools (e.g., the Minnesota School and the Missouri campus of the Forest Institute) or conversions to the PsyD of practitioner programs that had previously awarded the PhD degree. Partly because of growing acceptance of the PsyD and partly in response to pressure from their regional accrediting associations, several professional schools in California revised their programs in a two-track form, preserving relatively small PhD programs devoted primarily to education for applied research, and awarding the PsyD degree to the larger numbers of students enrolled in programs designed unambiguously as preparation for practice. This is the model originally proposed by the Clark Committee, implemented in the Illinois PsyD program, and kept in force in the Rutgers school, as well as the schools at Nova, Yeshiva, and Denver Universities. The Rosemead Graduate School, now affiliated with Biola University, was the first school in California to adopt the two-track pattern. More recently, the Fuller Graduate School, followed by the Los Angeles campus of the California School, and in 1991, the other three campuses of CSPP, at Berkeley-Alameda, Fresno, and San Diego, began to offer the PsyD to students preparing for professional careers, while maintaining PhD programs for students intending to pursue research careers.

TABLE 5.1
Establishment of Doctor of Psychology Programs From 1968 to 1991

Year	Institution
1968	University of Illinois (discontinued in 1980)
1970	Hahnemann Medical School (program now located at Widener University)
1971	Baylor University
1974	Fielding Institute
	Rutgers University
1975	Rosemead Graduate School (now affiliated with Biola University)
1976	Denver University
	Illinois School of Professional Psychology
	United States International University
1977	Central Michigan University
	Massachusetts School of Professional Psychology
	Wright State University
1978	Nova University
	Virginia Consortium in Professional Psychology
1979	Chicago School of Professional Psychology
	Forest Institute
	Pace University
	Oregon School of Professional Psychology
1980	American Institute of Psychotherapy (now affiliated with Forest Institute)
	Florida Institute of Technology
	New York University
	Wisconsin School of Professional Psychology
	Yeshiva University
1981	Hawaii School of Professional Psychology (now affiliated with Forest Institute)
	Indiana State University
1982	Antioch New England Graduate School
	George Mason University (converted to PhD in 1990)
	Spalding University
1984	Indiana University of Pennsylvania
	Hartford University
1985	Forest Institute, Missouri campus
1986	Pepperdine University
1987	Alfred Adler Institute
	Minnesota School of Professional Psychology (affiliated with the Illinois School in the American Schools of Professional Psychology)
1988	California School of Professional Psychology (CSPP) at Los Angeles (conversion of PhD practitioner program to PsyD)
1991	Georgia School of Professional Psychology (affiliated with the American Schools of Professional Psychology)
	CSPP at Berkeley-Alameda (conversion from PhD to PsyD)
	CSPP at Fresno (conversion from PhD to PsyD)
	CSPP at San Diego (conversion from PhD to PsyD)

SUCCESSES AND FAILURES: REFLECTIONS ON THE FIRST 25 YEARS

Each of the programs listed in Table 5.1 has a history of its own. The particular confluences of time, place, and person that led each effort on its course cannot be described fully in the space remaining. Attempted here is brief comment about some of the more conspicuous developments in the PsyD story, and a few tentative generalizations that the experiences of the first quarter century appear to justify.

The PsyD program at the University of Illinois was terminated in 1980. The most important conditions that led to this outcome were that the values of direct professional service, especially individual psychotherapy, were never deeply held nor widely shared by the faculty and administrators of the Illinois Psychology Department, and the administrative location of the program, in an academic department of a graduate college of a major research university, did not offer the autonomy and clarity of mission that a thoroughgoing professional program requires. A dissertation requirement was imposed by the Graduate College, and in time the requirement got out of hand. As the experimentalists, mathematical statisticians, biopsychologists, and clinical behaviorists who brought renown to the Illinois Psychology Department scrutinized PsyD dissertations, they seemed unable or unwilling to modify criteria to suit the projects that students in the practitioner program undertook. These were frequently ambitious field experiments of high complexity. The combination of problem difficulty and demand for scientific rigor led students into projects that took 2 and 3 years to complete. By the time the program was ended, the median time required to obtain the PsyD was 7.4 years.

After all this investment by faculty and students alike, substantial numbers of graduates went into private practice, devoting much of their time and energy to individual psychotherapy; an activity that few if any of the Illinois faculty approved. I paraphrase comments by the director of clinical training in charge when the PsyD program was discontinued: "No matter what we told applicants, no matter how carefully we described the preventive, community-oriented, behavioral emphasis in our program, students came in dreaming about professional lives as private practitioners of psychotherapy. Then they graduated and went out and did it. That was never what our program was designed to do."

The demise of the Illinois PsyD program is sometimes taken to mean that practitioner programs cannot survive in major research universities. The inaccuracy of this projection is shown by the evident prosperity of the programs at Rutgers and Yeshiva, both Class I research universities. The success of the Rutgers and Yeshiva programs seems due in large part to their location in relatively autonomous professional schools rather than academic departments. The PsyD program in school psychology at New York University (NYU), another major research university, also appears to be vigorous and durable, although many years of effort were required and many obstacles had to be overcome before Gilbert Trachtman and his colleagues managed to establish it. Attempts to develop a PsyD program in clinical psychology at NYU offer a demonstration on the other side, that is of the opposition to practitioner programs that is typical of research-oriented departments and typically defeats them.

Ideological conflict over the PsyD degree was intense in New York state. In a movement parallel with that of the council working to establish a school of professional psychology in New Jersey, a task force made up largely of practitioners from the New York State Psychological Association labored for nearly 5 years to create a freestanding professional school that would award the PsyD degree in New York. Their efforts were opposed by another faction, with objection to the practitioner degree led most conspicuously by Gordon Derner. Derner was an aggressive advocate of the scholar–practitioner model of education but a bitter opponent of the PsyD degree. Use of the degree, he believed, would damage the prestige of the profession.

The same division of opinion was represented among members of the New York Board of Regents, whose approval would be required for any new degree programs. A formal proposal for a PsyD program at Pace University, however, along with the activity at NYU and movement toward a graduate school of psychology that would grant the PsyD degree at Yeshiva University finally broke the deadlock. With support from the Secretary of the Board, the Regents approved the degree in March 1979. The program at Pace University was the first to be approved under the new ruling, followed shortly by the school psychology program at NYU and the Ferkauf Graduate School of Psychology at Yeshiva University.

Controversy over the degree has also been heated in other university settings. In New Hampshire, administrators and faculty seeking to establish the Antioch New England Graduate School of Psychology initially proposed award of the PhD degree, with strong encouragement from Gordon Derner, who was a member of their advisory board. Site visitors reporting to the New Hampshire Commission on Higher Education, however, made clear that the facilities, faculty, and intent of the Antioch program did not justify award of the PhD, although the necessary requirements for a professional program leading to the PsyD degree appeared to be met. Under these conditions, the Antioch team decided to "keep the ship and change the flag." Favorable recommendation by the New Hampshire Commission followed shortly thereafter.

A proposed program at George Mason University in Virginia bore most of the earmarks of a PhD scientist–practitioner program. Approval as a PhD program was denied, however, ostensibly on grounds that enough PhD programs were already operating in Virginia. In the face of apparently unbeatable opposition from educators at other Virginia universities, Alan Boneau and the George Mason faculty settled for approval of a program with clinical, industrial/organizational, and applied experimental components leading to the PsyD degree. After nearly 10 years of operation under that title, permission to award the PhD degree was granted by the State Council on Higher Education in Virginia.

The most successful university-based PsyD programs appear to be those that are organized within relatively autonomous academic units with a clear professional mission, as in the professional schools of Rutgers, Yeshiva, Wright State, and Denver Universities, or as departmental programs in regional or private universities where the emphasis on public service is strong and the demand for research production is not as consuming as it is in many of the major research universities. The program at Baylor has functioned quietly and effectively ever since its inauguration in 1971. The Virginia Consortium, Pace University, and Indiana State University, among others, all appear to be maintaining healthy PsyD programs.

In gauging prospects for success of a practitioner program, the importance of the institutional setting in which the program is located and of the value attributed to the practice of psychology in the surrounding community cannot be overemphasized. The histories of the program at Wright State University and of the program that was developed and maintained for years at the Hahnemann Medical School but was recently moved to Widener University offer vivid illustrations.

An account by the founder of the professional school at Wright State University, Ronald Fox (1986), reveals sharply the importance of cultivating political and community support in ventures of this kind. At the time Fox returned from the Vail conference, resolved to establish a professional school that would award the PsyD degree in Ohio, he was on the faculty of the Psychology Department at Ohio State University, and his first efforts were directed toward developing a professional school in his own institution. The actions that he took, however, were not confined to academia. His first step was to suggest to the president of the Ohio Psychological Association (OPA) the establishment of a committee, with Fox as chair, to study the desirability and feasibility of establishing a school in Ohio.

The OPA committee was duly established, incorporated as a separate nonprofit academy for education and research in professional psychology, in affiliative partnership with the OPA but not subject to supervision by the OPA Board of Trustees. They met with leaders of the Ohio General Assembly to secure advice on the cultivation of legislative support for the establishment of a professional school and secured the allegiance of the legislators as participants in creation of the school. The Academy found a welcome at Wright State University, the newest state university and one that did not have any other doctoral programs in operation. Not only persuaded by the soundness of the proposal, but almost surely motivated to attain the status of "doctoral degree-granting institution" within the higher education community, the Wright State administration offered the academy a home. Representatives from several universities and a number of psychology departments opposed creation of the program, but their efforts, according to Fox, were "poorly conceived and naively implemented." By ignoring state association affairs, leaders of existing university programs had lost touch with practitioners. By remaining aloof from the political arena, they had failed to earn the support of legislators.

When the University of Illinois closed its doors to PsyD applicants in 1980, the program at the Hahnemann Medical School became the oldest PsyD program in the country. It was organized as a Division of Psychology in the Department of Psychiatry. Relationships with the dean of the Medical School were cordial, and relationships with the chairman of the Department of Psychiatry were unusually close. The chairman of Psychiatry had worked with Jules Abrams, director of the Division of Psychology, to create the PsyD program, and held a sense of involvement and pride in it. He was later replaced by another chairman, Israel Zwerling, who had not only trained in psychiatry but had a doctoral degree in psychology. Zwerling and Abrams were instrumental in proposing a change in the name of the department from Psychiatry to Mental Health Sciences. The respect and support accorded to the administration, faculty, and students in the PsyD program in those years encouraged the development of a strong program that attracted several hundred applicants per year and became the second PsyD program to gain accreditation by the APA.

These conditions began to change dramatically when the program was about 17 years old. At that time, a new dean of the Medical School was appointed and was at the same time appointed senior vice president for academic affairs of Hahnemann University (no longer Medical School). Shortly thereafter, a new chairman of the department of psychiatry (as he consistently referred to the Department of Mental Health Sciences) was hired. In keeping with general trends in medicine and psychiatry, the mission of the university had changed. Education of nonmedical professionals was clearly subordinated to research, especially in the neurosciences and biological substrates of "psychiatric diseases." The autonomy that the PsyD program once enjoyed eroded quickly. On more than one occasion, the chairman of the psychiatry department attempted to change the PsyD curriculum. He made clear to the director of the Division of Psychology that he regarded clinical psychology as subordinate to psychiatry. These conditions struck a mortal blow to the morale of Abrams, his faculty colleagues, and students. They also threatened APA accreditation and the future of the program.

An effort was made to reorganize the division as an autonomous department in the Graduate School of Hahnemann University. The dean of the graduate school supported the move, but the chairman of the psychiatry department would not hear of it. The psychiatry chair was supported in this decision by the senior vice president for academic affairs, and the issue was closed.

Quietly, the search began for another aegis. Over the years, other universities in the Philadelphia area had approached the faculty and administration of the PsyD program, and contact was soon established with Widener University through the president of a third institution. Widener University, accredited by the Middle State Association of Schools and Colleges, was and is a rapidly growing institution whose major graduate educational mission is the training of practitioners in a variety of fields including law, education, nursing, health care management, and engineering. The general mission of the university was and is clearly consonant with that of the PsyD program. Negotiations to provide faculty appointments, physical space, additional library facilities, curriculum approvals, and other requirements were concluded rapidly but carefully, and in June 1989, the Hahnemann program moved en masse to Widener University as the Institute for Graduate Clinical Psychology, with its director an associate dean reporting directly to the dean of the Graduate School of Arts and Sciences.

Medical schools elsewhere have also offered fickle support for the education of professional psychologists. For years, clinical psychology and psychiatry worked together harmoniously at the University of Minnesota. A separate division of clinical psychology, within the psychiatry department but with all the autonomy psychologists required, was established there by Starke Hathaway. Hathaway and J. Charnley McKinley, chairman of the department of psychiatry, were co-authors of the original Minnesota Multiphasic Personality Inventory (MMPI). For a time, Hathaway was acting chairman of the psychiatry department. Over the years, however, equity in the relationship between psychiatry and psychology was seen to depend on the attitudes of medical administrators. In the 1970s, a proposal to develop a PsyD program in health psychology in the University of Minnesota medical school was squelched by a medical administration that some Minnesota psychologists have described as hostile, although ambivalent support from the academic psychology faculty also played a part in shelving the plan.

Besides academic departments and university-based professional schools, the main institutional settings for PsyD programs are freestanding professional schools. In every case, establishing these has been a demanding enterprise. As founders of independent professional schools, the organizers have faced formidable challenges in providing required resources. The physical plant, the library, the computer facilities, the faculty, and staff that are financed mainly by tax and endowment funds in universities are funded largely, in some cases almost entirely, by student tuition. This has meant either that tuition rates have been set at very high levels, or the quality of education has been so limited that regional and professional accreditation were difficult to attain.

Freestanding professional schools that award the PsyD degree are in double jeopardy, not only from economic constraints but also from the uncertainties that many still perceive in the PsyD degree. Despite these obstacles, 17 independent professional schools now award the PsyD degree in 10 different states. In many of the program plans, the PsyD was deliberately chosen as the preferred degree. In others, the practitioner degree was forced on the schools by state authorities who would only approve degree-granting privilege on condition that the PsyD rather than the PhD be awarded. The recent shift to the PsyD among professional schools in California appears to have been motivated at least as strongly by pressure from their regional accrediting agency, the Western Association of Schools and Colleges, as by conviction that a coherent professional program and a professional degree are appropriate for practitioners.

Practitioners in state psychological associations have usually provided the moving force for creation of the schools. Formation of new schools, as in Massachusetts and Oregon, as well as incursions from one state to another, as in extension of the Illinois School to Minnesota and of the Forest Institute to Missouri, have typically followed invitations from practicing psychologists in states whose universities have previously restricted doctoral education in psychology to their own small research-oriented programs. In nearly every case, the proposals to develop PsyD programs in independent schools have been opposed by university psychologists, usually on grounds that the university programs are already meeting the need for professional psychologists and often on grounds that preparation for the Doctor of Psychology degree is "unscholarly." Unlike academic psychologists, however, legislators and members of the general public on the executive boards of sanctioning agencies have found no difficulty in distinguishing between research production and scholarly education. They have recognized needs for competent practitioners in their communities, they have seen how poorly academic research programs meet those needs, and they have appreciated the public honesty of awarding a professional degree to practitioners of psychology.

Most of the programs they have approved, both inside and outside of universities, appear to be firmly established. Concerns about quality continue (Peterson, 1985, 1991) but are receiving more systematic and sustained attention through the conferences and related activities of the National Council of Schools of Professional Psychology than ever before in the history of our field. The assumption that location of a program in a prestigious university guarantees quality but at the same time prohibits close external evaluation lest the sanctity of academic freedom be violated is no longer accepted as readily as it once was. Neither is the assumption that all pracitioner programs are bad. Over the past 25 years, direct education for the practice of psychology and for the Doctor of Psychology degree, which is the strongest symbol of professional education in psychology, have been woven securely into the fabric of our institutions.

6
TWENTY YEARS OF PRACTITIONER TRAINING IN PSYCHOLOGY

Twenty years ago, Adrien Pinard, president of the Canadian Psychological Association, concluded his address to the Association as follows:

> I shall limit myself to summarizing in three propositions the tissue of commonplaces which make up the thread of my address. In the first place, I have called attention to the paradox that arises from the fact that the very large majority of psychologists are practitioners, while the model generally applied to the training of these practitioners is the scientist–professional model, a model essentially centered on scientific research. In the second place, I have tried to show that the generalization of this model is illusory and dangerous. It is first of all illusory because our so-called scientist–professionals, with the exception of a deluxe minority, are in reality either scientists who do not practice their profession or practitioners who do no research and who, by their own admission, are not even in a fit state to exercise their profession well. It is also dangerous, because the scientist–professional model cannot satisfy the multitude of

This chapter was originally presented as a Distinguished Professional Contributions award address at the 92nd Annual Convention of the American Psychological Association in Toronto, Canada, in August 1984. From *American Psychologist*, *40*, 441–451.

psychological services rightly demanded by the public, and because this model is a source of confusion and in fact deprives professional psychology of the very identity the model was supposed to give it. In the third place, I have proposed the institution of two different courses of psychological training, an academic course and a professional course specifying that these programs must both be at the doctoral level and must demand comparable requirements and be at the same time distinct and complementary. (Pinard, 1967, pp. 144–145)

In his talk, Pinard expressed some common concerns of his time. Following recommendations of the Boulder conference (Raimy, 1950), scientist–practitioner programs for educating professional psychologists were located in academic departments. Everyone who applauded that decision believed that the academic environment would provide the culture of scholarship required for a newly formed profession. Few foresaw, however, the extent to which research would come to dominate American universities in the years following World War II. When I was in graduate school at the University of Minnesota, the chair of the department was Richard M. Elliott, a scholar of great wisdom who deepened the knowledge and extended the vision of every student he touched. Elliott published practically nothing except a book called *The Sunny Side of Asia*, which he wrote after a walking tour of China. Today I cannot imagine a person with Elliott's qualifications receiving a faculty appointment at any rank in any major university. Shortly after I came to the University of Illinois, the director of our psychological clinic, a man who had done a great deal to organize services and was the chief practicum supervisor in the clinic but had published only two articles in his life, was promoted from associate to full professor. He would not stand a chance for promotion today.

The shifts in values that required productive scholarship of every professor were well advanced by 1964. As the emphasis on research grew stronger and stronger, the appreciation of mere reflective scholarship, good teaching, and humane public service declined. No longer could faculty in the most ambitious departments devote long hours to teaching or clinical supervision, to the neglect of research, and hope for promotion. No longer could students declare interest solely in practice and hope for admission to the best graduate programs. Yet most students who completed scientist–practitioner programs published no research. And few felt well prepared for the professional work they would spend their lives doing.

The titles of the following journal articles revealed the tensions of the time: "The Case of Clinical Psychology: A Search for Identity; (Kahn & Santostefano, 1962); "Psycholgy in Flux: The Academic–Professional Bipolarity" (Tryon, 1963); "The Crisis in Clinical Psychology Training" (Blank & David, 1963). In 1964, the American Psychological Association's (APA) ad hoc Committee on the Scientific and Professional Aims of Psychology, with Kenneth E. Clark as chair, was concluding its deliberations. The committee recommended a two-track system of education, one for researchers and one for practitioners (APA, 1967). The Chicago conference, remembered today mainly for its reaffirmation of the scientist–practitioner model of professional education, was only a year away, and preconference materials had already been distributed to participants (Hoch, Ross, & Winder, 1966). In Canada, similar activities were in progress. The address by Pinard (quoted in the beginning of this chapter) was one of the position papers for the Couchiching Conference on Professional Psychology. There, in 1965, most of the same issues that preoccupied the Chicago conference were addressed, and most of the same conclusions were reached (Webster, 1967). Although the academicians who dominated both conferences were willing to consider minor modulations of program philosophy, they did not agree that any fundamental change was needed. Instead, they congratulated themselves for doing what they had been doing and went back to continue business as before.

But neither articles, committees, nor conferences could solve the basic problems of the time. Many scientist–practitioner programs emphasized science so strongly that practice was not only neglected but disparaged. Most programs were tiny. In California, for example, at a time when the general population was increasing rapidly, when California society was in crisis over rural and urban problems alike, and mental health systems were expanding to proportions never seen before in this country, all the California universities combined were turning out fewer than 20 clinical psychologists per year. The public demand for competent practitioners was strong. The demand from students for access to the profession was growing strident. Demands from practitioners, who faced hopelessly unmanageable case loads, who were dissatisfied with their own training, and who saw no help available from the universities, grew more militant and better organized. University faculties, sure in their commitments to science and fundamentally preoccupied with their own concerns, did not respond to the pressures. The dam was bound to break.

The early stages of the practitioner movement in psychology have been chronicled elsewhere (Caddy & LaPointe, 1984; Dörken & Cummings, 1977; Peterson, 1982). Only a bare summary is needed here. In 1964, only one program in the country was devoted mainly to the education of practitioners in psychology. That was the program at Adelphi University. In 1965, the Fuller Graduate School of Psychology was established. The Illinois Doctor of Psychology (PsyD) program began in 1968. In 1969, the California School of Professional Psychology accepted its first class of students. Since then, the number of practitioner programs has risen sharply. By 1982, 44 practitioner programs were in operation, with 4,992 students enrolled (Caddy & LaPointe, 1984). Of the 44 programs, 20 are in universities, and 24 are in freestanding professional schools. Twenty-seven programs lead to the PsyD degree, and 17 to the PhD.

The growth curve shown in Figure 6.1 appears to be rising relentlessly, but there is reason to suppose that the increase in new programs will soon taper

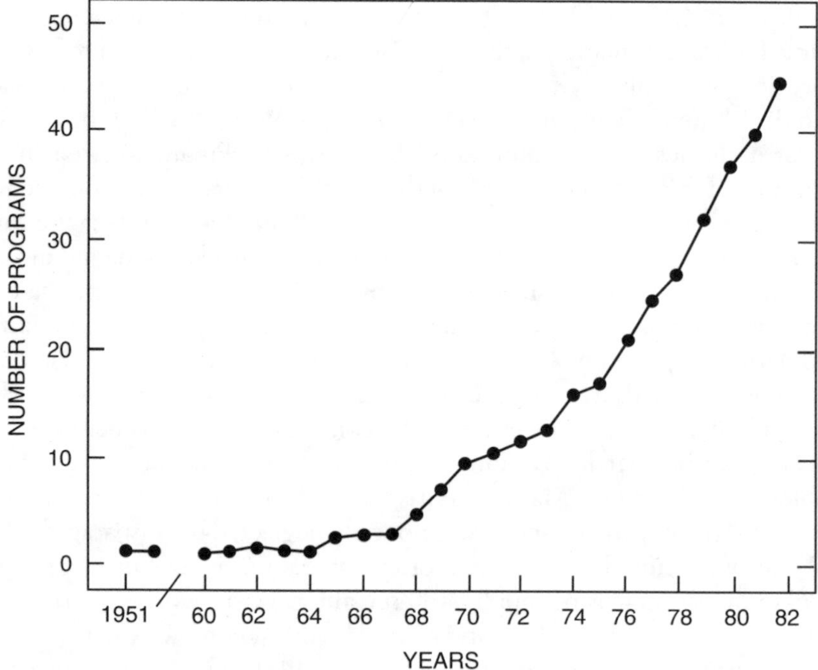

Figure 6.1. Increase in practitioner programs from 1960 to 1982. From "The Training of Professional Psychologists: Historical Developments and Present Trends," by G. R. Caddy and L. L. LaPointe in *Professional Practice of Psychology,* edited by G. S. Tryon, 1984, Norwood, NJ: Ablex Publishing Corporation. Copyright 1982 by Ablex Publishing Corporation. Reprinted with permission.

off. Unaccredited freestanding schools do not attract students as they once did, and the job market for graduates seems weaker than it was a few years ago. As any dean of an independent school of professional psychology will attest, development of a new school requires tremendous effort. It seems likely that most of the people interested in forming new schools have either already done so or given up. Some growth of PsyD programs will probably take place in small psychology departments in the years ahead, but the period of rapid increase in practitioner programs appears to be ending. Over the past 20 years, the professional school and the professional doctorate have become established in American psychology. What have we learned from the experience?

1. Major research universities will not establish practitioner programs in psychology. The Doctor of Psychology program at the University of Illinois failed. By now, the main reasons are clear. To the Illinois faculty, education for practice was never considered less demanding than education for research. It was always seen as equally demanding and in some ways more so. Specialization is justifiable and necessary for research. A practitioner facing problems as

they come from the public must be comprehensively trained. Preparing students not only for individual assessment and psychotherapy but also for a wide range of other skills, from neuropsychology to community intervention, requires an enormous investment of training resources. In the Illinois conception, especially as it developed after I left, professional psychologists were expected to contribute scholarly knowledge, if not scientific facts, to the discipline. The projects chosen by PsyD students were often more difficult than those elected by the PhD students, but demands for thoroughness and all possible rigor were not relaxed. By 1980, when the PsyD program was discontinued, the median time to completion was 7.4 years. Despite efforts by the Illinois faculty to describe the program accurately, many students entered dreaming of careers in the private practice of individual psychotherapy. They were annoyed by requirements that did not serve their personal goals and unsettled by faculty attitudes that attached little value to direct service through long-term individual treatment. They were not stupid. Why should they spend 7.4 years learning things they did not want to learn to obtain a PsyD when they could spend 5 years learning some other things they did not want to learn and get a PhD?

For faculty, the burdens of the program became too heavy to bear. Supervisory help from the local professional community did not materialize as expected. The task of clinical supervision fell mainly to full-time faculty, but in the research culture of the university time devoted to clinical supervision yielded few rewards. Many of the faculty had believed all along that a scientist–professional model of education, flexibly managed, could serve the aims of research and practice alike. Over the course of many discussions, that was the model to which they returned.

Despite the encouragement of practitioner programs by the Vail conference (Korman, 1976) few were attempted in research universities, and those that were proposed have rarely been sustained. An interfaculty program in clinical psychology and public practice ran for several years at Harvard but was put into moratorium when some of the administrators involved found it too expensive and too heavily ridden with conflict to merit continuation. The current program in counseling and consulting psychology at Harvard is housed in the Graduate School of Education. The Yale faculty endorsed the idea of explicit professional programs and the Doctor of Psychology degree, but neither the money nor the faculty commitment required to develop a professional program are in prospect, and the program in effect there is still a PhD program in clinical and community psychology. Twenty years ago, Paul Meehl returned from the meetings of the Clark Committee (APA, 1967) and presented the argument for outright professional education to Minnesota psychologists, but only a few of the other University of Minnesota faculty members supported the idea, and Meehl saw no point in pressing it. Later, a PsyD program in health psychology was formally proposed by clinical psychologists in the medical school, but conflicts with a new administration in the

Department of Psychiatry precluded attention to any new developments in psychology. At this time, the proposal is dormant and not likely to be revived.

At New York University (NYU), a PsyD program in clinical psychology was proposed informally as early as 1957. In the 1970s, a formal proposal was approved by the Psychology Department, the Graduate School of Arts and Sciences, the University Committee of Deans, and the Board of Trustees. At the last moment, the proposal was defeated by the clinical faculty, most of whom objected to the central role adjunct faculty were to have in the professional program. A PsyD program in school psychology was later established at NYU, but prospects for a parallel program in clinical psychology are remote.

These are anecdotes, but others could be told. Together they form a consistent pattern. The fact is that only 3 of the 44 practitioner programs in the country are in major *research universities*, as that term is defined by the Carnegie Council on Policy Studies in Higher Education (1976). These are at Rutgers, Yeshiva University, and NYU. The other universities with professional programs, such as Adelphi, Baylor, Wright State, and Denver, are not considered major research universities by the standards of the Carnegie Council, whatever the faculties may think about their reputations. The Carnegie rating system further divides research universities into Class I and Class II. Harvard, Stanford, Yale, the University of Michigan, and the University of California at Berkeley, along with other universities all would recognize, appear in the top group. A large share of Class I research universities do not even have scientist–professional programs in psychology, let alone programs for training practitioners. There is a very good reason for this. The primary mission of the first-class research university is research, not so much education and service, and the faculty in those institutions cannot afford to spend their time supervising practitioners in a minor profession.

For the most part, the major research universities of America have retained small, research-oriented scientist–professional programs in psychology. With only three exceptions, efforts to develop practitioner programs in research universities have failed. Given the incentives that govern faculty behavior, there is no reason to expect these conditions to change.

2. Education of most practitioners in psychology will take place in professional schools and small departments. Although graduates of scientist–professional programs in research universities are usually qualified to practice, the emphasis in those programs is on research, and the programs are very small. At this time, the number of students enrolled in university-based scientist–pratitioner programs and the number enrolled in professional schools appear to be about equal. As the new professional schools produce more graduates and as more practitioner programs are established in small departments, the numerical balance in the production of professional psychologists will clearly shift to practitioner programs.

Incentives for developing professional programs in small departments are substantial. Many departments already have master's programs in operation, but graduates of those programs face an uncertain job market. Faculties generally prefer doctoral programs to master's programs for the gain in intellectual stimulation and prestige doctoral programs provide. Universities in which the departments are located often have no doctoral programs in any field, so administrators are likely to support efforts to elevate their institutions into class of universities that grant doctoral degrees. Doctor of Psychology programs in universities attract students, graduates gain employment, and all the university-based PsyD programs that have applied for APA accreditation so far have been approved. These conditions are likely to favor development of more PsyD programs in small departments in the years ahead.

This worries me. Programs in professional psychology are not only not developing in the first rank of American universities, they are not developing in the second rank either. Professional programs are not seen at the University of Michigan but at Central Michigan University, not at Florida State University but at Nova, not at Columbia but at Pace University, not at Indiana University but at Indiana State University, not at the University of Kentucky but at Spalding College, not at the State University of Pennsylvania but at Indiana University of Pennsylvania.

The Conference Board of Associated Research Councils (CBARC) recently published a report on the scholarly reputations of universities (CBARC, 1983). If ratings of "faculty quality" in that survey are distributed and the positions of practitioner programs in psychology are noted, some interesting facts stand out. The first, already mentioned above, is that professional training in psychology has been abandoned entirely by many of the most prestigious universities. The psychology departments at Stanford, Harvard, Chicago, Princeton, and Northwestern Universities, all of which appear in the top quartile of the CBARC ratings, do not offer training for practice at all. The second fact is that those institutions that do offer direct education for practice do not fare well by the usual standards of faculty scholarship. Among 29 members, associates, and affiliates of the National Council of Schools of Professional Psychology (NCSPP), only one appears in the top quartile on the CBARC scale. One other is in the third quartile. Seven are in the bottom quartile. Twenty of the NCSPP members, who are training many if not most of tomorrow's practitioners, are not listed at all as qualified to educate scholars.

Conditions for access to the profession have changed radically since professional schools started to admit large numbers of students. Established professional schools that took part in a recent survey (Callan, Peterson, & Stricker, 1986) enrolled an average of 49 new students per year (Stricker, 1986). This is at least five times larger than typical entering classes in academic departmental programs. Not only are the numbers of students enrolling in professional schools larger than our field has known before, but the selection ratios are also different. Scientist–practitioner programs in prestigious universities receive several hundred applications per year. Some receive more; selection ratios of 1 : 100 are not unknown, and ratios of 1 : 15 are not uncommon. Standards for admission are still severe in most university-based professional schools, but freestanding schools admit higher proportions of applicants. The 12 independent schools that took part in the Callan et al. survey invited an average of 46% of applicants to enter their programs. Selection ratios ranged from about 1:3 to 2:3.

I have visited many schools of professional psycholgy and several small departments that are starting practitioner programs. The faculties usually impress me as bright, sincere, energetic people, dedicated to the education of professional psychologists in a scholarly way. Few are famous scientists. What this condition and the others mentioned above will do to our field is difficult to say, but it will not be the same as it was before.

3. The doctoral degree granted upon completion of graduate study depends on the administrative location of the program in which graduate study is done. Arguments about the proper degree for professional psychologists have been running on for many years. Those who support the PhD claim that it offers greater prestige than a professional degree and is more fitting because practitioners in psychology are really scholar–professionals (Derner, 1959; Stricker, 1975). Those who support the PsyD claim that it can be controlled by psychology as the PhD cannot and that it can be employed to certify professional competence in psychology as the PhD cannot (Fox, Barclay, & Rogers, 1982; Meehl, 1971; Peterson, 1976a, 1983).

The past 20 years have shown that rational arguments count less than some other conditions in determining which degree students receive at graduation. If the degree granted in each of the 44 practitioner programs identified by Caddy and LaPointe (1984) is related to the administrative location of the program, as in Table 6.1, it appears that use of the PhD for outright professional programs is mainly a practice of freestanding schools. Only three university-based professional programs (at Adelphi, the Fuller Graduate School, and the University of California at Davis) award the PhD degree. In most universities, the PhD is reserved for programs with research and scholarship as dominant objectives. Strictures, or the lack of strictures, imposed by state educational authorities also figure strongly in determining which degree will be allowed. All 14 of the PhD programs in freestanding professional schools are in California! In fact, with the single exception of Adelphi University, all the professional schools that grant the PhD degree for practitioner training are in California. There, regulations in higher education are unusually liberal, and the precedent established by the California School of Professional Psychology has been employed by other institutions to justify use of the PhD for practitioners.

Is the PsyD a second-class degree? Not yet, according to graduates who reported that the professional doctorate was more often seen as an asset than as a liability in seeking emploment in professional psychology (Peterson,

TABLE 6.1
Relation Between Degree Granted and Administrative Location of Program

Degree	Location of program	
	Independent school	University
PsyD	10	17
PhD	14	3

Eaton, Levine, & Snepp, 1982). Will the PsyD become a second-class degree? I fear it might, as more and more graduates come from single-purpose professional schools and small departments of uncertain reputation. In the race to poor repute, the PsyD will have stiff competition from the PhD. A professional school of humanistic studies run by 10 full-time and 40 part-time faculty, enrolling 794 students working toward PhDs in counseling, marriage and family therapy, and industrial/organizational psychology (Caddy & LaPointe, 1984) will not improve the value of the PhD. Probably our best hope is that the people who use psychological services will not know the difference, and that the distinction between PhD and PsyD will be just as mysterious and just as inconsequential as the difference between the DDS and the DMD in dentistry.

4. Graduates of scientist–professional programs and graduates of practitioner programs in psychology perform about equally well. The null hypothesis expressed in the sentence above has scarcely been proved. Carefully designed research to test the hypothesis has not been conducted. The few data now available comparing graduates of practitioner programs with graduates of scientist–professional programs either show small difference or no differences at all.

By now it seems fairly clear that students intending to enter careers of practice are more satisfied with practitioner programs than with traditional scientist–practitioner programs (Marwit, 1983; Peterson et al., 1982). Student satisfaction, however, says nothing about professional competence as measured by other means.

So far, internship supervisors have detected few differences between students from scientist–professional programs and those from practitioner programs (Shemberg & Leventhal, 1981; Snepp, 1983). Fully 50% of the supervisors in Shemberg and Leventhal's study, for example, saw no difference in the performance of PsyD and PhD interns; 25% thought the PsyDs were worse; and 25% thought the PhDs were worse. In Snepp's study, a tendency was observed toward greater "sensitivity" among PsyD students and more "scientific" attitudes among PhD students, but differences were small, and preparation in various skills was considered equally good for both groups.

Findings like these may give some comfort to those who feared that professional programs would do worse than scientist–professional programs in educating students. But professional programs are clearly justified only if they do a better job of preparing people for practice than traditional PhD programs have done. The PhD programs, conversely, should be evaluated with regard to the productive scholarship of graduates and the claims of devotees that students are well prepared for practice by the training they receive. Adequate comparative studies have not been done. The obstacles to sound research on these questions are formidable. The criterion problem (i.e., how to evaluate competence in professional psychology) is particularly difficult. I do not agree, however, that these difficulties preclude systematic evaluative research (cf. Stern, 1984). Psychologists are perfectly ready to assess human performance in other complex occupations and to evaluate educational programs in other fields. As the APA Task Force on Education, Training, and Service has recommended (APA, 1982), we need to turn our alleged skills in program evaluation upon ourselves.

5. Curricula of professional schools and scientist–professional programs are more alike than different. The self-study by the NCSPP cited above (Callan et al., 1986) concerned more than admissions. Methods for evaluating student competence, curricula, faculty characteristics, administrative organization, and psychological service centers were also described in detail. From analyses of the various curricula, a typical program in professional psychology was derived (Kopplin, 1986).

Mean credit requirements are shown in Table 6.2. APA accreditation criteria strongly influence professional school curricula. All the APA content demands in biological, cognitive–emotional, and social bases of behavior, in professional ethics; and in history and systems of psycholgy are met in the typical professional school program. Knowledge of personality theory, psychopathology, and human development is ordinarily required. Strong demands are set for professional activities of assessment and intervention (21 credits) and for supervised practicum experience (19 credits). Statisitcs, measurement, and research design are all required, and all but one of the professional schools requires a dissertation or project devoted to the scholarly study of an issue pertinent to applied psychology. Amounts of credit devoted to dissertation work are included in the general set of "additional required courses," which also includes courses in consultation, program evaluation, special projects, and advanced courses in any of the areas of the core curriculum.

How different is this from the content of most scientist–professional programs? Although comparable analyses of the curricula of departmental PhD programs have not been done, I recently attempted an informal study of the catalogs of ten highly regarded scientist–professional programs to see what was being taught in those programs today. When I coupled that information with the residual of my experience in reviewing programs for APA accreditation, my conclusion was that practitioner programs and scientist–professional

TABLE 6.2
A Typical Professional School Curriculum

Topic	Credits
Professional issues and ethics	3
Statistics and measurement	4
Research design	3
History and systems	2
Biological bases of behavior	4
Cognitive–emotional bases of behavior	3
Social bases of behavior I: Social psychology	3
Social bases of behavior II: Community and systems	3
Individual behavior I: Personality	3
Individual behavior II: Developmental psychology	3
Individual behavior III: Psychopathology	3
Individual behavior IV: Unspecified	3
Assessment I: General	3
Assessment II: Cognitive–intellectual	3
Assessment III: Personality	3
Intervention I: Individual psychotherapy	3
Intervention II: Behavior therapy	3
Intervention III: Group and family therapy	3
Intervention IV: Unspecified	3
Practicum	19
Additional required courses	25
Electives	8
Total	110

programs (not as idealized but as typically implemented in this country) do not differ much after all.

Scientist–professional programs also are designed to meet APA criteria, and so they contain the necessary substance for approval. Assessment, intervention, and supervised practica are all included, though emphasis on assessment is typically less than in practitioner programs, and I saw no departmental PhD program that included the 1,900 hours of supervised pre-internship practicum experience required at Adelphi and Baylor. Like the professional programs, the scientist–practitioner programs routinely require a 1-year predoctoral internship. As appropriate for programs designed to educate researchers, the academic PhD programs put a greater emphasis on research design and the conduct of research than any of the practitioner programs. The programs at Vanderbilt and Duke University, for example, not only require the usual courses in statistics and research design but also involve students in research apprenticeships from the beginning of graduate study. To a greater degree than practitioner programs, scientist–professional programs allow electives and encourage specialization. Students at Michigan State University, for example, are required to choose between curricula in child/family and adult clinical psychology, though some crossover is allowed. Students at Yale elect one of three subthemes in clinical psychology, health psychology, community psychology, or more traditional clinical psychodiagnosis and psychotherapy. Specialization in other scientist–professional programs is common, but even in this regard the distinction from practitioner programs is unclear. The Rutgers PsyD program in clinical psychology, for example, requires students to choose between behavioral and psychodynamic tracks, and a third emphasis, on organizational psychology, is under development.

In early formulations (APA, 1967; Peterson, 1966), the differences between research programs and practitioner programs were clear cut. The research programs were designed to educate productive investigators by engaging students in active research throughout graduate study. Professional training was not necessarily reduced in quality but was restricted in scope so that the specialized knowledge required for effective inquiry could be attained. Training for practice, on the other hand, was to be both thorough and comprehensive, to prepare psychologists for the full range of problems they might face in professional work. Practitioners were educated for the intelligent consumption of research, but the early program proposals contained no dissertation requirements at all.

As the professional programs evolved, however, emphasis on active scholarship increased, and some of the intellectual leaders of the professional school movement (e.g., Meltzoff, 1984) proposed no less an emphasis on scholarly inquiry than is found in most scientist–practitioner programs. The scientist–practitioner programs, for their part, no longer neglect training for practice, as they often did in the past. I have a distinct impression that training for professional service in the best scientist–practitioner programs is better today than it has ever been. In the longer history of applied psychology, the main contribution of the professional schools may be that they forced academic departments and organized psychology to take professional training more seriously than before. In the core of common knowledge, in practicum training for assessment and intervention, and in the requirements for internships and dissertations, the programs in professional schools and in academic departments are more alike than different. If one looks only at curricula, both types of programs seem to be educating scholar–professionals after all.

6. The main differences between practitioner programs and scientist–professional programs lie in the attitudes and interests of faculty and students. The mission statements of scientist–professional programs in academic departments are clear about the emphasis on research in their programs.

The 1984 Duke University clinical program description stated,

> We do not conceive of our mission as the training of mental health professionals, but rather the goal is to train scholar–professionals who have the capacity to transform and better our approaches to mental health related phenomena.

According to the mission statement in the 1984 clinical program description of the University of Illinois,

> we expect all of our students to develop competence in, and an understanding of, both the scholarly and applied aspects of the field. . . . Given the above emphasis, the program is not recommended for those who wish to pursue exclusive professional practice careers.

This is different from the acceptance of professional application for its own sake as expressed in the mission statements of professional schools. According to the mission statement in Adelphi University's 1984 catalog, "The professional school . . . accepts unequivocally the career goal of the students, whether it is clinical practice, research, or teaching." Wright State University, in Ohio, stated in its 1984 graduate catalog that "it is the mission of the School of Professional Psychology to . . . educate and train qualified individuals . . . for quality practice in professional psychology."

The two kinds of institutions accomplish their objectives in different ways, including the kinds of faculty members they recruit. No first-rank scientist–practitioner program in the country will accept as a full-time faculty member anyone without a record of production in research, and the values attached to faculty performance are predominantly those of scholarly contribution. Professional schools engage scholars too, but complement their ranks with people whose lives are devoted primarily to professional service. In the freestanding schools, practitioners form most of the faculty. In university-based schools, practitioners are usually hired on an adjunct basis. Either way, role models for professional careers are provided to students, and the value of practice is affirmed in its own right.

Faculties create the cultures within which graduate education takes place. Although the curricula of academic departments and professional schools do not differ widely, I propose that there are some important differences between the cultures of the two kinds of institutions. Gregory Kimble (1984) has recently done some interesting work on the values and beliefs of psychologists, following the line of thought C. P. Snow (1964) articulated in distinguishing between the scientifc and humanist cultures in Western society. With apologies to Charles Osgood, Kimble constructed a device he called the Epistemic Differential. The test consists of statements describing differing views on a range of philosophical issues with which psychologists are perennially concerned, such as the predictability of behavior, relations between nomothetic and idiographic laws, and the relative advantages of data and theory in methodological strategy. Factor analysis defined a coherent scientist/humanist dimension, and the scores of members of several APA divisions were compared. Large differences, significant at the .00001 level, were found. Members of Division 3, Experimental Psychology, expressed views sharply on the side of science. Members of Division 32, Humanistic Psychology, fell to the other side. Members of Division 29,

Psychotherapy, were nearly as humanistic as the humanists (Kimble, 1984). So far, no one has compared the faculties of professional schools and academic departments using Kimble's measure, but I will be surprised if substantial differences do not appear when the study is done.

The interests and values of students resemble those of faculty. When Roger Knudson and I examined the interests of students in several clinical psychology programs we found two massive factors, one of interest in research and the other of interest in practice. Students preparing for careers of research and those preparing for careers of practice differed widely in the expected direction (Peterson & Knudson, 1979). Some of the differences are so obvious no studies are needed to demonstrate them. Any site visitor who reviews a program for accreditation will sooner or later get to talking with students about their interests. In the academic departments, students discuss the research they are doing. In the professional schools, students talk about the therapies they are learning.

More than attitudes and interests are required to make a culture. A work culture is formed by a group of people laboring together toward common objectives. A research culture is created by a group of investigators who share the values of science, probe into the questions that intrigue them, dig out the facts, frame ideas and findings into coherent conceptions, talk with each other, and work with each other to find out what is going on in the world—all in an environment that encourages inquiry. The departments of physics at Berkeley or Princeton show us what a research culture can be. In psychology, the Harvard group under Murray in the 1930s, the Yale group under Hull in the 1940s, and the Stanford group (I hesitate to name a single leader) in more recent times show what I mean by a research culture.

The culture of practice is different. There a group of professionals are doing their best to provide services to the public. They are engaged in working out the puzzles of the individual case, talking these over with colleagues, despairing over their failures, enjoying their successes, exulting now and then when particularly stubborn problems yield to the solutions they have engineered, designing new programs together, working these into the community, and helping people right now with the best professional service they can offer. The Mayo Medical Center shows what the culture of practice can be. In psychology, Albert Ellis's Institute of Rational–Emotive Therapy and the Psychological Center at the Fuller Graduate School are starting to show what can be done to take psychological services to the people.

Many academic departments bring students into the culture of research. Few of them provide comparable socialization in practice, though many provide satisfactory training for professional work. Professional schools bring students into the culture of practice. Few provide comparable socialization in research, though professional schools that maintain active research programs can provide cultures of research as well.

7. Under some conditions, the cultures of science and practice can be

blended. The kinds of science and practice prevalent in 1964, when Pinard delivered his diatribe against the scientist–professional model of education, defied integration. At that time, any "scientific" project that was not empirical in substance and experimental in method stood little chance for approval or publication. "Practice" consisted mainly of individual psychotherapy, indeterminately related to individual assessment procedures of questionable value. Most of the research of the time was irrelevant to practice, the practice of the time was invulnerable to research, and each activity went on in isolation from the other. Over the past 20 years, the definition of acceptable scholarly work has been extended. During the same time, the profession has changed in ways that allow scholarly investigation to improve it. These are the conditions required for the blending of science and practice.

The past 20 years have seen a considerable liberalization of methodological constraint in psychological inquiry. Kimble (1984) wrote about an "easy acceptance" of topics for research that would have been out of bounds in earlier times (p. 838). "Mental imagery, the distinction between remembered and imagined, voluntary behavior, self-awareness and self-control, conceptually driven processing, helplessness and coping, risk taking, metaphoric expression, and inferential processing are a few of these topics, all of which are identified by phrases that catch important ideas in the humanist tradition" (Kimble, 1984, p. 838). In the behavioral tradition of professional psychology, the development of single-subject designs and the successful implementation of field studies have allowed systematic inquiry in areas of clear practical importance. Among titles of doctoral proposals listed by Leitenberg (1974) in describing the scientist–professional program at the University of Vermont are "The Prediction of Medical Rehabilitation Outcome," "A Contingency Management and Fading Procedure for the Modification of the Classroom Behavior of Institutionalized Delinquents," "The Generality Issue in a Head-Start Behavior Modification Program," and "Changes in Interaction Patterns in Multiple Family Therapy." Barlow, Hayes, and Nelson (1984) recently completed an analysis of the issues that divide scientists from practitioners in psychology and proposed an integrated model of applied research that includes clinical observation, generation of new intervention procedures, generation of new measurement procedures, single case studies, clinical analogue studies, short- and long-term outcome studies, evaluation of training and dissemination methods, and evaluation of field efficacy. In the view of Barlow, Hayes, and Nelson, responsible practitioners must employ combinations of these procedures to be accountable, and by the systematic accumulation of knowledge through replicated case studies and other means practitioners may contribute to science as well.

Outside the boundaries of science as conventionally conceived lie the disciplines of humanistic inquiry. The interpretive studies of historians, for example, are not usually regarded as science, but they are not intuitive art either. A disciplined historian has strong concern for such issues as the validity of report and the coherent interpretation of scattered fragments of fact. In literature, the writing of biography requires careful attention to accuracy of account, reconciliation of disparate reports, and elaboration of coherent themes that unify the life of the subject. Some of the humanities require discipline as firm as any science. Thoughfully conceived and carefully executed, inquiries of these kinds can produce an order as compelling as many an experimental series and often more useful for understanding some of the processes a clinician needs to comprehend. The proper base for practice in psychology is not science but disciplined knowledge. The scholarly activity required to build that knowledge may take many forms. Instead of restricting inquiries to suit our methods, we must design methods to suit the problems we face as practitioners.

As science changes, so will practice. Three surveys (Callan et al., 1986; Garfield & Kurtz, 1976; Peterson et al., 1982) show that professional psychologists spend more time doing individual psychotherapy than any other single activity. I regard the practice of psychotherapy as a perfectly honorable and fairly useful way to make a living, but there is no reason to suppose psychologists do better at it than people from several other professions, including some whose services come cheaper than ours. If professional psychology is to serve the public effectively and efficiently, it will help to broaden our scope from individuals to groups and organizations, to shift our orientation to include prevention as well as treatment, and to extend the settings in which we work from mental health centers to the full range of environments in which human dysfunctions may occur and in which psychological knowledge may be applied to improve human function. Assessment remains a critical skill for professional psychologists, but it cannot be restricted to the assessment of individual personality. We also need to study groups and organizations in natural settings to find out how they work, what can go wrong with them, what can be done to improve them, and how to evaluate any improvements we have attempted. A professional psychology conceived in this way—broad enough to accommodate the problems we address, based on disciplined knowledge, and linking conception, assessment, and intervention as systematically as the human condition allows—can be accountable and self-corrective and thereby more useful to society than much professional activity is today.

The argument for extending the scope of professional psychology has been stated most recently by Sarason (1981) and Levy (1984). Many of the ideas Sarason and Levy expressed so well are embodied in the charters of several schools of professional psychology. How much we actually know about the grand range of problems we have staked out is another matter, but a reasonably firm knowledge base for professional psychology has been established (Peterson, 1976b), and a professional psychology linked with the broad-ranging disciplines of inquiry proposed above offers every promise of improving in the future.

Education for practice is not less difficult than education for research. In some regards, it is more difficult. Knowledge of fact and theory must be just as thorough, and the range of knowledge required for practice is greater. Practitioners must not only understand the facts and concepts of psychology, but they must also know how to apply them in helping others. Frank Hawkinshire, of New York University, has drawn my attention to some ideas of his mentor, W. H. Cowley, about the aims of professional education. Cowley (1960) distinguished among three kinds of education, which he called *logocentric*, *practicentric*, and *democentric*. Logocentric literally means "centered in knowledge." A logocentrist is concerned with advancing the boundaries of knowledge without concern for practical affairs. Practicentric education is concerned with the skills of practice in applying knowledge to solve problems. Democentric education, in Cowley's definition, is concerned with interpreting knowledge for the public at large, but the meaning of the term would not be violated if the *demos* were taken to be students who enter our schools, and the democentric emphasis in education a concern for the personal development of the people we hope to influence.

Education of scientists is dominantly logocentric and probably must remain so if the science is to advance. Education of professionals is dominantly practicentric and probably must be so if the skills of the profession are to be fully taught. I do not know what we can do to advance the personal development of students. Most of them are well formed when they come to us. We can, however, stop quenching their concern for others in a cold objectivity that does not suit our discipline in the first place. We can stop requiring hypocrisy of them, as we do by refusing entry to the profession unless they pretend interests they do not have. If we can create environments in which proper regard is given to disciplined knowledge, the skills of practice are taught and respected, and the integrity of students is not impaired, it may not matter whether we work in professional schools, large departments, or small departments. We will all be giving students all we can.

7

PsyD PROGRAMS: EARLY IDEALS, FACTUAL OUTCOMES, CRITICAL CONCERNS, AND INSTITUTIONAL REALITIES

EARLY IDEALS

We set out bravely. The announcement of our program in the *American Psychologist* began with the following paragraph:

> We are going ahead with plans for a professional program leading to the Doctor of Psychology degree in clinical psychology. Now, as before, we intend to prepare clinicians for work at the highest levels of professional competence in the study and change of disordered behavior. Free of constraints in the academic tradition of the PhD, and of such costly irrelevancies as the intensive study of biological medicine in psychiatric training, we plan to prepare professional clinicians, better than we have in the past and better than any other discipline, for positions of central leadership in the so-called mental health field. We believe we know enough to do this now, and the program is underway. (Peterson, 1968b, p. 511)

Next came the familiar litany of reasons for our decision to move ahead with the program: importance of maintaining the distinction between nomothetic research and idiographic professional action, recognition that most clinical psychologists entered careers of research or practice and rarely combined the two except by using practice as an arena for research, efficiency of a two-track program that allowed both choice of emphasis and opportunity to combine research and professional training for those who chose to do so, importance of a professional degree to certify competence in professional psychology. Next came a summary of the program we had hammered out over the previous 3 years.

> The program as we have designed it is not a totally separate program, off to the side and completely distinct from the PhD program. Students are admitted in clinical psychology, period. There is no demand to decide the first year between research and service careers, because all students do the same things the first year. Their experiences will include a proseminar in general psychology, an introduction to clinical psychology, training in quantitative methods and research design, and courses in personality theory and behavior disorders.
>
> The second year all students will take a year-long sequence in behavior assessment, or psychodiagnostics as we used to call it, as well as courses in social development and a didactic survey of approaches to clinical behavior modification. By this time, however, students will have to choose either to complete a master's thesis, which is required in the PhD research program, or to take additional course work in preparation for a professional career. The courses for Doctor of Psychology candidates deal with basic medicine for clinical psychologists, community psychology, educational counseling, and the special education of exceptional children.
>
> In the third year the separation between programs grows wider, though there still are common elements. All students will complete a two-semester practicum in clinical psychology, and all students will take two laboratory courses in clinical psychology, ordinarily in individual psychotherapy and in behavioral desensitization procedures. In this year, PhD students must also complete four units of work in a minor field, while Doctor of Psychology students can enter additional clinical labs. This is where some very important clinical training will take place, and limitation of time and class size will restrict the labs almost exclusively to professionally oriented students. The laboratories, as we are planning them now, will offer continued training in individual treatment procedures (PhD students only have time for one semester), operant methods with clinical populations, group therapy, community action, the assessment of brain dysfunction, clinical personality tests of the traditional kinds (PhD students are rather lightly exposed to these in the required clinical assessment course), and two special education courses in the diagnosis and remediation of learning disabilities.

> The fourth-year PhD students will complete a dissertation, while PsyD students will complete an internship with varying proportions of experience in a local community clinic, zone centers for children and adults, and at least one more traditional hospital setting.
>
> Graduates of the PhD program who decide after all to learn more about professional clinical work can take a postdoctoral internship and be right where the products of Boulder-style programs have always been. Better yet, they can spend 2 years picking up the clinical labs they missed and complete an internship to meet requirements for the Doctor of Psychology degree. Doctors of Psychology who want to obtain PhD degrees as well can complete the necessary research and language requirements in 2 additional years. (Peterson, 1968b, p. 513)

The work we had done to plan the program showed in our description, but so did my inexperience. We were not nearly as "free of constraints in the academic tradition of the PhD" as I thought at the time. I did not grasp the significance of the graduate college demand for a "report" following the internship, nor did I anticipate the extent to which the Illinois faculty would interpret the demand as tantamount to a dissertation requirement. No mention of the PsyD dissertation appears in the article. I have since come to regard the dissertation as an important part of professional education in psychology, but in the early days of the Illinois program, I did not think that way. In my thinking, every case would become an exercise in disciplined inquiry. Many investigative projects, over a wide range of clients and settings, would be conducted over the course of graduate education. Following graduation, Doctors of Psychology would continue the "clinical studies" they had learned to do in their graduate training. Some of the findings would be of sufficient general interest to merit publication, but most would only serve the individual, group, or organizational clients with whom the practitioners were immediately concerned. I did not yet have Stricker and Trierweiler's (1995) language for the role of the professional psychologist, but my clear intent was to educate practitioners as "local clinical scientists."

Our aims went beyond a new educational model and a new degree. We were never so pretentious as to say so, even among ourselves, but by our example we hoped to inspire radical change in the profession itself. The profession we envisioned would be settled firmly on a scientific foundation. Clinical psychology, as commonly taught and practiced in the 1960s, was not a science-based profession. At the time, clinical practice was generally conceived as "applied personality theory." Though efforts had been made to restate Freudian concepts in the language of learning theory (e.g., by Dollard & Miller, 1950; Mowrer, 1950; Shoben, 1949), the disciplinary base for clinical practice was still largely limited to neo-Freudian dynamic psychology, and the technology that could be built on that foundation was inherently restricted. "Diagnosis" still consisted mainly of inferential construction of the "personality" of the individual case. "Treatment" still consisted mainly of individual insight-oriented psychotherapy.

A small but significant body of critical investigations of both the diagnostic and therapeutic aspects of professional function had produced disquieting results. A series of studies on the reliability of test-based diagnosis (e.g., by Kostlan, 1954; Little & Schneidman, 1959; Silverman, 1959) showed expert diagnosticians to disagree radically in their formulations about human personality. Meehl's (1954) critique of the clinician as a predictor of significant human outcomes was unsettling to many practitioners, and his suggestion that they devote more time to psychotherapy was little help, for psychotherapy too had become a questionable enterprise (Eysenck, 1952; Levitt, 1957).

Even if the outcome and validity research of the time had produced more favorable results than it did, a clinical profession founded solely or primarily in individual dynamic psychology was doomed from the start to economic futility. Little but individual psychotherapy could come of it. The cost–benefit balance for long-term individual psychotherapy was bound to be prohibitive. For lasting, widespread benefits of professional work, assessment and intervention at the group and organizational levels were needed.

A profession is only as good as the intellectual discipline on which it is founded. The conceptual basis for early clinical psychology was too heavily burdened with inappropriate medical metaphors, too vague in its definitions, too narrow in its scope, and too weak in its effects to offer any serious hope for generally effective professional services. More than new techniques were needed. A new way of thinking about the human condition was required.

The new paradigm did not begin to emerge in clearly visible outlines until 10 years or so after the Boulder conference. As is often true of developments of this kind, it came both from the professional field and from the scientific laboratory. In his practice, Joseph Wolpe (1958) developed systematic desensitization as a way of reducing phobic anxiety, along with other learning-based methods for dealing with clinical problems. Outcome research on systematic desensitization quickly followed (e.g., Paul, 1966) and for the first time a strongly effective, clearly communicable method for dealing with an important clinical problem was available to the profession and to the public. However questionable the theoretical presumptions underlying the process of systematic desensitization may have been, they were at least stated in the language of testable psychological science, and the relationship between application and basic discipline was firmer than it had been before.

Around the same time, several psychologists began to apply the principles and methods of operant conditioning to clinical problems. The early outcome reports were encouraging. Whatever questions may have been raised about the generality and durability of effects, the phenomena under consideration could at least be examined dependably, the discipline in which clinical applications were rooted had the marks of psychological science, and the basis for an authentically scientific approach to the study and functional improvement of human behavior had clearly begun to emerge.

Ironically, the most visible pioneers in forming a scientifically based psychological profession were not scientist–professionals of the Boulder mold. Joseph Wolpe was a practicing psychiatrist. B. F. Skinner was a laboratory experimentalist. But the intellectual climate fostered by the scientist–professional concept was receptive to the ideas such people as Wolpe and Skinner offered, and the clinical psychologists who adopted the new ideas contributed strongly to their development. Less than 15 years after the appearance of Wolpe's *Psychotherapy by Reciprocal Inhibition* (1958), the core principles of behavior modification had been defined and experimentally examined (e.g., by Bandura, 1969), the phenomena of "mental illness" had been construed in the language of behavioral psychology (e.g., by Ullmann & Krasner, 1969), clinical "diagnosis" had been defined as the application of behavioral methods to the study of human problems (e.g., by Peterson, 1968a), and a wide array of behavioral procedures for dealing with human problems had been developed (e.g., by Lazarus, 1971).

A carefully tested, widely applicable body of procedures for studying and changing human behavior was not and still is not available, but by the late 1960s the definitions needed for developing those procedures had become reasonably clear, a few procedures had been tested and found effective by acceptably rigorous research, and the flow of new procedures appeared to be steady enough to warrant an outright declaration of professional independence. In designing the first PsyD program, we hoped to change much more than the way professional psychologists were trained. By our example, we hoped to encourage transformation of the profession itself. Ours would be the first truly science-based professional program in the history of the discipline.

The organizational location of the program was important in our thinking. We knew that freestanding professional schools were on the way in California and probably elsewhere. We feared that these would lack the resources and quality controls that universities provide. We did not believe that a professional program should be implemented except in partnership with a strong research program. But we had also seen the way in which the culture of research could drown the culture of practice, and we wanted to show that a professional program of the highest quality could be established in a first-class research university.

Except for replacing my naivete with hindsight, I would not change much if I were to design the Illinois PsyD program today. The rationale for the program, its basic structure, and its definition as an educational experiment that called for continuing empirical appraisal still seem sound to me. Even the understanding that we would abandon the program if it failed (Peterson, 1968b, p. 516) was sadly prescient.

STUDIES OF THE FIRST PsyD PROGRAM

Just as we expected of our students, we guided our plans by collecting systematic data on the questions that concerned us. One of the first questions was that of employability of our graduates. Would anybody hire a PsyD with the education and training we were building into the program? I obtained a strong local answer to that question before any students were admitted. In a survey of employers in human service agencies in Illinois, I described the training Doctors of Psychology would receive and asked whether employers would hire one. Answers were overwhelmingly positive. Respondents frequently added qualifying comments like, "My God, yes! This is exactly the kind of psychologist we need in our agency." If results had gone otherwise, I would not have gone ahead with the program.

Our long range concerns, however, were not local but national. The issues of greatest concern were the radical departure from convention in the structure of our program and award of a professional degree to our graduates. We wanted especially to know whether the academic opposition to the PsyD degree that had dominated the Chicago conference was shared by students, practitioners, and a broad sample of prospective employers. At the very start of the program, therefore, when it still would have been simple to reroute students into our PhD track should results encourage us to do so, we conducted a survey of attitudes toward practitioner programs and the PsyD degree.

We asked two questions of all respondents. "Everything considered, do you approve or disapprove of the Doctor of Psychology program?" (check marks requested) and "Why?" (open space for free response). Depending on the sample involved, we asked variable third questions concerning possible actions respondents might take in reference to the program and its graduates.

Data were sought from faculty and students from the Universities of Illinois, Minnesota, and Michigan, from a random sample of members of the APA Division of Clinical Psychology (Division 12), and from participants in the 1965 Chicago conference on the professional preparation of clinical psychologists. Over all, more than two thirds of the respondents said they approved of the PsyD program. Qualifications of the response were quite rare. Those that appeared usually restricted approval to the experimental program at Illinois and withheld judgment about the program as a general development—for example, "I approve of the training *experiment* you are doing at Illinois, but I would like to wait and see the results before promoting Doctor of Psychology programs on a nationwide basis." Pertinence of training to job function was the most common reason for approving the program. The most common reasons for disapproval had to do with public acceptance of the degree and the effects programs of this kind might have in reducing the status of clinical psychologists.

Members of Division 12 were asked, "If you were in a position to hire a psychologist holding the Doctor of Psychology degree, would you hire one to join your staff?" Of the 302 respondents, 75% said yes, 13% said no, and 11% were undecided. Participants who had attended the Chicago conference were asked how they currently viewed the idea of PsyD programs. At the conference, most had voted merely to "recognize" practitioner programs, whereas a minority were prepared to "encourage" them, and only a few (6) voted for "endorsement." In our survey, most of the respondents voted for "endorsement"; "encouragement" was second and "recognition" came in a weak third.

A report of the study (Peterson, 1969) was published in the first issue of *Professional Psychology*, the first APA journal devoted directly to issues in the practice of psychology. Results offered some collegial encouragement to our effort but could not answer the basic behavioral and organizational questions by which the functional progress of the program might be measured. By the time three cohorts of students had been admitted, we had a sufficiently large sample to obtain systematic answers to some of the questions of greatest concern to us. We had wondered how many students would apply for admission to a program leading to the PsyD degree and found that applications to our clinical program increased more than threefold when the clear option of training for practice was introduced. We wondered whether applicants who declared intentions in the direction of the PsyD would be as well qualified as those inclined toward the PhD program and found that they were not by the usual standards of grades and test scores. The differences were small, however, and the expanded pool of applicants allowed us to select supremely well qualified students for graduate study in professional psychology. We were concerned about performance in the program, especially in the "hard science" components concentrated in the first year, and found that the grade point averages of PsyD students were numerically higher than those of PhD students, though both groups did very well and not one of the average differences between groups, either in didactic courses or clinical work, was statistically significant. We wondered about stability in choice of program. Students who entered as prospective PsyD candidates were welcome to move over to the PhD program if developing interests encouraged a shift, though we neither encouraged nor discouraged program changes. Over the first 3 years of operation, three PsyD students did in fact move to the PhD program, but during the same time five students entered the PsyD program from PhD programs in the department, three from the clinical PhD program, and one each from personality and social psychology. Again, we saw nothing but encouragement in our findings (Peterson, 1971).

Four years later, our first graduates had entered professional jobs, the program was fully accredited by the APA, two other PsyD programs were in operation at the Hahnemann Medical College and Baylor University, the Vail conference on patterns and levels of professional training in psychology had been planned and funded, and another evaluative review of the Illinois program was in order.

By this time, the volume of applications had increased still further despite efforts on our part to be firmly realistic with candidates about their chances for admission. We were receiving upward of 500 applications per year and admitting fewer than 20 of those for the combined PsyD and PhD programs. Students performed excellently throughout. On several indices of academic and clinical performance, we compared the 42 PsyD students we had admitted since 1968 with the 41 PhD students we had admitted during the same period and found that means for PsyD and PhD students were nearly identical over all comparisons.

As the program evolved, some changes occurred. The program grew more flexible than it had been in the original design. Both PsyD and PhD students exercised broader choices in their education than we had expected. PhD students did not follow the rather tightly confined research track we had laid out for them. Typically they signed up for several more of the clinical labs than were required to qualify for the PhD degree. All but one elected to complete an internship. With the utmost clarity, they showed us that their interest was not in an exclusively research-oriented education. They wanted, and we cheerfully provided, the education and experience embodied in an enriched Boulder-style, scientist–practitioner program. For their part, the PsyD students undertook more ambitious projects for their "reports" than we had anticipated. Most of the projects constituted major efforts to evaluate professional services in some way, engineer improvements in the services, and evaluate the effects of the innovations. The projects still differed from traditional PhD thesis research in that all were clearly relevant to professional work in some way but rarely offered the closely controlled design and extensive base of systematic data that most scholars would demand for "research" in our field. It seemed to us that the PsyD projects expressed the kind of critical attitude and innovative spirit creators of the Boulder model intended to instill in clinical psychologists but that had been so weakly manifested in the past.

At the time of our study, only four people had completed all requirements for the PsyD degree, but three others had taken professional jobs with the expectation, later fulfilled, of completing their final reports on the job. All of the graduates were employed in public agencies. All had positions of considerable responsibility, and several were eagerly hired before graduation by employers who wanted them to organize human service programs of one kind or another.

We asked our graduates, "To what extent was your credential as a PsyD an issue in your employment?" According to their answers, the degree did not matter greatly one way or another in getting jobs. As had been anticipated by the earlier survey, employers were more interested in the professional experience and work capabilities of candidates than in the letters behind their names.

A preliminary version of our report (Peterson & Baron, 1975) was completed just before the Vail conference that took place in July 1973. I sent a copy to everyone who had been invited to the meeting. At the time, of course, I did not foresee the eventual termination of the Illinois program nor appreciate the force of the conditions that would bring it to a close.

FURTHER STUDIES IN PROFESSIONAL PSYCHOLOGY

At the Vail conference, I was assigned to the task group on training settings and patterns that drafted the resolutions recognizing the legitimacy of professional schools and the PsyD degree. When the resolutions were approved by the conference as a whole, I felt that my main goal as an organizer of practitioner programs in psychology had been accomplished. At the same time, troubles were brewing in my department back home. For the first time in my experience at Illinois, we were working through some political problems. I grew tired of the pettiness of it all. Worse than tired, I became impatient and disgruntled. By the time the report on the Illinois PsyD program was published, I had resigned as director of training and returned, as I thought, to a career of teaching and research. When I read in the *APA Monitor* that Rutgers University had established a school of professional psychology and would award the PsyD degree to graduates of its programs, I felt a twinge of avuncular satisfaction but no sense of personal involvement. I barely noticed that Rutgers was searching for a dean.

At the APA convention the following August, Jack Bardon and I fell into a conversation about the new school at Rutgers. Jack and I had worked together in the same task force at Vail. He asked whether I had considered sending in my resume. I had not, but I told him I would think about it. A short time later, I mailed my vita to the search committee. One thing led to another, and in September 1975 I came to Rutgers as dean of the Graduate School of Applied and Professional Psychology.

Once again in a position of visible responsibility for educating professional psychologists, I returned to the study of practitioner programs with revitalized interest. By now, I had plenty of company in the educational enterprise, and all subsequent studies were collaborative efforts. The first had begun while I was still at Illinois. It was suggested by Roger Knudson, an assistant in the research on interpersonal relationships that Stephen Golding and I were doing. Knudson and I were both curious about the interest patterns of professional psychologists. I had long suspected that the low research productivity of professional psychologists had less to do with their training than with the demands of their jobs and with their interests. I suspected that psychologists, like any other people, would devote discretionary time to work they enjoyed, not what their teachers in graduate school had told them they ought to do. So, Knudson and I asked, what do clinical psychologists like to do? What do they hate to do?

In our study, we used a work preference inventory that had been constructed previously (Peterson & Baron, 1975) by examining the functions involved in the clinical laboratories that provided practicum training in our program and adding some items that described teaching and research activities. The inventory was sent to a random sample of Division 12 members and to clinical psychology students in two large midwestern universities besides our own at Illinois. We received nearly complete returns from graduate students and from 65% of the Division 12 members.

Factor analyses of the 25-item inventory revealed a clear two-factor structure. Highly coherent, orthogonal factors of interest in practice, on the one hand, and of research, on the other hand, appeared. Means and standard deviations of scores on the two factors were then calculated for each group of students and for occupational subgroups of APA clinical psychologists. On the average, both students and established psychologists reported stronger interests in practice than in research. Very few people said they disliked clinical work, though positive interests in service were strongest among the Illinois PsyD students and privately employed clinical practitioners. Among APA clinicians, those in private practice and those who worked in public agencies showed similar interests. On the average, they enjoyed practice but were indifferent toward research. Of all the groups examined, only university faculty members showed a stronger average interest in research than in practice. The contrast between Division 12 practitioners and academicians paralleled that between Illinois PsyD and PhD students (Peterson & Knudson, 1979).

Evaluating an educational program ultimately requires assessment of competence on the part of the people who have completed the program. As everybody who has tried to measure competence in the practice of psychology knows, that is hard to do. At least, however, we might approach more satisfactory measures by examining what supervisors *say* they observe in evaluating competence among trainees, by studying the attributes they claim to consider when deciding whether a student is competent enough to be given a passing grade in a practicum course, recommended for an internship, or otherwise certified as proficient in the practice of psychology. Brenna Bry and I did some work along these lines (Peterson & Bry, 1980).

The study was done in our professional school at Rutgers, which at the time employed 14 full-time faculty members, 20 adjunct faculty members, and 68 field supervisors who participated in training students over a wide range of professional skills. In the first year of the study, all supervising faculty were mailed a list of the 126 students who had completed at least 2 years of professional training. The supervisors were asked to identify the students with whom they had worked closely and to rate each student as *outstanding, competent, mediocre,* or *incompetent*. Then they were to select the best of the outstanding students and the worst of the incompetent or low mediocre students and write down the characteristics of the students that had determined judgment of them as good or poor professional psychologists.

Among trainees considered most competent, high intelligence stood out as the most frequently mentioned characteristic, followed closely by various interpersonal and motivational qualities. In describing the least competent trainees, lack of knowledge and intellectual density were mentioned most often, followed by various personal disturbances that appeared to interfere with sound professional functioning.

In the second year of the study, the lists of descriptors were combined into a single rating schedule of 28 items, and the resulting "professional competence inventory" was sent to supervising faculty for use in rating another cohort of trainees. Factor analysis of the schedule yielded four dimensions: responsibility (integrity, conscientiousness, etc.), warmth (compassion, openness, etc.), intelligence (articulateness, clarity of thought, etc.), and experience (technical skill, self-sufficiency, etc.). Factor scores were correlated with ratings of general competence separately for supervisors who described their theoretical orientations as psychodynamic, behavioral, or eclectic. The correlations were all positive, quite high, and fairly evenly distributed over factors and viewpoints. In general, supervisors who claimed to subscribe to different theoretical orientations looked to the same qualities in appraising professional competence among their trainees (Peterson & Bry, 1980).

As PsyD programs developed across the country after the Vail conference, questions continued about the kinds of work graduates were doing, how well they did the work, and how their training and degree were received by others. By the summer of 1980, 21 PsyD programs were in operation. Nine of these had produced a total of 273 graduates, and a nationwide survey of the career experiences of Doctors of Psychology was both desirable and feasible.

Three Rutgers graduate students joined me (Peterson, Eaton, Levine, & Snepp, 1982) in designing a questionnaire to yield several kinds of information. One set of items concerned the professional activities in which graduates were engaged: their job titles, institutional affiliations, balances of agency work and independent practice, and distributions of time spent in various activities. Another set of items concerned experiences in obtaining employment, joining professional organizations, and gaining licensure or certification as professional psychologists. The items were especially directed toward determining whether Doctors of Psychology had experienced any difficulties related to the PsyD degree as they entered the professional community. Respondents were asked to indicate degrees of satisfaction or dissatisfaction with professional psychology as a career and with the graduate education they had received. Several of the items in the inventory were drawn from a previous survey of PhD graduates of scientist–practitioner programs in clinical psychology (Garfield & Kurtz, 1976) and thus allowed comparison between PsyDs and PhDs.

The proportions of people working in hospitals, outpatient clinics, and independent practice did not differ much across the two samples. A larger fraction of PsyDs than PhDs were working in the community mental health centers of the time. As expected, more PhDs were employed by universities, though many people might not have expected nearly 10% of the Doctors of Psychology to hold jobs in universities and medical schools. The great majority of PsyDs, most of the remaining 90%, were in situations in which professional service was the dominant occupation.

As expected, PsyDs spent more time than PhDs in direct professional services such as psychotherapy and clinical assessment. Next to no time (less than 2%) was spent by PsyDs in research, but this seemed less remarkable than the fact that only 7% of the time of PhD clinicians was devoted to research, however strongly the values and skills of research might have been emphasized in the scientist–practitioner programs from which they came. About 46% of the time of PhD clinical psychologists and 69% of the time of Doctors of Psychology was spent in professional activities. Both PhD and PsyD psychologists spent substantial amounts of time in supervision and administration, however little preparation they might have received for those responsibilities.

When the PhD clinicians were asked to indicate degrees of satisfaction or dissatisfaction with graduate training, 77% expressed some degree of satisfaction with the education they had received. Garfield and Kurtz interpreted this to mean that the PhD programs "must be doing something right" (1976, p. 5). On the same scale used by Garfield and Kurtz, 96% of the PsyDs indicated some degree of satisfaction with their training. Significantly and substantially more PhDs than PsyDs were dissatisfied with their graduate education.

Only 12 of the 184 PsyDs who took part in our study reported any difficulty, related to the degree, in seeking employment. For the most part, the problems they reported were questions of information: "Some people did ask if the PsyD was equal to a PhD" and, "Initial unfamiliarity with the degree." In a few cases, clear attitudinal opposition was encountered: "The chief psychologist, a traditionalist who was partial to the PhD, was against hiring me" and, "There were a few hostile PhDs." The great majority of respondents, however—94% of them—reported no problems whatsoever, and many of those wrote comments to say that the PsyD was an asset in gaining employment: "The PsyD degree turned out to be an advantage in the sense that I could document my range of clinical experience," "Potential employers were impressed by the extent of my supervised experience," and, "The practical experience I had was a definite asset in job seeking."

At this stage in our studies, fears about perception of the Doctor of Psychology degree as a second-rate credential appeared to be unfounded. Whether the questions we asked in our survey would be answered the same way today and in the future can only be determined by continued study. We were prepared to acknowledge and adapt to negative findings if any had shown up, but all of our early results were positive. They appeared to justify our decisions and encourage others to follow our lead.

CRITICAL CONCERNS

The PsyD program at the University of Illinois was discontinued in 1980. I have already discussed that matter in chapter 5, but there is more to the story. After I left Illinois, several successive directors of clinical training continued to track the careers of graduates of the PsyD program. Although all graduates in the first cohort had taken jobs in public service agencies and most PsyDs in following years continued to do so in their first postdoctoral positions, more and more of the graduates later left their jobs in human service agencies and went into private practice. In practice, they spent most of their time doing psychotherapy. Our program had not been designed to produce more psychotherapists. If that was the main outcome of all our efforts, there seemed to be no more point in continuing the program than there had been in sustaining PhD programs the graduates of which did no research.

Few of the faculty who remained at Illinois after I left were as sympathetic as I was to psychotherapy as a career choice. I did not believe that professional training programs should be devoted exclusively or even primarily to psychotherapy as the core of professional work, but I believed that clinical psychologists should be well prepared to take on the responsibilities of psychotherapy. If some of our graduates, doctoral degrees and licenses in hand, should decide to leave relatively low paying, bureaucratically encumbered jobs in public agencies and go into private practice, who could blame them? The pay was better, their lives were easier, and they were amply qualified to do the work.

Who indeed could blame the Illinois faculty for relieving themselves of the unrewarding burdens of the PsyD program? All of the people I knew on the Illinois clinical faculty were highly responsible teachers. They insisted on close supervision of students in all professional activities. When we planned the PsyD program, we had hoped to gain strong supervisory contributions from practicing psychologists in the community. Those contributions did not materialize as expected. The directors of the clinical program found few practitioners in the Champaign-Urbana region whose professional commitments or supervisory skills the university faculty could trust. So the main burden of clinical supervision fell to full-time professors, and when the time came to decide about a promotion or a pay raise all those hours spent in clinical supervision did not count for much. The academic faculty who made the pay and promotion decisions might offer an appreciative nod to a clinical teacher who spent 8 to 12 hours each week listening to therapy tapes and discussing them with students, but that accomplishment did not score anywhere near the mark reached by procurement of a large competitive research grant or publication of a series of frequently cited articles in a prime scholarly journal.

The dissertations attempted by PsyD students and approved by the graduate college faculty committees were not easier to supervise than PhD dissertations. Many were more difficult to supervise. Many of the PsyD projects were large-scale field studies, the dependent variables of which resisted measurement, the independent variables of which were impossible to control, and the implementation of which was often impeded by public inertia or beset by outright political opposition. Most of the studies were excellent local science, but the findings were rarely of general interest, and few of the reports qualified for publication in mainstream scientific journals. For the faculty, the net effect was a heavy burden of supervisory responsibility with limited payoff in advancing their own careers. In reverting to a smaller, research-oriented PhD program, they made what was, for them, a rational choice.

However persuasive ideological arguments for direct education in professional psychology may have been, and whatever our outcome studies may have shown, the calculus of costs and benefits to clinical faculty in the academic departments of research universities did not encourage establishment of PsyD programs in those institutions, and few programs were developed there. Instead, as noted in several chapters of this book, the growth of practitioner programs took place mainly in small departments and freestanding professional schools of variable quality.

Very few of the PsyD programs that formed after the Vail conference followed the Illinois pattern of cooperative partnership with a strong PhD program. I suspect that some of the authors of those programs did not understand our insistence on comprehensive, science-based education. Others may have understood but disagreed with our ideological position. They had their own ideas about the nature of professional psychology and requirements for the education of practitioners in our field. As a result, the programs they created vary widely in substance and quality.

So far, no one has proved that the new PsyD programs, as a group, are inferior to PhD programs or the PsyD programs that preceded them. No one has shown that they are superior, either. The procedures required for decisive appraisal have not yet been developed. All we have so far are self-reports and global ratings by supervisors. Results of the studies done to date, however, should not be ignored. Crude as they are, they are our only alternatives to parochial experience and ideological prejudice. Performance comparisons by internship supervisors (Shemberg & Leventhal, 1981; Snepp & Peterson, 1988) have failed to show any significant differences between trainees from PsyD and PhD programs. Applicants over all appeared to be better prepared for internship than they had been in the past, and equal proportions of PsyD and PhD students showed some deficiencies. These findings should give pause to any internship directors considering policies that categorically exclude or offer preference to PsyD candidates for training in their agencies. Decisions about acceptability for internship, like those for professional employment, are best made on an individual basis.

Other studies have shown, however, that admission to research-oriented

PhD programs is, on average, four times more selective than admission to PsyD programs (Mayne, Norcross, & Sayette, 1994), that completion of PhD programs in clinical psychology takes, on average, 1.5 years longer than it takes to get a PsyD (Gaddy, Charlot-Swilley, Nelson, & Reich, 1995), and that faculty–student ratios in freestanding professional schools, most of which now offer the PsyD degree, are substantially lower, on average, than in PhD programs and university-based PsyD programs (Caddy & LaPointe, 1984). These facts offer presumptive grounds for fearing that some of the PsyD programs that have been established since the Vail conference leave something to be desired by way of quality.

We also know that the numbers of psychologists receiving doctoral degrees from professional schools are proportionally much larger than those receiving PhD degrees from the academic departments of research universities (Stricker & Cummings, 1992). In absolute numbers, more practitioners are coming through the PhD programs than from all the professional schools and programs combined. No substantiating data support the elitist claim that the PhDs are better prepared for professional work. Our profession is still numerically tiny compared with such well-established professions as medicine, nursing, and social work. If and when we develop new roles—as proposed in the final section of this book—present numbers will fall far short of those required to meet public demands for psychological services. Nevertheless, the perception that we are currently overproducing poorly educated practitioners is widespread. This is the main functional concern shared by everyone who is dedicated to the highest levels of excellence in the preparation of psychologists for professional careers.

Another concern is more symbolic than functional, but it is even more deeply felt. That is the fear that professional psychology, in moving to direct education for practice and the PsyD degree, will compromise its identity as a science. This was the fear that impelled the architects of the Boulder model to insist that clinical psychologists be scientists first and practitioners second, that moved participants at the Chicago conference to reaffirm the values of the scientist–practitioner pattern of education, that encouraged most academic psychologists to ignore or repudiate approval of professional schools and the PsyD degree by the Vail conference, and that has inspired many thoughtful educators (e.g., Belar & Perry, 1992; Dawes, 1994; McFall, 1991, 1996; Perry, 1979; Wiens, 1986) to oppose practitioner programs and the professional doctorate in psychology.

The arguments vary in substance and stridency, but they sound a common alarm. According to the critics, whatever credibility psychology may claim rests on its identity as a science, and any actions that jeopardize that identity endanger not only the quality of the work psychologists do but the public image of the discipline and the fundamental ideological unity of the field. Among the more commonly quoted anti-PsyD arguments is the comment by Ericksen that, "Insofar as professional psychology becomes pinched off from scientific psychology it will be taking one clear backward step toward becoming a second-class service technology" (Ericksen, 1966, p. 953) and the following statement that Bertram Brown, a psychiatrist, made while he was director of the National Institute of Mental Health:

> Psychology, as a profession, has inherent in it a very strong scientific base about the nature of the human mind. If it splits into practitioners, doctors of psychology who do not necessarily have training into the nature of science, the nature of scientific methods, some training in doing research, it will become just another competing profession in the human problems arena along with social work, nursing, marriage and family counseling and a host of other professions. . . . [I]t will be changing the nature of the profession itself. (Brown, 1980, quoted in Wiens, 1986, pp. 53–54)

Those who oppose professional schools, practitioner programs, and the PsyD degree are concerned about the loss of scientific identity and disciplinary control. According to these critics, psychology as a science is valued. Psychology as a science–profession is acceptable, especially when it is primarily devoted to the aims of science. Psychology as an independent profession, however, is not acceptable. If we lose our hold on the PhD and all it represents, the critics fear, we may drift away from our scientific moorings to be lost in a sea of near-professions, following the tides of popular demand and technical fashion wherever they might carry us.

INSTITUTIONAL REALITIES

When our Founders framed the Tenth Amendment to the Constitution of the United States, assigning authority over education and other undesignated powers to the states, they set the conditions for the diversity we see today in the educational practices of our society. In most other countries, educational uniformity is maintained by some kind of governmental agency. In North America, several Canadian universities considered establishing PsyD programs. Formal proposals to do so were submitted by York University and a consortium made up of Lakehead University and the Universities of Minnesota and Wisconsin. However, the proposals were not approved by the Ontario ministry of higher education, and the development of PsyD programs elsewhere in Canada has been a slow and difficult process.

In the United States, requirements for establishing doctoral programs vary from state to state and change from time to time. The liberal conditions that prevailed in California in the 1960s and 1970s, for example, allowed practitioners to establish freestanding professional schools, recruit students, and award the PhD degree to graduates. Recent changes in regional accreditation policy now require most of the California professional schools to grant the PsyD degree to graduates of their professional programs. Efforts to develop a freestanding professional school in New Jersey were blocked by the state's department of higher education, whose standards for doctoral programs required either a large monetary endowment or affiliation with a university. In most states, requirements for the establishment of doctoral-level practitioner programs in fields like psychology are rather vaguely defined. If a group of practitioners want to open up a freestanding professional school and can claim a public need, offer credible documentation to support the claim, define plans for facilities and administrative management, and list credentials of prospective faculty, they can usually succeed in accomplishing their aims. If counseling psychology faculties in small university departments decide to add more time and additional training to master's programs and award the PsyD degree to graduates, there is little to keep them from doing so. Before the Vail conference, the strongest restraining force on such developments was the collective sanction of the academic community in psychology. Once the gates were opened at Vail, there was no way to stop the flow of new PsyD programs. By now, most of them are well established. They will not be phased out, as some critics have proposed. For better or for worse, most of the PsyD programs now in operation are here to stay.

In describing the rapid expansion of PsyD programs after the Vail conference, I did not intend to suggest that the creation of new programs was easy. Each state and every college imposed its own controlling conditions, rational or irrational, on educational developments under its jurisdiction. Any faculty determined to establish a PsyD program could look forward to many hurdles, difficult bureaucratic negotiations, political opposition, including "dirty tricks," from academic faculty running PhD programs in the area, and a long pull of hard work. Nor did I intend to suggest that the faculties who designed the post-Vail programs typically came forward with the weakest proposals they could hope to slide past the governing agencies whose approval they required. Most of the people I know who founded PsyD programs carried admirable dedication and high ideals to the creative enterprise, and most of their proposals were laboriously and thoughtfully developed. In my description of the formative process I intended only to show that variations in regulatory control over higher education in the United States of America allow more diversity in educational opportunities, and carry greater risk than in any other postindustrial nation I know. Without the freedom to experiment that our laws allow, there would be no PsyD programs in the United States. Another consequence of our freedom, however, is a greater range in quality. The realistic imperative now before us is not to get rid of one kind of program or another, but to improve the quality of all our programs, PsyD and PhD alike, and trust other forces to eliminate those that fail to do so.

Quality control of education in the United States depends on voluntary establishment of internal standards and voluntary participation in our system of accreditation. In the case of practitioner programs in psychology and the PsyD degree, the development and exercise of both kinds of controls has been labored and complex. The continuing story is told in the following section of this book. In our free-market society, economic conditions also exert powerful influences on education, especially at the graduate level. Doctoral students who could once look forward to lucrative careers in the private practice of psychotherapy must now face the realities of managed health care and increased competition not only from increasing numbers in their own field but from other disciplines the practitioners of which offer similar services.

Under these conditions, practitioners are likely to be more cautious than they were in the past to establish new, freestanding professional schools. If any schools now in operation continue to offer little more than training for psychotherapy, if they offer only the clinical components of traditional PhD programs but leave out training for research, economic forces are likely to drive them out of business. Students aiming for careers in professional psychology will still find the best available preparation for their life work in strong science-based practitioner programs, but as costs and competition increase, students will be more wary than before. Enlightened by studying the extensive materials on graduate study available from the APA, examining a wide range of options including those represented in this book, and close personal scrutiny of institutions bidding for their applications, students will not be as ready as they once were to accumulate large debts to enter the profession of psychology. PhD programs that offer preparation for research careers but disavow any intention of training psychologists for practice will be no more attractive to students interested in professional careers than narrow, poorly staffed programs leading to the PsyD degree. One result, I hope and believe, will be a winnowing out of weak, inappropriately designed educational programs. Another result, I also hope and believe, will be the redirection of professional services to meet the most pressing needs of our society, close scrutiny of the services to discard those that do not work and maintain those that do, and continuing innovation to offer an ever extending array of services to clients under the changing conditions that our fluid society is bound to present.

Critics who argue that our profession must not abandon its base in science are correct. That is our special strength in the broad field of human services. The demands of a science-based profession, however, do not require every practitioner to contribute general knowledge to science nor hold the PhD degree. They do require every practitioner to acquire comprehensive knowledge of psychology and the flexible but rigorous skills of disciplined inquiry. As a community, psychology can learn to get along with less interprofessional derision, less enthusiasm for fratricidal politics, better communication, and more active cooperation than we have seen in the recent past. Fears that the development of psychology as a profession will somehow lessen or destroy psychology as a science are irrational. Whenever the professional forces grow too strong, the forces of science come into play. The journal *Professional Psychology* becomes *Professional Psychology: Research and*

Practice. A new organization, The American Association of Applied and Preventive Psychology, is formed to ensure preservation and development of the scientific foundations of professional work. The professional and scientific factions in psychology are now defined with enough clarity, and have reached sufficient size and strength, to advance their distinctive aims with steady confidence and unremitting energy. At the same time, practitioners and scientists need to combine their efforts in serving the larger society. Without science, our profession is not merely weak, it ceases to be a profession. Without our profession, scientific psychology could avoid the human morass, but it would not confront the most exciting challenges of our time. Each needs the other, not as a rival but as a partner.

III

QUALITY CONTROL IN PROFESSIONAL EDUCATION

INTRODUCTION

QUALITY CONTROL IN PROFESSIONAL EDUCATION

A recent study of issues of importance to members of the APA identified "standards for curriculum and program quality for education and training at the doctoral level" (Oakland, 1994, p. 884) as the most important of the 32 issues included in the survey. Although those issues are complex and concerns may take many forms, the central focus is clear. Vigorous critiques of professional education and various exclusionary political actions leave little doubt that the heart of the concern is the threat to quality that many APA members perceive in the rapid growth of programs expressly designed to prepare psychologists for professional careers, and especially the spread of programs beyond research universities to freestanding professional schools and small departments with limited resources and shallow traditions of research. The demand for quality control, always firm, has now grown strident.

In American higher education, the primary locus of quality control is internal. Quality, or the lack of it, is mainly determined by the program itself. In chapter 8, I describe seven conditions that I consider essential for attainment of high quality in the education of professional psychologists. I hope faculty appraising their own programs and students choosing locations for graduate study will find these guidelines useful. A preliminary version of the statement was presented in 1993 as a keynote address for a National

Council of Schools and Programs of Professional Psychology (NCSPP) conference on clinical training. In revising the paper as a book chapter, I have extended some of my comments, especially those concerned with the several kinds of organizations in which graduate education in professional psychology is conducted. Some of these amendments were drawn from a paper titled "Organizational Dilemmas in the Education of Professional Psychologists" that was originally presented in 1983 at the first NCSPP conference on quality in professional psychology training. My views on these issues changed very little over the intervening decade.

American academicians concerned with graduate education often protect their academic freedoms with such fierce intensity that they resist all forms of encroachment on their autonomy, from licensing boards, accreditation committees, or any other external agencies. Consensus among peers is often sought, however. In American psychology, standards that have been endorsed by broadly representative training conferences are widely accepted. National conferences at Boulder and Vail, Colorado, for example, have had strongly visible effects on professional education in our field. Beyond these, numerous conferences on direct education for the practice of psychology have been sponsored by NCSPP. The history of the council and a summary of its conferences are presented in chapter 9.

As is appropriate for a science, academic psychology resisted the external reviews and the risks of inappropriate standards that are inherent in any form of program accreditation throughout its first half century. When psychology officially acknowledged its identity as a profession at the end of World War II, however, the constraints of accreditation were accepted as matters of financial interest as well as public responsibility. Since then, the accreditational system has grown rapidly in size and has changed several times in its organizational structure. Chapter 10 describes the history of accreditation in American psychology.

8

ESSENTIALS OF QUALITY IN THE EDUCATION OF PROFESSIONAL PSYCHOLOGISTS

In several ways, I consider the development of professional schools and programs that has taken place over the past 30 years a laudable accomplishment. From detailed, case-by-case study of the careers of graduates of our programs at Rutgers, I know that the graduates are doing the work they were trained to do. They are all employed, over a wide range of settings, in a great variety of activities, working with clients who offer an enormous range of challenges and opportunities. After reading the resumes of our graduates, I did not feel ashamed of a single one of them, and I felt proud of the many who are fulfilling our highest ideals for effective, innovative professional service. I believe, and hope the collective studies we are doing in the National Council of Schools and Programs of Professional Psychology (NCSPP) soon will show, that many other schools are doing as well. I am pleased by the work of NCSPP as an organization, especially the unrelenting self-scrutiny and demand for quality that we have imposed on ourselves. In our beginning, we were a handful of men, all white men, brought together in part to meet an organizational requirement for some training grants that never materialized. Now, after many conferences, hundreds of other meetings, many thousands of hours of individual work, and impressive diversification by gender and ethnicity, we are as strong a voice as any to be heard in matters related to the education of professional psychologists.

I am heartened by the extent to which psychology as a corporate discipline has acknowledged the legitimacy of professional service and educational programs designed to prepare psychologists for careers of practice. Fifty years ago, the professional aims of psychology were officially excluded from the APA constitution. Thirty years ago, programs specifically designed to educate psychologists for professional service did not exist, and only one program declared preparation for practice as its main emphasis. Today, the Practice Directorate stands alongside the Science Directorate as an integral part of the APA structure, and the first head of the Education Directorate was once dean of a professional school. We have come a long way from our beginnings, and we have much to celebrate in our progress.

In other ways, however, the growth of professional schools and the spread of the professional doctorate worry me as much as they disturb our harshest critics. I am haunted by the fear that too many professional schools and PsyD programs will be cobbled together in the wrong places, by the wrong people, for the wrong reasons. Establishment of the Doctor of Psychology degree has opened a door to the development of doctoral programs in many institutions that would not stand a chance of gaining approval for graduate education at the doctoral level in other fields. The attractions are strong, especially if a master's degree program in some area of psychological service is already in place. Plenty of well-qualified students will apply, including a built-in subset from the master's program. Faculty will gain the satisfactions that come with involvement in a doctoral program. College presidents can brighten the luster of their institutions, often advancing them to university status, by supporting development of doctoral programs. Top administrators are especially tempted to go ahead if they think they can do the job cheaply. Flexible as standards must be to allow desirable variation, accreditation should not be out of reach, and even if it is, accreditation of postsecondary educational programs is technically voluntary in the United States. For many considering the creation of doctoral programs in professional psychology, there is much to gain and little to lose, whether or not the programs are of the highest attainable quality.

Except, as loss in the longer range, academic excellence and public benefit. The last thing in the world our society needs is an oversupply of poorly trained professional psychologists. What we need is a sufficient supply of carefully chosen, thoroughly educated practitioners; creative development of new services, in part by the practitioners themselves; scrupulous evaluation of those services; and a constant renewal of our discipline through imaginative conceptualization and sound research. There is nothing wrong with the establishment of practitioner programs in small colleges and independent professional schools as long as the people running the programs do a first-class job of it. But our world has no use at all for PsyD programs that are little more than clinical PhD programs without research. Mediocrity will kill our movement. It will help nobody else. In my opinion, anyone who perpetrates a PsyD program or professional school without planning at least to seek APA accreditation should be charged with unethical conduct.

From a long history of telephone conversations and correspondence with people considering establishment of professional schools and programs, I am forced to the uneasy conclusion that many people do not grasp the essentials of a strong doctoral program in professional psychology. These days, many NCSPP leaders are getting the kinds of inquiries I have received over the years. "What does it take to establish a professional school or a PsyD program?" The first reply to people who ask that question is another question. "Do you intend to meet the APA standards for accreditation?" If the answer is no, tell them to reconsider. If the answer is yes, advise them to contact the APA Office of Program Consultation and Accreditation for all the information and help that office can provide, and then join NCSPP to gain the counsel and support needed to travel a long, hazardous road. Professional schools and programs are still a minority among educational institutions in psychology. We should welcome more good members. But we should not encourage efforts that are doomed to mediocrity by low aspirations and unreadiness to commit the resources needed to do the job.

Within our council, the most important move we can make is to set a higher standard of quality than we have ever set before. Accreditation is only a first step. We must move beyond to a level of excellence we are only beginning to realize. How to do that is a challenge to everybody who takes on the responsibility of educating people for the practice of psychology. We will not find a *single* way to meet our goals. We have already found many ways to meet many goals, and the proof of success for any school or program will lie in attainment of its goals, not in speculation about prerequisite conditions. However, we have been in the business of training practitioners in psychology for more than a quarter of a century now, and our experience offers some fairly definite indications about the essentials of quality in our field. As widely diverse as our programs may be, some common conditions must be met if we are to do the best possible job of educating professional psychologists. Here are the main essentials as I see them at this time.

AN ENCOURAGING CULTURE

The first condition is a social culture in which both the commonalities and the differences between scientific research and professional practice are understood, and practice is valued for its own sake. Despite some important similarities between research and practice, the differences are profound. Scientists aim above all to advance general knowledge; practitioners aim above all to help their clients. Scientists choose problems to investigate; practitioners address the problems clients bring to them. Scientists control conditions of inquiry; practitioners cannot exclude the complexities of natural life. Practitioners in psychology can be regarded as local scientists, but no more so than physicians or engineers, and critical differences between the aims and demands of research and practice must be acknowledged.

An encouraging culture for the education of professional psychologists requires that practice be valued for its own sake. It is above all in this regard that many programs in major research universities fail. How can one tell whether professional work is valued in an educational program? Some time ago, when practitioner programs were just beginning, Paul Meehl (1971) suggested some clues. I have added a few items from my own experience and made a little test of the signs.

- Does the catalog description say that the program is designed to produce researchers rather than mere practitioners? Score minus 10.
- Do faculty members speak of practice almost entirely as an arena for research or as a valuable activity in its own right? Subtract 5 in the former case; add 5 in the latter case.
- What kinds of practice, if any, do the faculty do? Score 5 if some of the faculty practice some of the time; add 10 if all of them are engaged in some form of practice.
- At promotion time, is the amount and quality of professional service considered, along with research and teaching, in evaluating faculty contributions? Score 10 if it is; −10 if research is really the only thing that matters.
- When students are chatting in the lounge, do they talk about the cases they are seeing and the service projects they have undertaken or almost entirely about traditional forms of research? Score 5 if they talk about service; 10 if you hear enthusiastic discussion of apparently effective innovations; −5 if almost all you hear is talk about confirmatory research.
- Do faculty speak with pride of a graduate who has designed and managed an evidently successful public service program but never published any formal research? Score 10.
- If someone you love needed psychological help, would you send him or her to a graduate of the program? Score 20.

If the total falls on the negative side, you may be considering one of the best research programs in the country, but you are looking at a poor choice for education in the practice of psychology. If other conditions are well met, the higher the positive score the better the chance for an excellent professional education.

In affirming the values of practice, I do not disparage science. Ever since psychology broke away from philosophy little more than 100 years ago, researchers have been working to establish our field as a science. Most historians agree that we have made considerable progress along this line. No one can dispute successfully the importance of sound research, both basic and applied. No one can legitimately require the immediate practical application of all research. Yet the worship of research for its own sake, the *scientism* that is widespread in American universities, must be challenged.

Again, Meehl's ideas are provocative. In a paper titled, "The Seven Sacred Cows of Academia: Can We Afford Them?" he (1979) defined a set of assumptions that appear to be devoutly believed by most academics, but have never been documented, may well be false, and cost a lot of money that might be more wisely spent if alternative assumptions were allowed to prevail. One of the assumptions is, "Most research published by college professors is worthwhile." Noting that the average journal article in the social sciences is read by fewer than 50 people, and that the usual fate of theories in the social sciences is neither empirical refutation nor scientific permanence but a slow fade from scholarly attention as researchers get bored and turn to other topics (cf. Meehl, 1978), Meehl said, "I think it is fair to say that the great majority of papers published by professors of psychology (at least in the 'soft' areas) and sociology have no enduring value either as bricks in the edifice of theoretical knowledge or as contributions to the solution of any practical problem" (1979, p. 19). The problems of poor dissemination and low impact are not limited to the soft sciences. Enrico Fermi, on hearing a colleague describe some unexciting but methodologically sound studies in physics as "bricks in the edifice of science," is reputed to have said that most of them were "just bricks lying around in the scientific brickyard" (Meehl, 1984, p. 13). The distinguished historian of science, Derek J. de Solla Price, after studying citation patterns in scientific journals, estimated that approximately 10% of published articles are not cited at all and 50% are cited fewer than five times in the ensuing decade. His report ends with the following lament. "I am tempted to conclude that a very large fraction of the alleged 35,000 journals now current must be reckoned as merely a distant background noise and as very far from central or strategic in any of the knitted strips from which the cloth of science is woven" (Price, 1965, p. 515). Since Price conducted his survey, the number of scholarly journals published worldwide has more than doubled. It seems likely that the increase in informational volume, the sheer glut of poorly integrated facts flowing into journals and through electronic media today, has reduced still further the impact of most of the material that is put into print.

Good research is indisputably valuable, but there is nothing holy about it. The common concurrence of reverence for research and contempt for practice is damaging to our field and a disservice to the public. We need a strong profession as much as we need a strong science, and in order to have a strong profession we must provide an educational culture in which professional service is deeply and consistently esteemed. It is inherently impossible to educate self-respecting, confident, creative practitioners in a community in which authorities see research as the only truly valuable kind of work for psychologists to do, who insist on primary devotion to research among the students they admit to their programs, and who regard the full-time practitioners among their graduates as failures.

A COMPREHENSIVE, RIGOROUS CURRICULUM

I will not attempt to define the substance of predoctoral education in professional psychology. NCSPP has made considerable progress along these lines in its conferences and written documents (Bourg et al., 1987; R. Peterson et al., 1992; R. Peterson, D. Peterson, Abrams, & Stricker, in press). For this occasion, I will only offer four reminders. The first is that the curriculum for the education of professional psychologists must be comprehensive. The needs of the human community are wide-ranging. Biological, individual, interpersonal, and organizational processes are all involved in human functioning. Practitioners who expect to meet the needs of the community must be prepared for systematic inquiry and intervention at any of those levels and to shift from one to another as the condition of the client requires. Scientists can afford to focus more narrowly. Indeed, any investigator who aims to advance knowledge in any field of inquiry has to understand everything that is already known about that field and move beyond established knowledge to an original contribution. This usually requires a degree of specialization that is unacceptable in the education of practitioners.

The second reminder is that the problems students meet in graduate school have to resemble the problems they will meet in their professional careers if we are to maximize transfer of the skills students learn in training to the practical settings they will be working in later on. This holds for research requirements as much as for clinical experience. Practitioners need to learn generalizable strategies of inquiry that suit the kinds of conditions they are likely to face in practice. The dissertation and other investigative exercises should represent the ecology of issues that career practitioners are likely to encounter in their daily lives.

The third reminder is that the professional curriculum must be rigorous. Education for practice is not easier than education for research. In some ways it is more difficult. Professionals have to master knowledge over a wider range than scientists do, and they must also learn the skills of assessment and intervention by long practice under close supervision. The challenges practitioners face are as demanding as those of science, and educational preparation to meet those challenges must be just as demanding or more so.

The fourth reminder is that the evaluation and improvement of curricula is a never-ending responsibility for educators of professional psychologists. With Roger Peterson as first editor, my colleagues and I have prepared two summary statements of the NCSPP model of education for practice in psychology (R. Peterson, D. Peterson, & Abrams, in press; R. Peterson, D. Peterson, Abrams, & Sticker, in press). This work is the product of numerous conferences and untold hours of work by the people in the member institutions of the council. In my opinion, it is the strongest statement to date on standards for the education of professional psychologists. But I am not entirely content with the consensually endorsed curriculum as it currently stands, and I hope nobody else is either. Our goal is to teach professional psychologists the very best that they need to know to practice psychology effectively for the rest of their lives. As our educational operations are functioning today, we are clearly not doing as well as we might in this regard. I am not talking just about your school. I am talking about my school as well, and about the educational preparation of professional psychologists nationwide. For this argument, one example will prove my point.

It should be obvious that we must teach our students treatment methods whose efficacy has been thoroughly documented by rigorous outcome research. Yet the Task Force on Promotion and Dissemination of Psychological Procedures (APA Division of Clinical Psychology, 1995) has shown that only a fraction of graduate students in clinical psychology are currently trained in the use of these procedures. We need to change that as soon as possible, despite our inertia, over any ideological resistance we might encounter, and however much it may cost. And then, as reflexive appraisal continues, we will find something else to change. The process never ends.

AN EXPERIENCED, DIVERSE, PRODUCTIVE FACULTY

Faculty members must be skilled in the practices they teach. If I go in for a surgical operation, I want the surgeon who wields the scalpel to have been trained by someone who has done a great many operations of that kind, and I want my own surgeon to have had a good deal of practice too. I want someone who has encountered and surmounted the common problems that arise in my kind of ailment and developed the creative versatility required to manage any special challenges my case may present. I do not care much if he or she has ever written an article in a scientific journal. I want my surgeon to know where to cut, how to cut, and how to sew me up again, and I want my doctor's teacher to know the same, only more so. In a comparable way, I want to be assured that anyone I see for psychotherapy or organizational consultation has a convincing history of successful experience, and I'll bet most critics who argue that training and experience do not matter in the education of professional psychologists look for the same qualities in seeking help for themselves or their loved ones. Practice must be taught by seasoned, skilled practitioners. If they cannot be hired as tenured faculty because they haven't published any research, they need to be hired in an adjunct capacity and given an honored role in faculty affairs.

Attaining the comprehensiveness essential to professional education requires a wide diversity among faculty, not only in gender and ethnicity but in conceptual orientation, substantive knowledge, and professional expertise. This means that the faculties of professional schools must either be large or uncommonly versatile. Tiny departments cannot do the job. In converting master's programs to PsyD programs, some planners may be tempted to offer only the limited clinical training that is provided in the most heavily research-oriented PhD programs and form their distinction from the latter principally by gutting the research requirement. Adding a couple of new members to a five-person faculty, offering release time to one of those to run a clinic, and adding another half-time secretary may allow legal operation of a PsyD program and attract some students, but it will not offer the best professional education our discipline can provide.

The faculty collectively must not only be experienced and diverse, they must also be productive. I do not hold with the requirement, nearly universal nowadays among the high-prestige academic departments I know, that every faculty member must be an active, grant-procuring researcher publishing a high annual quota of articles in prime journals. I do believe, however, that every first-class professional school must include among its faculty an active, visible contingent of contributing scholars. In psychology as in medicine, law, engineering, pharmacy, and every other profession, the best professional schools need to be wellsprings of critical inquiry and innovation. Some of the faculty need to be leading the field in their own specialties. Without this stimulation and excitement, the schools stagnate intellectually and in time cease to be professional schools at all. They become trade schools, turning out technicians.

In institutions in which voluminous research productivity is not a necessary qualification for employment, special administrative measures may be needed to encourage scholarly enterprise among faculty. Some of the member institutions of NCSPP have established centers for research, on process and outcome of practice itself and in the vast, untamed wilderness of human problems that practitioners face every day but about which little systematic knowledge is available. Big Science researchers avoid many of these problems, largely because they do not allow the levels of control and precision demanded by most major grant agencies. In professional schools, opportunities are wide open not only for traditional forms of applied research but for exploratory work of many kinds, for methodological and theoretical analysis, replicated case studies, descriptive and quasi-experimental field studies, for disciplined inquiries over the full range of scholarly topics that must be considered in a comprehensive profession. In institutions in which research traditions are not already well established, however, the schools themselves must usually contrive creative ways to provide the necessary supports.

INTELLIGENT, CARING, TOUGH-MINDED STUDENTS

Practitioners who are actively seeking to meet the most pressing needs of their communities never know exactly what kinds of problems they will encounter next. If they are to manage each problem sensibly, they must often bring pertinent aspects of complex information together in novel ways and adapt the knowledge flexibly to the complex, ever-changing situations they confront. That is a definition of intelligence, and average or bright-normal intelligence is not enough to meet the challenge. Mayne, Norcross, and Sayette (1994) have shown that it is four times as easy to get into a PsyD program as it is to get into a research-oriented PhD program. Whatever reservations one may harbor about the conventional criteria for admission—GRE scores, grades, quality of undergraduate institutions, and the like—a shift of the kind and size that Mayne et al. describe does not encourage hope that we are elevating the intellectual quality of students coming into the field. A very high level of fluid intelligence is required for effective performance in the practice of psychology. Allowing anything less among our practitioners would be disastrous.

The emotional demands of practice are severe. By definition, many clinical patients are socially difficult, some are downright offensive, and a few are dangerous. Any practitioner who takes on the job of organizational or community change will inevitably meet conflicting demands and political frustrations that try the soul. To live with the uncertainties and aversions that are part of daily professional life, to do the best one can, and to take satisfaction in the relationships formed and the satisfactions gained through practice requires a special set of interests, values, and personal qualities.

By now, a large literature has accumulated on personality characteristics, interest patterns, and cognitive styles of psychologists. With impressive consistency, the studies show that the constellations of vocational interest, emotional disposition, and cognitive style displayed by researchers and practitioners in psychology are different (Frank, 1984). The patterns correspond to the distinction between scientists and humanists that has been conceived in one form or another at least since the time of Aristotle, popularized by Snow (1959), and applied to the cultures of research and practice in psychology by Kimble (1984) and others. The two constellations are not positively correlated. Instead, they are negatively correlated or orthogonal. Scientists may practice, and some practitioners may do research, but lifelong devotion to a career more commonly requires the dominant choice of practice or research. For students entering the field, the choice is most likely to be congenial, and ultimately most beneficial to the public, if it is congruent with the prior inclinations of the student.

Although humane concern for the well-being of others is frequently associated with fuzzy liberalism as a social attitude, it is not necessary to professional psychologists to be muddle-headed in the practice of their discipline. Indeed it is especially important for practitioners to be incisively critical in their consideration of new procedures if they are to avoid the ideological fads and technical fashions that sweep continually through the field. Fortunately, the analytical skills required for thoughtful comparison of alternative conceptions and critical evaluation of research can be taught. Basic intellectual abilities, however, cannot be injected into dull minds by any known means. In my experience, trying to inspire a passion for research in someone whose strongest interests lie in the challenges of practice or trying to instill in a brilliant but not particularly compassionate researcher the caring concern for other people that professional service requires is almost equally futile. Instead of counting on graduate training to convert people from one temperamental pattern to another, it is better to start from admission with students whose hearts are in the right place, who are keenly intelligent, and who are genuinely interested from the beginning in the kind of work they will be doing the rest of their lives.

Nobody can claim to know exactly how to conduct the predictive operations needed to bring the very best practitioners into graduate study, though it is reasonable to assume that decisions for admission should be based on careful examination of academic performance records and test scores as well as behavior in interviews and work-related situations. When the pool of scholastically qualified applicants is large, and faculty give the time and attention needed to select students as carefully as they can possibly manage, attrition rates through graduate study fall close to zero. I consider it demographically likely that many of the people who apply for admission to doctoral programs in professional psychology are poorly qualified for useful careers in the field, so I am immediately suspicious of any program that admits a high fraction of its applicants. In admitting students to graduate study, we need to examine carefully the conditions that matter most in professional work, employ the most effective assessment procedures we can contrive, and be closely selective in our choices.

AN APPROPRIATE ORGANIZATION

For nearly 20 years after the Boulder conference on training in clinical psychology (Raimy, 1950), only one kind of organization was available for doctoral education in professional psychology. Anyone who wished to enter the field in a state of full grace had to attend a PhD scientist–practitioner program in an academic psychology department. Today, at least ten kinds of organizations are in operation, all training people for careers in professional psychology. In addition to departmentally based PhD programs, students may enter practitioner programs within university psychology departments (e.g., the PsyD program at Baylor University), university-based professional schools (e.g., the School of Professional Psychology at Wright State University), clinical programs in autonomous graduate schools linked with a larger educational organization (e.g., the Department of Clinical Psychology in the Antioch New England Graduate School), freestanding professional schools (e.g., the Massachusetts School of Professional Psychology), departments of professional psychology (e.g., the Department of Clinical Psychology at the University of Florida), programs in medical schools (e.g., the Division of Psychology in the Northwestern University Medical School), schools of professional psychology within theological institutions (e.g., the Graduate School of Psychology at the Fuller Theological Seminary), consortial arrangements involving several institutions of higher education (e.g., the consortium of Old Dominion University, the College of William and Mary, the Eastern Virginia Medical School, and Norfolk State University in Virginia), and external degree programs (e.g., the PsyD program in the Fielding Institute).

Each kind of organization was created for a special set of reasons and shows some features that distinguish it from all the others. Given the varying demands of our society, the complexity of our discipline, and the differing needs of students, multiple structures for professional education in psychology are likely to continue. However, most students who are becoming professional psychologists today are receiving their education in one of three kinds of organizations—namely programs within academic departments, freestanding professional schools, and university-based professional schools. The three organizational forms share a primary goal—education for practice in psychology—but they are structurally quite different, especially in regard to the supports that maintain them and dominant agencies of control.

Departmental Programs

Clinical programs in academic departments are organized in parallel with other graduate programs, in experimental psychology, social psychology, human development, and other areas. The department, in turn, is administratively parallel with other departments within a superordinate college, usually a college of sciences and arts. Because all professional programs in psychology are at graduate levels, the program typically falls under the governance of a university-wide graduate college. The financial support for the program, and ultimately the controls, come from above. If the director of a clinical program in an academic department wants to institute a new course or hire a new faculty member, he or she must have the endorsement of the head of the department. If consequences for the rest of the department are entailed, as they typically are when limited resources have to be divided among several programs, the director must also obtain the sanction of an advisory or executive committee representing the other programs in the department. University-wide quality control is exercised mainly by policies and procedures for the award of degrees. Where the PhD is granted, many of those conditions center on the dissertation, and rules for approval of the dissertation and award of the degree are usually stipulated by the graduate college.

The advantages of this organization are several and substantial. The program shares the resources of the university. The bulk of financial support comes either from the legislative appropriation of tax money in public universities or the proceeds of endowment in private universities. Less than half, about 40% in most state universities, is drawn from student tuition. The general facilities of the university, including such expensive ones as physical plants, libraries, and computer systems, are immediately available. A core faculty is stably present as tenurable professors within the university community. Because the degree carries the name of the university, some quality standards more general than those of the program itself are necessarily imposed. In the most prestigious universities, active scholarship is emphasized, standards are stringent, and pressures toward high quality performance are strong.

All of these conditions are geared to the education of productive scholars, and it is this objective that departmentally based PhD programs are especially well suited to meet. As organizations for the education of professional psychologists, however, departmental programs leave much to be desired. The most serious problem with academic departments as organizations for educating practitioners in psychology is that most of them are predominantly devoted to the aims of science rather than to the aims of professional service. Most of the highly prestigious private universities do not have professional psychology programs at all. Princeton never established a clinical program. Stanford and the University of Chicago discontinued theirs. Northwestern moved its clinical psychology program out of the academic department and into the medical school. Yale has a clinical program, but it is more noteworthy for educating researchers and conceptualizers in community change than for preparing comprehensively trained practitioners. The prize for ambivalence about the missions of science and practice in psychology goes to Harvard, which has established and then disbanded its clinical, counseling, and public practice programs six different times. No program in professional psychology is currently in operation at Harvard University.

The research emphasis in the scientist–practitioner programs of most large public universities is nearly as strong as it is in the most highly regarded private universities. Many of the programs in state universities claim to be balanced in their emphases on research and practice, and some may be. In the top ranks of American research universities, however, faculty members are hired mainly for their research qualifications, and promotions are based mainly on scholarly contributions. The incentives and evaluations guiding the careers of students go the same way. Visible, respected role models for the practice of psychology are scarcely to be seen among the faculty.

Freestanding Professional Schools

Independent professional schools avoid exclusionary emphasis on research and the commonly concurrent denigration of practice by locating themselves entirely outside universities. In autonomous professional schools, the values of professional service can be affirmed without subsidiation to the values of research. Faculty members can be hired and rewarded for their contributions to the aims of professional education and to practice itself. A curriculum that reflects the demands of the profession can be installed at an accepted loss of the academic freedom that science requires but with the promise that graduates will know what professional psychologists need to know. A school organized expressly to educate professional psychologists, and therefore free of the inherent contradictions, inappropriate pressures, and limiting constraints of the PhD culture can, in principle, do an excellent job of educating practitioners.

However, freestanding schools suffer some practical disadvantages when compared with alternative organizations for educating professional psychologists. Some of the most serious limitations are economic. I am not sure just how much it costs to educate a professional psychologist at the doctoral level, but I am sure the cost is high. As near as I can estimate, the costs of good professional education and good research education differ very little. In general, well-funded programs are likely to offer better education than poorly funded programs. No one can reasonably claim a perfect correlation between the amount of money invested in education and the quality of education students receive. But neither can anyone sensibly deny substantial correspondence between the financial support that undergirds educational operations and the level of excellence the programs can attain.

Most freestanding professional schools in psychology today obtain more than 90% of their income—and some closer to 98%—from student tuition. If the costs of graduate education in professional psychology are as high as they appear to be, and if the schools continue to be as dependent economically on student tuition as most of them now are, only two solutions to the problem of financial support are evident. Either students are charged very high prices, or the quality of education is reduced. If tuition rates are very high, many students who could offer the most vital benefits to our society will be excluded from the profession. If costs are cut, the quality of education will decline. I do not know what a minimally adequate student: faculty ratio is, but I think it is safe to assume a rather high positive correlation between small ratios and quality of education. At Illinois and Rutgers, the ratio of students to full–time-equivalent faculty is 7:1. I do not know how many clinical cases a supervisor can manage. I get mixed up when I have to keep track of more than 9 or 10. I do not know how many dissertations a professor can advise at the same time. I can handle 5 or 6. I cannot handle 25. How many qualified dissertation supervisors can autonomous professional schools support?

Substantial economies can be obtained by hiring practitioners as part-time professional faculty. As adjunct professors, the practitioners bring a wealth of knowledge and skill to the educational organization at relatively low cost. However, a faculty made up entirely or predominantly of part-time people cannot offer the continuity, stability, and institutional identity required by an effective educational organization. Some full-time people are needed and the best ones command high salaries. If research is an institutional objective, as I believe it must be in the best professional schools, released faculty time for research must be written into the budget. A financial grant agency within the school is very helpful and possibly essential. The facilities needed for active scholarship, such as a research library, space and equipment for labs and studios, and a computer system must be provided. All this costs money, and as long as freestanding professional schools depend mainly on student tuition for their financial base, either the price for students will continue to be high, the quality of education will be low, or more creative solutions to the problem than I have seen so far will have to be found.

The safeguards of quality that are built into the budgeting process in strong universities—annual review by administrative superiors, internal and external performance reviews—must be deliberately constructed in freestanding schools. For collegiate- and university-level review agencies, independent professional schools often substitute a board of trustees or similar agency. Boards of trustees in freestanding professional schools are cursed with complex and severe responsibilities. Not only must they monitor quality, they must also serve as community support groups. Most board members I have met are kind-hearted people. When the demands for quality and support come into conflict, the temptation to relax quality standards can be very strong.

Once students enter the school, they gain a voice in policies and procedures of performance evaluation. I have never met a student seriously intent on graduating from a bad program, so student involvement of this kind usually works to the benefit of all concerned. However, schools that are entirely or mainly dependent on student tuition for financial survival are especially vulnerable to problems of quality control. It is difficult to fire one's employer.

University-Based Professional Schools

The third main kind of organization for the education of professional psychologists is the university-based professional school. Because these are established in parallel with other graduate and professional schools, the line of support and control between the school and the central administration of the university is direct and unencumbered. This makes an enormous functional difference in the way the school operates as compared with a departmental program. In matters of general policy, the dean joins a council of other deans, not a committee of program directors, who speak to a department chair, who consults with at least one and usually two deans, who then assemble with other deans to negotiate with central administration. The dean of a professional school can go right to the top in seeking resources and influencing policy.

When a professional degree is awarded, the school itself is the degree-granting unit. The school itself can therefore exercise controlling influence over policies and procedures for conferring the degree. This is one of the main organizational advantages of the PsyD over the PhD in the education of professional psychologists. In most American research universities, policies for award of the PhD are controlled by a graduate college, following guidelines established by such agencies as the Council of Graduate Schools in the United States. These policies have become increasingly uniform and firm in recent years. The PhD is to be awarded for scholarly contribution to knowledge, not for any other purpose. If a professional program is to culminate in a doctoral degree within such a university, and if inappropriate conditions for award of the degree are not to be imposed, there is no alternative to use of a professional degree.

A professional school, clearly organized to meet the objectives of professional education within a major univeristy, has all the advantages of support and quality maintenance of programs in academic departments and other advantages as well. Faculty are qualified and encouraged to do all the kinds of research that are done in the clinical programs of the best departments, but students and faculty are also free to explore the wider range of problems that practitioners encounter but are unsafe topics for PhD dissertations or the research programs of young, untenured professors. A professional school obviously needs active professionals to do the teaching. Some valuation of professional work for full-time faculty members and engagement of community practitioners as part-time faculty members can be justified in a straightforward manner. For exactly the same reason that every medical school needs a teaching hospital, every professional school in psychology needs a large, active psychological center as an agency for public service, teaching, and research. The need is obvious, and the call for support can be justified with clarion assurance.

So far, I have seen no disadvantages in university-based professional schools. At Rutgers University, the Graduate School of Applied and Professional Psychology is one of the jewels in the university's crown. Our school attracts more applicants than any other graduate program in the university. Our faculty, both full-time and part-time, have collectively won an impressive array of honors, not only for professional contributions and public service but also for research. All graduate and professional programs in Rutgers University are evaluated periodically by a multidisciplinary committee of distinguished scholars. Ratings are linked with priorities for financial support. Our clinical PsyD program is one of the very few programs that received the very highest 1a rating by that committee. The Rutgers school of applied and professional psychology is the only one I am personally qualified to describe, but it is not the only good one in operation. I doubt that there is a single university-based professional school in NCSPP that would not be glad to place its own brag sheet on public display.

When site visitors examine our school for APA accreditation or the external review that Rutgers requires of all graduate programs every 5 years, we are sometimes asked why we don't "return to the mainstream"—in other words, revert to a PhD scientist–practitioner program in our academic department. When the question comes to me, it is usually followed by some play on the metaphor (Are you sure *you're* in the mainstream? Maybe we are all drifting down little tributaries; haven't glimpsed the mighty river yet; don't even know it's there). Metaphor aside, however, the question is important. Illinois dropped its PsyD program; why not Rutgers?

We could, of course, go that way. The Rutgers psychology department is strong. For the most part, relationships with faculty in the department are respectful and friendly. Several members of the department are active in the work of the school, and several of the faculty in our school are also active in the department's PhD program in clinical psychology. But the fundamental aims of a research department and a professional school are not the same. Conflicts inevitably arise. During the year in which this chapter was written, the chair of the department proposed a major reorganization within the departmental unit. To make room for relocation of personnel, he proposed that the Graduate School of Applied and Professional Psychology be disbanded or privatized. Citing Dawes' (1994) *House of Cards: Psychology and Psychotherapy Built on Myth*, he wrote, "It is not clear to me why the Univerity should be involved at all with a psychotherapy-related professional school . . . why taxpayers should subsidize an unnecessary route to licensing for private practice and third-party payments." Except for the research for which several internationally visible faculty of the professional school are noted, the manifold activities of the faculty and students in our school were not mentioned. None of our community programs, none of our work in schools and business corporations, none of our enterprises in organizational behavior, nothing, in short, that was anything other than traditional controlled research, appeared to have a place in the chair's system of values. To me, his trivialization of practice was more blatant than usual but scarcely new to my experience. In past years, other departmental chairs have voiced similar views. Many influential faculty members in the department simply do not believe that psychology has anything to offer as a profession. The current chair, with whom I have a personally respectful and tolerably cordial relationship, merely demonstrated once again why professional schools rather than departmental programs are an organizational necessity. For the Graduate School of Applied and Professional Psychology at Rutgers University, abandonment of the autonomy conferred by our administrative status and our privilege as a degree-granting unit would be institutionally suicidal.

It is wrong to translate local experience into public policy, but that is not what I intend by my illustration. The contradictions between the aims of science and practice are inherent in the disciplines themselves. The cultural conditions that require us to maintain a professional school at Rutgers are not unique to this institution. At different times and in different forms, related conditions have led to the creation of comparable organizations at Adelphi, Denver, Wright State, Widener, and Yeshiva Universities, among others. For the education of professional psychologists, university-based professional schools provide more appropriate cultural values, a more coherent sense of professional identity, and a more salutary balance of support and quality control than any alternative organization. In the long run, I do not see how psychology can be any different from law, medicine, dentistry, pharmacy, nursing, architecture, business, journalism, or any other profession in finding university-based professional schools the most effective organizations for educating practitioners. As James McKeen Cattell said more than a half century ago, "There will not . . . be a profession until we have professional schools" (Cattell, 1937, p. 1).

AN INTEGRATED SERVICE, RESEARCH, AND TRAINING FACILITY

George Albee has repeatedly noted that we cannot continue training our students in the house of medicine and expect them to become psychologists (e.g., Albee, 1966, 1970). The psychological clinics affiliated with most PhD programs in clinical psychology are also grossly insufficient to establish our professional identity and meet the educational needs of our discipline. Just as every medical school needs a teaching hospital, every school of professional psychology needs a psychological center, administratively controlled by the school, offering a range of services as broad as the field itself, conducting research to improve the services, and providing a setting in which students can develop skills through observing faculty and practicing under faculty supervision.

The center needs to be much larger and the range of activities more diverse than is commonly seen in the psychological clinics of departmentally based scientist–practitioner programs. Not all of the work that is done under the aegis of the center will take place within the facility that houses it. Much of it must be done through cooperative affiliation with other agencies in the community. Service and research contracts with schools, hospitals, mental health centers, correctional facilities, business corporations, and other agencies, always involving the faculty and students of the school, can provide high quality services to the public at relatively low cost and provide the school with access to the populations and settings in which necessary professional experience can be gained and useful field research can be conducted. The center is more properly conceived as an administrative organization than as a building, though a building is needed too. The physical facility should be large, attractive, conspicuously identified with the school, and seen by the public as the place to go whenever professional services of the highest quality are required.

If psychological centers are well managed, and the services and research they provide are of high quality, they can become economically self-sufficient and even turn a profit. In 1994 to 1995, for example, 22 projects, involving nearly all of the students in our school and supervised by 15 faculty members, were managed by the Rutgers Center for Applied Psychology. The total income from projects, contracts, and grants was well in excess of $1 million. Most of the money was used for student support, staff salaries, and extra pay for faculty, though some of it was used to buy equipment and rehabilitate one of our satellite facilities. A few thousand dollars remained in the account at the end of the year. The Center for Applied Psychology at Rutgers University is only 6 years old and is still growing. I presume some centers established earlier at other schools would show more impressive balance sheets than ours.

The principal returns from a psychological center, however, are not financial. The main values of the center are functional and symbolic. Functionally, the centers are needed to provide the service, research, and training that professional schools must offer. Symbolically, the centers are needed to define the professional identity of our discipline.

EFFECTIVE MEANS FOR CREDENTIALING STUDENTS AND ACCREDITING PROGRAMS

The doctoral degree is the most clearly valid ticket of admission to the profession of psychology, and control of the degree is the most effective means of improving the quality of psychological practice. State licensure cannot assure high quality. To avoid restraint-of-trade litigation, licensure laws are written to accommodate people from varying educational backgrounds who do some of the work that professional psychologists do at the lowest admissible level of competence. The nature of our profession does not allow construction of a test of professional knowledge comparable to bar examinations in law or specialty boards in medicine. I cannot foresee a time when any imaginable test battery will replace direct observation and critical evaluation of performance over the full range of activities and settings in which professional psychologists are engaged. No situation except graduate training provides ethical sanction for the kinds of observations that need to be made, the opportunities and resources needed for evaluation of many kinds of performance by many observers in many situations, and the obligation to withhold the qualifying credential if satisfactory performance is not displayed. Our most powerful leverage for improving the quality of professional education in psychology lies in the systematic monitoring of cumulative performances throughout graduate study and in maintaining stringent standards of excellence for award of the degree.

We need to give the right degree. Use of the PhD, a credential that tradition and formal policy define as a mark of contributory scholarship over all the arts and sciences, is appropriate for graduates of research-oriented programs. As a credential for practitioners, however, the PhD misdirects the focus of effort from the client to the discipline, misplaces authority for control of the degree, and fails to identify the body of knowledge and skill that the practitioner is prepared to offer the public. Like every other profession, psychology needs to use its own degree, as it now is doing for its practitioner programs, with only a few anachronistic exceptions.

Finally, we need the most effective means we can devise for evaluating and accrediting professional programs. Accreditation has no place in science. Science embodies its own correctives, and the people most concerned with scientific matters are other scientists, who are perfectly capable of evaluating the products generated by their colleagues. Scientists may enjoy forming elitist academies in which they can congratulate themselves for their purities, but they need neither protection nor interference from external accrediting agencies. In fact, the free pursuit of knowledge essential to science requires scientists to oppose the demands and constraints of professional accreditation with all the force at their command.

Educational institutions purporting to qualify professionals for public practice, however, must subject their programs to accreditational review. The specifications, demands, and constraints inherent in accreditation do not need to stifle innovation. All professions are in continual flux. Policies and procedures for accreditation must allow diverse institutional forms to accommodate the special constituencies we need to serve and take full advantage of local resources. The policies and procedures must include systematic means for revising program content as new conceptions and improved procedures are developed. At any given time, however, the interests of the profession as well as the public are best served when each program has to be described as specifically as possible, conditions for approval are defined as clearly as they can be, and standards are set as high as available knowledge allows.

Throughout its preprofessional phase, organized psychology resisted all threats of program accreditation so successfully that no system of accreditation was ever set in place. Accreditation began when it was forced on the APA by the Veterans Administration (VA) as a condition for receipt of VA training funds. The first accreditation review took place in 1947. It was based entirely on survey information provided by the applicant organizations, and it was accomplished by a small committee of academicians. All the programs in the country were evaluated in a single day. Of the 40 applicants, 29 were approved.

We have come a long way in the ensuing half century. The December

1995 issue of the *American Psychologist* lists 300 accredited doctoral programs, 437 internships, and 224 members of the APA who aided a recently expanded accreditation committee by conducting site visits and performing other accreditational activities during the 1994 to 1995 academic year. Our accreditation system has not only become larger, it has become more diverse and more representative of the constituencies that have a stake in the process. The most recent changes in the structure and function of the APA accreditation system promise an order of review that is at once more fair and more stringent than we have ever known before. Students, schools, and the public all stand to gain from the changes.

At its best, however, accreditation can never do more than set a bottom limit on the quality of programs. The professional psychology of the twenty-first century must move beyond its current preoccupation with psychotherapy to a versatile array of services in education, health care, business management, government—every arena in which human beings as individuals, in groups, and as members of organizations are subject to dysfunction and have a chance to function better. Our job is to provide psychological services to the public, effectively and at reasonable cost. We cannot hope to do this well unless we aim for a higher level of excellence in educating practitioners than we have reached so far. Within the larger academic community, we who are primarily concerned with the education of professional psychologists are a minority, both numerically and culturally. We are often stereotyped. Common characteristics are assumed. Differences are ignored. Without inquiry, we are reflexly regarded as inferior. Like other cultural minorities, we will have to do better than the dominant majority to be seen as equal.

9

ORGANIZING FOR QUALITY: THE NATIONAL COUNCIL OF SCHOOLS AND PROGRAMS OF PROFESSIONAL PSYCHOLOGY

In the summer of 1976, there seemed good reason to predict that a Democratic administration would replace the Republicans whose reputation had been tainted by the Watergate scandals of the Nixon years. In psychology, rumors were heard that federal support for the education of human service professionals might begin to flow again, but some of us also heard that eligibility for support would be limited to disciplines that incorporated an organization of professional schools whose purpose was to emphasize quality in professional education.

Nicholas Cummings, one of the founders and first president of the California School of Professional Psychology (CSPP) was president of the American Psychological Association (APA) that year. Whether the rumors about federal money were uppermost in his mind I cannot say, but, whatever the reason for his action, he invited representatives of the 19 professional schools then in operation to a day-long meeting before the APA convention in August 1976. We would meet, said Cummings, to consider creation of a council of professional schools to facilitate and coordinate the work of member institutions and advance the cause of professional psychology as a whole. As president pro tem, Cummings convened the meeting, charged us with the first of our tasks—defining a "professional school"—and conducted a voice election by which Gordon Derner became acting president. Cummings then withdrew.

GETTING STARTED

The following year, the group met for the second time and formally named itself the National Council of Schools of Professional Psychology (NCSPP). Derner was officially elected president. Never one to worry much about democratic procedure, Derner appointed an executive committee with Paul Clement as vice president, Maurice Zemlick as secretary–treasurer, and me as member at large. I was later assigned the task of chairing an ad hoc committee to draft the first bylaws of the organization. The bylaws have since passed through several revisions, though their central intent has never changed. The title of the organization now includes "programs" as well as "schools" though the acronym NCSPP has been retained, and the abbreviated acronym SPP is used to designate departmental programs as well as schools designed to educate people for professional service in psychology. According to the bylaws now in effect, the purposes of NCSPP are to

1. Gather and disseminate information regarding SPPs,
2. Develop standards for the education and training of professional psychologists,
3. Provide a forum for the exchange of information about SPP functioning,
4. Provide liaison with others involved in the education and training of professional psychologists,
5. Provide consultation on SPP development and maintenance,
6. Monitor and influence public policy with regard to the education and training of professional psychologists,
7. Foster research, development, and application in appropriate areas of psychology and work toward the solution of significant problems of human welfare,
8. Develop quality assurance methods based on empirical evaluation,
9. Engage in such other pursuits as are not inconsistent with those specified above.

Early meetings were devoted largely to go-arounds in which each representative would tell how things were going in his—or far less commonly, her—organization. Those of us whose programs were fairly well established usually reported our latest accomplishments. Representatives of schools just starting out, hoping for applicants and worried about accreditation, also noted any progress they could claim but at the same time voiced their trepidation and sought the support they needed to continue their efforts. Discussions about degrees, PsyD versus PhD, and organizational structures, freestanding versus university-based, were at first frequent and sometimes heated but soon grew tiresome as ideological positions were repeated by their advocates and hopes for consensus faded from view. At one point, Bruce Weiss, dean of the Massachusetts School of Professional Psychology, proposed a moratorium on talk about preferred degrees. Weary participants agreed, and our meetings became more productive after that.

During Derner's two-term presidency, an important concern of the council was to gain visibility and political position, in part through membership in key agencies of the APA and other organizations. Among other involvements, Derner served as liaison to the APA Education and Training Board. In 1978, I was asked to join the board's committee on accreditation, and I chaired the committee in 1980, the year I was elected as the second president of NCSPP.

FOCUS ON QUALITY

During my term, I focused on action to improve the quality of professional education in psychology. So did others. Joanne Callan, then dean of the San Diego campus of CSPP, organized the first NCSPP conference on "quality control and the training of professional psychologists." The conference, which took place in La Jolla, California, in 1981, and the proceedings of which were later published under the title, "Quality in Professional Psychology Training: A National Conference and Self-Study" (Callan, Peterson, & Stricker, 1986), seemed to all of us a great success. After it was over, I placed the following memorandum in the NCSPP newsletter:

> To: Members, Associates, and Affiliates of the National Council of Schools of Professional Psychology
> Subject: Helping each other improve the education of professional psychologists
>
> The San Diego conference gave us a good start in addressing some of the issues that concern us as educators of professional psychologists. Now we need to do more. We can all learn from each other. Each of us can profit from the experiences of the others. If we can collect our ideas and integrate them sensibly, we should be able to say what professional psychology is and can become better than any of us can do alone, and better than any other group has done so far.
>
> It seems to me we need a series of conferences, with full and functional participation of our entire group, on each of the issues that concern us. We need to consider matters of curriculum in close detail. We need to work out better ways to select candidates for admission. We need to create psychological centers that go beyond anything most of us have developed so far. We need to evaluate competence in professional

psychology more effectively than before. We need to find other ways of financing the education of professional psychologists. We need to consider the kinds of administrative organizations that will work for us. In all of this, all of us will have contributions to make. We need to find a way of getting those contributions expressed, exchanged, discussed, and synthesized so that not only each of our programs but professional psychology as a whole will be the better for it. If we do our job right, what is good for professional psychology will also be good for the discipline and for people generally.

Here is a specific proposal that may help move us in these directions. I have already talked with several of you about the proposal. What follows is therefore already a group product that embodies ideas from several people.

1. Let us conduct a series of day-long conferences, on at least the following issues:
   a. Curriculum
   b. Admissions
   c. Evaluation of professional competence
   d. Selection and evaluation of faculty
   e. Developing effective psychological centers
   f. Administrative organization, including financial supports and executive controls
   g. Professional schools as research centers

   (You can think of additional items, but this is a start.)
2. As a basis for discussion, let us begin with a thorough exchange of descriptive information, from each participant to all the others. . . .
3. The conferencé itself can then be devoted to specific agenda items such as . . . the common properties of the programs as they now stand . . . the special features of particular programs . . . and steps to make the programs better. . . . It would probably be best to separate into small groups to discuss the several agenda items, and then come together for general discussion and synthesis.
4. The participants at each conference should include those from each program most directly involved in the function with which the conference is concerned. . . .
5. An annual conference might be scheduled for the day prior to the start of APA [convention]. . . . We may want to schedule additional midwinter meetings too. . . .
6. The outcomes of the conferences should be published so that our collective statements are available to the entire field.

The memo ended with a questionnaire asking about preferred topics and schedules for the meetings. Enthusiasm for further conferences was high. Many additional topics were suggested. With close agreement, members preferred to schedule conferences on quality during the midwinter months, apart from the meetings before each APA convention, which would now be devoted mainly to organizational concerns.

Since then, eight more conferences have taken place. The pivotal Mission Bay conference (1986) was the first meeting systematically designed to articulate the key elements of education in professional psychology. From this conference came the second NCSPP volume, *Standards and Evaluation in the Education and Training of Professional Psychologists: Knowledge, Attitudes, and Skills* (Bourg et al., 1987). Several basic principles were affirmed: the importance of educating professional psychologists in programs that were explicitly and primarily devoted to practitioner training, a strong commitment to expanding cultural diversity within our schools and in the profession at large, and continuing commitment to evaluation of professional competence among students and of educational effectiveness among programs. The bodies of knowledge, skill, and attitude and the core competencies required for the practice of psychology were spelled out more thoroughly than ever before.

The Mission Bay Conference was followed by a series of conferences that explicated various elements of the professional school model. A typical conference process had developed. For each meeting, a number of critical issues in professional psychology were identified. Then the executive officers of NCSPP designated committees to study and organize relevant information, bring together a set of working papers, and design a midwinter conference for the larger membership. The participants at the NCSPP conferences were representatives of the member institutions and their invited guests. Other influential people who were not members of the council or came from fields outside of psychology were sometimes invited to offer keynote speeches.

The conference on ethnic diversification in psychology education and training (1989) sharpened the awareness of many white male administrators of professional programs about the need for ethnic diversification in all aspects of professional psychology. Not incidentally, the conference was held in Puerto Rico, where the white male majority who ran most of the programs and held most of the executive positions in NCSPP experienced themselves as an ethnic minority. Although other conferences also moved the organization toward better understanding of cultural issues in our field and beyond, many long-time members of NCSPP would say that the Puerto Rico conference was a dramatic turning point for them in building ethnic and racial diversity into the structure of their programs. From this conference came *Toward Ethnic Diversification in Psychology Education and Training* (Stricker et al., 1990), the third in the NCSPP series and the first published through a contract with APA Books.

A conference on curricula at San Antonio, Texas, in 1990 extended the professional model of education that had been outlined at the Mission Bay Conference. The written product of the San Antonio conference was a book titled *The Core Curriculum in Professional Psychology* (R. L. Peterson et al.,

1992), the fourth in the NCSPP series. Expanding on the Mission Bay resolutions, the San Antonio conference articulated each of the professional core curriculum areas in further detail, clarified the social nature of professional psychology, and emphasized the need for multiple ways of knowing in the disciplined inquiries of the local clinical scientist.

A conference on women's issues in professional psychology, at Tucson, Arizona, in 1991 (Magidson, Edwall, Kenkel, & Jackson, 1994), immersed the still primarily male leadership of NCSPP in issues often identified as feminist. Conferees considered, among other concerns, the problem of underrepresentation of women in leadership positions in psychology and other professions, the inclusion of women's issues in curriculum and training, and a broad range of questions about the roles of women in our rapidly changing society. This conference, along with the previous one on ethnic diversification, indelibly changed NCSPP as an organization. Prior to these meetings, one or two male administrators typically represented each program. After the Tucson conference, two more delegates from each member institution could attend the meetings, provided that each one brought ethnic or gender diversity to the delegation. Standing committees on gender and ethnic diversity were formed, and respective chairs became members of the NCSPP executive committee.

A conference on evaluation in professional psychology, held in the Bahamas in 1992 (Grip, 1994), was designed to work toward new models for evaluating professional competency of students in professional psychology. The concern of the conference foreshadowed the current focus of the APA Committee on Accreditation on the evaluation of outcomes (APA, Committee on Accreditation, 1996) but produced more by way of redefined questions than convincing answers. Most members of NCSPP, like most members of the APA accreditation committee, would probably agree that the thorough and accurate assessment of individual professional competence in psychology is more realistically seen as a goal for the future than as a well-settled accomplishment. A conference on clinical training in professional psychology in 1993, the second La Jolla conference, focused on the practicum and internship. In opposition to proposals that the internship in professional psychology require a second postdoctoral year, NCSPP recommended maintaining the internship, whatever its length, as a predoctoral experience (Forbes, Dutton, Farber, Polite, & Tan, 1994).

REFLECTION AND INTEGRATION

At this stage in the evolution of the council, members felt a need to review the wide-ranging array of issues and resolutions considered in the preceding seven conferences. By this time, the mass of materials we had accumulated had begun to seem bewildering, and a metaconference was planned to bring coherence to our successive discussions and lists of resolutions. Summaries of prior conferences and a new set of preconference papers designed to focus attention on the social responsibilities of psychology as a profession were distributed to participants. The conference took place in Cancun, Mexico, in 1994. Two statements have since been prepared to articulate the NCSPP model of education in professional psychology: One is a book, *Standards for Education in Professional Psychology* (R. Peterson, D. Peterson, & Abrams, in press), and the other is a journal article titled "The National Council of Schools and Programs of Professional Psychology Educational Model" (R. Peterson, D. Peterson, Abrams, & Stricker, in press).

A brief historical review of the kind that appears in this chapter cannot provide a coherent summary of the substance and philosophy of education that NCSPP has collectively endorsed. The statements cited in the previous paragraph are intended to provide that summary. Correspondence between the consensually approved NCSPP position and the conception I have presented in this book is reasonably close, but readers should not assume that the views of the author and of all members of NCSPP are perfectly isomorphic. Considerable disagreement still prevails, for example, about preferred degrees, the importance of dissertations, and the relative merits of freestanding and university-based professional schools. There is much room for discussion on other matters as well, from the values of various techniques to emphases on constructionist and empiricist epistemologies. One of the main blessings of the council is the freedom that we all feel to differ on issues of these kinds, yet stand together in our insistence on the value of direct education for practice in psychology, the centrality of disciplined inquiry, the role of the professional psychologist as local clinical scientist, and other core principles.

Annual conferences continue. The need for rational integration of our deliberations was accompanied by need for another empirical self-study. The number of members now in the organization, and the track records collectively amassed, allow a far more comprehensive and systematic examination of our programs than could be attempted in the first evaluative review (Callan et al., 1986). With full participation of members, a study that includes a survey of graduates, interviews with program leaders, reexamination of curricula, and evaluation of the extent to which conference resolutions have actually been implemented in the programs of member institutions is currently under way.

Plans for the self-study were a central element in a conference titled "Standards for Education in Professional Psychology II: Where Are We? Where Are We Going? And How Do We Let People Know?" that took place in New Orleans, Louisiana, in 1995. A conference titled "Innovations in Professional Psychology Education and Practice: Preparing for the New Millennium," in Clearwater, Florida, in 1996, focused on ramifications of changes in the health care system for education in professional psychology. A conference on educating psychologists for collaboration with other professions took place in 1997. Through it all, NCSPP has continued to serve its constitutional purposes of self-scrutiny, mutual support, and cooperative action in improving education for the practice of psychology.

In August 1996, the council celebrated the twentieth anniversary of its founding. By coincidence, the meeting took place in Toronto, the site of the first assembly in 1976. Few of the founding members were present, but among new and old participants alike reflections on the development of the council were common topics in the informal conversations that were interspersed among the business sessions. It seemed to many of us that the organization had moved through two broad phases in its evolution and was on the threshold of a third.

The first few years, roughly from 1976 to 1981, were devoted primarily to organizational matters—defining purposes, settling structure, offering mutual support, and accepting new members until a critical mass was reached. This could be called the *formative* phase of development of the council. The second phase began with the first conference in La Jolla in 1981, the self-study that was initiated there, and the decision to continue conferences and self-studies in the future. These actions signaled the beginning of the *evaluative* phase of development.

The activities that dominated the first two phases continue. Some changes in organizational particulars are made at nearly every meeting and will no doubt be required in future meetings as well. Dedication to evaluation is never-ending. By now, however, the basic structure of the council is firmly defined, and the emphasis on evaluation has at once provided the base of knowledge needed for confidence in the mission of the council and the mechanisms required for unrelenting examination and improvement of educational operations. The work of the council over the first 20 years provided constituents with a sense of stability, strength, and unity of purpose—the internal assurance required to reach beyond the council to psychology as a whole and the public at large.

Direct education for practice in psychology has not gained widespread, wholehearted acceptance in psychology as a scholarly discipline, and the work of professional psychologists, as members of NCSPP understand it, remains largely unknown or misunderstood in the ken of the general public. These conditions form the grounds for increasing emphasis on constructive affiliations with other organizations, both within and beyond psychology. Affiliative attitudes have been present all along, but it seems fair to call the recent surge in activity beyond the council as the beginning of a *collaborative* phase in development of the organization.

Affiliations within psychology typically take the form of liaison arrangements. By now, NCSPP has established liaison agreements and has regularly sent representatives to meetings of the APA Board of Educational Affairs, the Council of University Directors of Clinical Psychology, and the Association of State and Provincial Psychology Boards. Many members of NCSPP are also members of other organizations in psychology, particularly the several APA divisions concerned with the practice of psychology, and leaders in NCSPP often gain positions of prominence in the other organizations as well. Understanding and acceptance of professional schools and programs, however, is far from universal. A report by Roger Peterson on his experience as NCSPP liaison to the Council of University Directors of Clinical Psychology and the APA Board of Educational Affairs offers some direct illustrations.

> Though NCSPP and professional psychology have many friends, there are psychologists out there who know little about us, and quite a few who are suspicious and even antagonistic. In the best circumstances, there is forthright, collegial respect and curiosity. Other times skeptical attitudes toward professional psychology seem to have a shadowy presence in the discussions of the meetings themselves; they can appear more directly over dinner or in the bar after the meetings.
>
> So what are worst questions like? Here are some real examples:
>
> "How many students do you admit?" "How can any place train a hundred new students a year?" "Are any NCSPP schools actually accredited by APA?" "Why should there be different accreditation standards for you folks?" "Now the schools in your group, don't they admit just about every applicant?" "Do you have any faculty who are not part time?" "Do your students learn anything about research?"
>
> Such questions are so frequent that my blood pressure hardly rises much above normal any more. . . . I am constantly surprised to find that otherwise informed people haven't thought or read much about professional education. (R. Peterson, 1995, pp. 3, 6)

In his report, Roger then cited some straightforward, noncombative, factually informative answers that he typically offered to correct the gross assumptive errors the questions imply, and in a later memorandum added, "If there was ever a time in the history of psychology when we need to build bridges, have integrated strategies, speak with other psychologists with different perspectives, it is now."

Like professional psychology as a whole, NCSPP faces a challenging future. Until now, education for practice in psychology has shown all the characteristics of a new growth industry. The market among students willing to pay high prices for a doctoral ticket of admission to the profession has appeared to be, if not entirely unlimited, far short of saturation. For the most part, students have gained ready access to internship training and have enjoyed full employment following graduation. In NCSPP, all comers have been welcome, as long as they declared primary devotion to the values of professional education and intent to seek APA accreditation. Conferences and other activities have moved cheerily along in a spirit of egalitarian acceptance, social amity, and economic optimism. How well this mood can be sustained in a changing market remains to be seen. Apprehension about employment gives new pause to prospective applicants for graduate study. Already, difficulties in placing students in APA-approved internships have led to proposals for voluntary restraint in admitting students to NCSPP programs. As opportunities for training and employment change further in the years to come, the spirit of cooperation and creativity that has pervaded the council in the past will be tested as never before.

10
ACCREDITATION IN PSYCHOLOGY

In 1937, James McKeen Cattell, by most lights the founder of applied psychology, was asked to write the lead article for the first issue of the *Journal of Consulting Psychology*. Fifty years before, Cattell had been appointed professor of psychology at the University of Pennsylvania. Now he was asked to look back on that half century and set down his thoughts about the development of psychology as a profession. He wrote about the learned professions in general, the evolution of psychology, the establishment of the American Psychological Association (APA) in 1892, the uses of psychology during World War I that put applied psychology "on the map and on the front page," and he insisted that professional schools and professional standards were required to establish psychology as a profession (Cattell, 1937).

Among his comments, Cattell admitted that he had made a mistake, not in advocating professional applications of psychology—he held to that mission proudly throughout his life—but in predicting how rapidly psychology would grow as a profession. In a previous address, in 1917, on the 25th anniversary of the founding of the APA, Cattell had noted that 272 of the 307 members were engaged in teaching, 16 in applications, and remarked that the latter group might outnumber academics by the 50th anniversary of the APA in 1942. By 1937, it was already apparent that his prophecy would not be fulfilled. Ever resilient, Cattell simply repeated his prediction, only this time he advanced the prophetic date to the 75th anniversary of the APA. On this second bet, he was still off the mark, but only by 5 years, and in the opposite direction. Not in 1967, but in 1962, the number of psychologists employed in professional work surpassed the number employed primarily in teaching and research (Tryon, 1963).

The fractional increase has continued ever since. According to the best estimates available from the APA Office of Demographics, the number of psychologists currently employed in independent practice, schools, hospitals, clinics, and other human service settings is approximately double the number employed in universities, colleges, medical schools, and other academic settings. The number engaged in independent practice alone appears to be slightly greater than the number in all academic settings combined. Over this past century, psychology has changed from a discipline defined purely as a science and composed entirely of academicians to a discipline that acknowledges its identity as a profession as well as a science and whose substantial majority is now made up of practitioners.

The transition has not taken place without turbulence. Tensions between the incompatible ideals of free scientific inquiry and responsible professional service have bedeviled our discipline from the beginning and remain to this day. Many people are talking about challenges in these changing times. To me, the most fundamental challenge for psychology in the twenty-first century is to advance the public benefits our discipline can offer, not by denying certain irreducible conflicts between the aims of science and the aims of practice, and not by trying to suppress either science or practice in favor of the other, but rather by turning the inevitable tensions between our scientific and professional forces into constructive use for the benefit of the people all psychologists must ultimately serve.

For the first half century of the existence of psychology as an identifiable discipline, no system for accrediting psychology programs was seriously considered, much less implemented. Psychology was conceived as a science. Educational programs were designed to prepare students for careers of scholarly research. Many psychologists went into practice anyway, mainly because that is where the jobs were, but no systematic education for professional work was available to them. Efforts to define professional training programs began with Lightner Witmer's address to the APA in 1896 (Witmer, 1896/1907) and continued in individual efforts by Wallin (1911), Mitchell (1920), and Crane (1925), among others. A few internships sprang up around the country, beginning with Henry Goddard's program at the Vineland Training School in New Jersey in 1908, but for the most part psychologists who took professional jobs in the early part of this century had to bootleg their training by taking any pertinent course work their universities happened to offer and arranging apprenticed professional supervision wherever they could find it.

In those days, full-time professional psychologists were clearly and officially second-class citizens. Membership in the APA required a record of postdoctoral research, published and of acceptable quality, a demand that few full-time practitioners could meet. Efforts to specify curricula, set standards for training, and develop public credentials of professional competence were routinely defeated, and any proposal to accredit academic programs would have been hooted down on grounds that accreditation was both unnecessary and pernicious. Accreditation was considered unnecessary because science is public and embodies its own correctives; pernicious because external constraints inhibit the free pursuit of knowledge.

In its early years, organized psychology in America treated professional psychology much as a new family in an established neighborhood treats an eccentric, marginally loony relative. Uncle Harry isn't exactly crazy. He just doesn't behave appropriately. He has some talent. He even manages to bring a pretty good income into the household. But you can never be sure what he is going to do. Doesn't seem to be dangerous. More embarrassing than dangerous, but you never can tell, and what will the neighbors think? We can't say it to his face, but to tell you the truth, we're ashamed of him. Can't lock him in a closet. Don't want to kick him out into the street. We'll just have to work around him the best way we can.

These conditions sorely distressed practitioners working outside of the academy. In their disaffection, they organized their own association, the American Association for Applied Psychology (AAAP) in 1937, and among other actions began to publish their own journal, the *Journal of Consulting Psychology*. It seems to have taken a common enemy and a war to bring psychologists together again. In 1943, a joint convention of the APA and the AAAP was held, and a committee, headed by Robert Yerkes, was appointed to draft a new constitution. The APA constitution then in effect defined the purpose of the organization as "the advancement of psychology as a science." The corresponding statement in the new constitution read, "The object of the American Psychological Association shall be to advance psychology as a science, as a profession, and as a means of promoting human welfare" (Wolfle, 1946, p. 3). To accommodate the diversity psychology had come to represent, a divisional structure was created for the various special interest groups in the association (18 at the time), a new journal, the *American Psychologist*, was established to provide a vehicle for discussing professional as well as scientific issues, and dues were raised from $10 to $15 per year.

Attention was focused on the education of professional psychologists as never before. While the APA and the AAAP were still separately organized, a joint subcommittee on graduate internship training, with David Shakow as chair, had laid out conditions for the selection of students, academic requirements, and practicum experience in highly specific detail. In one of the most cautious understatements our discipline has ever seen, the report suggested that "It is not entirely inconceivable that the development of a considerable group of soundly prepared clinical psychologists would have an appreciable effect on the future of psychology as a whole" (APA & AAAP, 1945, p. 243).

The need for accreditation of university programs and internship centers was clearly stated, but the actual establishment of a mechanism for accreditation did not come about until the U.S. government, with a call to noble mission in one hand and a bag of money in the other, required the accountability that psychology had so far failed to provide for itself. The mission was to provide psychological services for the 16 million veterans returning to civilian life from World War II. The money was to provide financial support to graduate students in clinical psychology, and not incidentally, consulting fees to academic faculty. In December 1945, the APA Board of Directors received a request from the Veterans Administration (VA) to provide a list of institutions that possessed adequate facilities for training clinical psychologists at the doctoral level. Those on the list would be eligible to receive financial support. Those omitted would not get any money.

Thus inspired, APA sprang into action. In fact, a considerable amount of preparatory work had already been done. During the preceding months, the APA Committee on Graduate and Professional Training had been gathering fairly extensive data about graduate training programs with special reference to clinical faculty and practicum facilities (Sears, 1946). Forty universities had returned the information requested, and in September 1946, the committee sent the VA a list of 22 institutions that provided "adequate" training, according to their standards. The following year a second review was conducted, on request from the U.S. Public Health Service as well as by the VA. By this time, 29 institutions had met the criteria (Sears, 1947). These, the first public, discriminative program evaluations ever done by the APA, were conducted entirely on the basis of survey information provided by the applicant institutions, and the decisions were made by the Committee on Graduate and Professional Training that had been appointed by the board of directors. The review reported in 1947 took 2 days—1 day to reconsider the standards by which judgments were to be made and 1 day to evaluate the programs and determine which were to be approved.

None of the institutions denied approval appealed their exclusion. Those were the days when students who failed academically blamed themselves for not studying hard enough or even for being too dumb to master the assigned material. Psychology departments behaved in a comparable way. Faculty would decide whether they had what it took by way of interest and internal resources to develop a clinical program along the lines defined by the APA committee, and if they elected to go ahead proceeded to hire the faculty, add the course work, and organize the practicum and internship arrangements needed to do the job.

Once it became clear that the governmental agencies offering support and requiring evaluative judgments of academic programs were not imposing inappropriate bureaucratic demands nor threatening academic freedom—but instead were asking organized psychology to define its own standards, set up its own procedures, and reach its own decisions about the quality of the programs they were asked to review—the leaders in American psychology were committed to the task of accreditation and took their responsibilities very seriously.

A new APA Committee on Training in Clinical Psychology, with David Shakow as chair, examined the previous joint APA/AAAP report on internship training and revised it to meet the situation they now were facing. Some sections in the earlier report were deleted, including one proposing serious consideration of a professional doctorate, such as the Doctor of Psychology degree, rather than the PhD. Other sections were added. The importance of research and the concept of the clinical psychologist as scientist–practitioner were emphasized more strongly than before. The report of the Committee, now generally known as the Shakow Report, was published in 1947 (APA, 1947). The Boulder conference on training in clinical psychology (Raimy, 1950) essentially ratified the substantive core of the Shakow Report but served an important additional function in unifying the community of psychologists around the scientist–practitioner concept of professional training.

In accreditation, site visits began in 1948, with expenses paid by a $2,500 appropriation by the APA and a $12,000 grant from the U.S. Public Health Service. Accreditation of counseling programs began in 1950. Accreditation of predoctoral internships began in 1956. The decision to accredit school psychology programs was approved in 1967, though implementation of the plan was delayed until 1971. Through the 1950s and into the 1960s, the size of the accrediting operation increased dramatically. From a few dozen clinical programs in 1947, the number had soared by 1968 to some 95 programs in 75 universities and 100 internship programs. The name of the review committee was changed several times, from the Committee on Training in Clinical Psychology to the Committee on Doctoral Education in 1952 and the Committee on Evaluation in 1954, but no significant changes in the size, composition, or function of the group were made. The size of the committee fluctuated between 9 and 12 members. Participants were drawn almost entirely from senior university faculty personnel. Rules of procedures required at least one member of the committee to visit every university program that applied for review.

In the late 1960s, the situation reached crisis proportions. Accreditation of internship sites had become almost meaningless. Among 100 agencies on the approved list for 1966 to 1967, 69 had not been visited in 10 years and about 25 had never been visited at all. Despite these omissions, members of the Committee on Evaluation were still called away from their home institutions for accreditation business for an average of 20 days per year. Wholesale resignations from the committee resulted (APA, 1970).

The Education and Training Board proposed to reduce the workload by eliminating the accreditation of internships and thinning out the university schedule by extending the time between reviews for well-established programs. The proposal was vociferously rejected by the Council of Representatives in 1967. Instead, the council directed the Education and Training Board to continue evaluating internship agencies, to continue evaluating clinical and counseling programs at current levels, and to move as quickly as possible to evaluate doctoral programs in school psychology.

The accreditation machine was caught, as they say, between a rock and a hard place—required by higher authority to sustain and expand their operations but stuck with an outdated organization and deprived of the resources needed to do the job. Central Office staff, made up at the time of Alan Boneau and William Simmons, estimated that conducting accreditation as decreed by the council would cost upward of $100,000 and that sizable fees to participating organizations would be required. In light of this and other considerations, the Council of Chairmen of Graduate Departments of Psychology asked that any assessment of fees be postponed for a year so that they could build the necessary funds into their budgets and proposed appointment of a blue-ribbon panel to examine the process of accreditation in all its ramifications.

The panel, which came to call itself the APA Commission on Accreditation, was duly appointed. Arthur MacKinney became its chair. The commission recommended that evaluations, including site visits, be conducted by ad hoc review panels, that provision be made both for advisory consultation with programs seeking accreditation and for appeal of decisions by programs denied approval, and that the costs of accreditation be borne in part by the institutions under review and in part by the APA, with help from any grant agency that might be persuaded to support the operation. They also recommended changing the name of the decision-making group to its current form, the Committee on Accreditation (APA, 1969).

The task of accreditation had grown not only in size but in complexity. Freestanding professional schools were springing up in California and proposed elsewhere. The Illinois Doctor of Psychology program had been established and became the first entry in the newly formed category of provisional accreditation. The Chicago conference on the training of clinical psychologists (Hoch, Ross, & Winder, 1966) had been a good deal more disputatious than any of the previous conferences, and the Vail conference on levels and patterns of training in professional psychology (Korman, 1976), destined to be more contentious still, was not far in the future. Education in professional psychology was again in rapid transition, and continuing review of the accreditation process was clearly required.

Another task force was established in 1976 to revise criteria in consideration of ideas expressed at the Vail conference and the emergence of professional schools of psychology. The group, chaired by Louis Cohen, did its best to balance some of the excesses of the conference against the more conservative inclinations of the academic community. The report of the task force was completed in September 1978 and published in the *APA Monitor* in April 1979. Among other changes from previous criteria, the practitioner model of education and the Doctor of Psychology degree were recognized as legitimate, along with the scientist–practitioner model leading to the PhD. The principle of affirmative action to extend cultural diversity among students and faculty was endorsed, but no specific requirements were set, on the assumption that site-visit teams would be alert to the issue and in a position to make appropriate judgments.

Again, the volume of work for which the Committee on Accreditation was responsible had mounted beyond the capacity of the group as then organized, and the committee had fallen far behind in its schedule. Meredith Crawford was called out of his second retirement to direct the Office of Accreditation, and he brought his well-practiced organizational skills to bear in revising procedures for selecting, enlarging, and training the pool of site visitors on which reviews depended. He drafted the first edition of the *Accreditation Handbook*, on which all site visitors now depend. In meetings of the committee, he showed members how to conduct fair and expeditious reviews.

When Crawford retired yet again, he was replaced by Paul Nelson, who in his second career has managed accreditation through a time when massive organizational changes were occurring within and beyond the association, including creation of the Education Directorate, breakaway establishment of the American Psychological Society, and the extra work occasioned by special events like the celebration of the centennial anniversary of the founding of the APA.

In June 1984, still another task force was appointed to conduct a review of the entire accreditation process. Sandra Scarr served as chair until 1988, when Jill Reich became chair and served through completion of the report in April 1989. The major recommendations of the task force—to enlarge the accreditation committee substantially and to select members in a way that represents the major consituencies of the APA—are now in effect.

I will close with a few reflections. We have come a long way since Robert Sears and a small group of colleagues could review all the clinical programs in the country in a single day. The December 1991 issue of the *American Psychologist* listed 273 accredited doctoral programs in professional psychology and 398 internships. Three hundred seventy-one members of the association took part in site visits or other accreditation activities during the 1990 to 1991 academic year. The volume of work has not changed materially since that time. Our accreditation system has not only become larger, it has become more diverse. From a time when academicians did the whole job, we have attempted representation of our entire community. In its expanding size and diversity, accreditation reflects the discipline at large. I find no evidence in my review that accreditation has stifled innovation in any sector of our field, as many once thought it would and as many still fear it might. Our science has proceeded to explore every conceivable human activity, including many once thought to be beyond the reach of systematic investigation. Our practitioners have moved into fields once forbidden, and if they think they can do some good are ready to enter any arena of human enterprise whatsoever. Our educators have pressed their innovations forward wherever they believed they had to go. Accreditation has followed, to see to it that anybody claiming to train practitioners is doing an effective job of it. In the increasing emphasis on program enhancement, it functions as a supportive consultant, not as a dictatorial authority.

Throughout the history of accreditation in psychology, we have been blessed with the contributions of a legion of talented, dedicated men and women. When crises arose, the people who were needed came forward, took hold, and brought us through. I do not know of any discipline, science or profession, whose members are more critical of themselves than psychologists are. Perhaps that is because we have been arrogant enough to take on this impossible job—understanding the human process and trying to improve it—but at the same time modest enough to appreciate our own frailties. At some level, we all seem to know how selfish and narrow we can be, so we are spendidly skeptical of one another. In fundamental ways, accreditation in psychology and psychology as a discipline mirror the trials and opportunities that confront our society as a whole. We are a community of many colors, many faiths, many histories, and many aspirations. If we are to prosper, we must acknowledge the differences among our diverse groups and take pride in our separate identities but at the same time hold always to our respect for one another and the search for excellence in everything we do.

IV

THE FUTURE OF PROFESSIONAL PSYCHOLOGY

INTRODUCTION

THE FUTURE OF PROFESSIONAL PSYCHOLOGY

The first three chapters in this part were all written as preconference papers or addresses for the National Council of Schools and Programs of Professional Psychology (NCSPP) conferences of 1994 and 1995. In 1989, well before those conferences were scheduled, I had retired from my dean's job at Rutgers University. Once again, I had planned to let professional psychology go its own way and devote my energies to other pursuits. My interest in our profession, however, has never abated. When my friend Jules Abrams, director of the Institute for Graduate Clinical Psychology at Widener University and president of NCSPP in 1993 to 1994, asked me to rejoin the council as an active participant in planning and conducting the meta-conference that he had conceived and I have described in chapter 9, I could not resist. After all of the work of preceding decades, it was time to take stock, reflect on our efforts, and look to the future of professional psychology in light of the changing needs of our society.

Chapter 11, "Making Psychology Indispensable," was originally prepared as a keynote address for the NCSPP conference of 1994. In the chapter, I argue that professional psychology must move beyond traditional preoccupation with psychotherapy to cautious but courageous disciplined inquiry into the most serious problems in our society if we are to improve our usefulness and prosper as a profession. Disciplined inquiry, of the kind I have described in this book, requires an epistemology that is sufficiently comprehensive and flexible to engage the full range of issues a biopsychosocial profession must confront, but at the same time sufficiently rigorous to provide reasonable safeguards against error. In chapter 12, Roger Peterson and I outline "ways of knowing" that a useful profession of psychology can sensibly employ. The chapter was first prepared as a preconference paper for the NCSPP meeting of 1994. Chapter 13, "The Reflective Educator," was originally written as a preconference paper for the NCSPP meeting of 1995. There I note that the education of professional psychologists is itself a profession. When this truth is taken seriously, critical analysis of our own educational process, full-scale disciplined inquiry to elucidate and improve the education of professional psychologists, stands out as an urgent responsibility, still poorly met by most educators in our field.

Through the time these chapters were in preparation, the divisions between scientific and professional factions in psychology seemed to be growing deeper and more angry than ever in my recall. Never before had I broadcast unsolicited papers to colleagues, but this time I did, in hope of helping to bridge some of the divisions. Along with a letter expressing my concerns about the difficult times psychology was facing and the need to work together in meeting the challenges before us, I sent preprints of the papers that now appear in the following three chapters to some 40 colleagues I had come to know and respect over the years. In the letter, I described my correspondents as "influential in the intellectual and moral leadership of psychology." Alphabetically arranged, the list of names starts with George Albee and ends with Arthur Wiens. Anyone who does not recognize the names on the list has not studied psychology. The response surprised me. Letters came from people I had not seen in years. Several people sent me reprints of articles they had written, and long lapsed correspondences were resumed. Two of the papers, here chapters 11 and 13, were invited for publication in appropriate journals. Chapter 12 is also scheduled for publication in the book on standards for education in professional psychology that Roger Peterson, Jules Abrams, and I are preparing.

These are challenging times for psychology. Threats from outside the field are sharpened by schisms within. I comment on the topic of division and union in our discipline in the final chapter of this book. Some of my remarks were taken from a lecture, "The Gift of Diversity," that I gave at the APA convention in New York City in August 1995. For the most part, however, chapter 14 consists of near-random thoughts that come into my mind as I reflect on the 50 eventful years that professional psychology and I have gone through together, after all so short a time, so small a world, so different from the world we once imagined, yet how strong the basic structures. Occasionally, I peer into the haze that clouds the future.

11

MAKING PSYCHOLOGY INDISPENSABLE

Professional psychology has grown enormously in the United States during the past 25 years. Over this time, the number of licensed psychologists has increased by more than 300%. By now, almost 65,000 psychologists are licensed to practice in one or more states. This number is more than twice that of total membership in the American Psychiatric Association. According to estimates by Shapiro and Wiggins (1994), almost 70% of current members of the American Psychological Association (APA) are primarily involved in the practice of psychology. The same authors show that 7 of the 8 largest APA divisions, starting with Clinical Psychology (Division 12), Independent Practice (Division 42), and Psychotherapy (Division 29), and ending with Health Psychology (Division 38), Clinical Neuropsychology (Division 40), and Counseling Psychology (Division 17), are all devoted to professional concerns, especially health care. Practically all of this development in the

This chapter was originally prepared for an NCSPP conference on Standards for Education in Professional Psychology: Reflection and Integration, in Cancún, Mexico, in January 1994. A revised version was published in *Applied and Preventive Psychology*, 5, 1–8, accompanied by an article by Richard M. McFall titled "Making Psychology Incorruptible," pp. 9–16, and a following statement by me titled "Making Conversation Possible," pp. 17–18.

professional side of our discipline has taken place since World War II, and much of it has happened since the Vail conference on Levels and Patterns of Training in Professional Psychology in 1973. Within a biological generation, psychology has moved from a relatively minor position in the health care industry to become the largest provider of doctoral-level mental health services in the nation.

The size and speed of the increase pleases some and alarms others, depending on whether they see it as the normal adolescent growth spurt of a young profession or more like a cancer. In the following remarks, I suggest that neither complacent approval nor horrified denunciation of the creature we have produced should motivate our efforts to improve the profession of psychology. Instead, we need to take a sober look at the way our society and our profession are changing, and set directions for effective development in the years ahead. I begin with some of my deepest concerns.

THE CULTURAL PAROCHIALISM OF PROFESSIONAL PSYCHOLOGY

A thought that sometimes troubles me in the dark hours before the dawn is that the United States of America is the only country in the world that has a large, doctoral-level profession of psychology. Every other first-world nation has physicians and lawyers, engineers and teachers, but no other country in the world has large numbers of professional psychologists with PhD and PsyD degrees attending to its psychological concerns. Psychology is active as a science in most other culturally advanced nations, although as a science too, psychology is much larger in the United States than anywhere else. Professional psychology, or as it is often called, "applied psychology," is also active in many other countries, but not at the doctoral level. The international survey of psychology by Rosenzweig (1982) and the descriptions of psychology in other countries that appear from time to time in the *Annual Review of Psychology* show that education for professional practice outside the United States is typically at the master's level. So the first question that troubles me is this: If Japan, Germany, and every other civilized country in the world can get along without a large force of doctoral-level professional psychologists, might not ours?

Insofar as graduates with PhDs from scientist–practitioner programs spend their lives providing health care and other professional services, the question holds as much for them as it does for Doctors of Psychology. So does another question: How did we come to be the only country in the world to enjoy the blessings of a large doctoral profession of psychology? In this case, the answer lies in a sequence of historical events whose general outlines are well known but some of whose particulars are not well known. Most psychologists recognize that the rapid expansion of professional psychology in the United States after World War II can be attributed largely to the Veterans Administraion (VA) training program in clinical psychology, which provided financial support, training opportunities, and readily available jobs to thousands of students of my generation and the generations to follow. Some psychologists are also aware that the adminstrators of the VA, pursuing the demands for accountability that are inherent in all forms of governmental benevolence, issued the "request" for identification of qualified clinical programs that required organized American psychology, after a half century of political paralysis, to standardize education for practice and establish a system of accreditation to assure quality in its professional programs (cf. Peterson, 1992a). Few psychologists seem to know, however, about the peculiar circumstances that brought the VA training program in psychology into being.

Prior to 1946, none of the "psychologists" in the VA held doctoral degrees. They were technicians, titled "psychometricians," at the baccalaureate or master's level. They gave tests. The treatment of psychiatric patients was entirely controlled by the medical profession. Malarial inoculation for syphilitic paresis, metrazol, insulin, and electroconvulsive shock for schizophrenic and manic–depressive disorders, and prefrontal lobotomy for the psychotically unruly were the order of the day. Any psychotherapy that was offered to the inmates of VA hospitals was done by neuropsychiatrists.

During the war, American clinical psychologists gained a reputation for competence not only as diagnosticians but as psychotherapists, assisting hard-pressed psychiatrists in treating battle casualties. The involvement of psychologists as therapists was encouraged by the chief of neuropsychiatry in the U.S. Army Surgeon General's Office, one William C. Menninger, an early advocate of the "team approach" that included psychologists as essential, high-status participants in the diagnosis and treatment of psychiatric disorders. I do not know who was in charge of neuropsychiatric affairs in the military services of other countries, but it is unlikely that any of them encouraged the advancement of psychology as a quasipsychiatric profession as enthusiastically as Colonel Menninger did. Only one British agency, the Maudsley Institute of Psychiatry, offered training in clinical psychology, and the head of clinical psychology there, Hans Eysenck, opposed involvement of psychologists in psychotherapy as a matter of principle. Psychology was science. The central functions of clinical psychology were assessment and research. The practice of psychotherapy was "essentially alien" to those pursuits (Eysenck, 1949). Eysenck did not come to advocate treatment as a legitimate activity for psychologists until later, and then only when "therapy" was preceded by "behavior" rather than "psycho."

Professional psychology got no special encouragement among our military adversaries either. At the very time American psychologists were developing tests and their secret statistical weapon, the stanine, to select aircraft pilots, the Germans stopped using tests for that purpose. Hitler wanted to use appointment to the glamourous Luftwaffe as a reward for service in the Hitler youth corps, and the Prussian generals who dominated the German high command wanted their sons and nephews to receive dirrect appointments to the air force without prejudice from any battery of aptitude tests. So, through a perfectly unique combination of personalities and political conditions, American psychologists came out of the war in greater numbers, with higher status, and a more clearly established role in health care than did psychologists of any other country.

The big leap in professional psychology, of course, did not take place during the war but after it, largely through the VA training program in clinical psychology and the related programs that followed. Every other warring nation had veterans, but none of the others mounted anything like our VA program. Why and how did we? For a detailed answer to that question, I refer you to an account by Dana Moore (1992). Here I will mention only a part of the story that is decisive in understanding how American clinical psychology, as we know it today, got its most important boost.

With 16 million veterans returning from the war, the need for huge increases in health care personnel was obvious to everyone who considered the situation. As one of several responses to the emergency, Congress passed Public Law 293, which established the VA as a major medical training agency. Affiliative relationships were formed between VA hospitals and medical schools. Residency programs were established for physicians. Initially, psychology was not included in the plan. Psychology was not generally regarded as a health care profession. Psychology was not so much as mentioned in the law.

In the early months of 1946, only three doctoral-level psychologists were employed by the VA. One of them was James Grier Miller, who held an MD and a PhD in experimental psychology from Harvard University and had served in the war. This is the same James Grier Miller who became known to many psychologists later on as the author of living systems theory (Miller, 1978). Miller wanted to bring more clinical psychologists into the VA service, and he saw a provision in the law that gave him a way to do so. The law allowed payment of part-time staff on the VA scale. Miller proposed that trainees in clinical psychology be hired as part-time staff, and that their assignment be service-related training in the skills of their profession. He was encouraged in this interpretation by the VA's first consultant in psychology, George Kelly. Miller gathered some respected signatures on a petition to support the proposal, obtained the approval of the head of the VA, General Omar N. Bradley, and with the help of many other people set the VA training program in clinical psychology in motion.

As a young trainee who entered the program in 1948, I knew nothing of this. I knew that the program was new, and I sometimes wondered why I could only work 39 hours per week when I wanted to make some extra money during vacation periods, but for the most part I took the program for granted. I was, however, as grateful for it as I was for the GI Bill that had allowed me to complete my undergraduate education. As I look back on the whole scene now, it seems to me a monumental fluke. And then I ask my second question: If the VA training program, which did more to determine the size and shape of professional psychology in the United States than any other single creation, came into being by one set of historical accidents, might not some others, say sudden, politically guided changes in our health care system, take us out?

MAKING PSYCHOLOGY INDISPENSABLE

In reflecting on our history, some comfort can be found in the realization that every novel creation that ever happens is a kind of fluke. The peculiar combination of elements and energies that produced life on this planet might have happened somewhere else, but so far we have seen no sign of it. Biological life, as we know it on earth, is possibly unique, and must at least be exceedingly rare in the physical universe. An extraordinary combination of hospitable climatic conditions, fresh water, edible vegetation, and relative freedom from effective predators was required to allow evolution of the human species. And of course every social invention, including the Roman Empire and the U.S. government, grew out of its own particular circumstances of time, place, and person. Whatever cosmic design may govern it all, every novel condition that we take for granted in our lives today began as a kind of fluke.

But no matter, here we are. We might as well make the best of the situation. Unlike the dinosaur, we can exert some control over our own future. Our lonely position as the only large doctoral profession of psychology in the world can work to our advantage, but only if we turn ourselves to the genuine advantage of the people we are hired to serve. American inventions have often led the world. If we create a profession that is indispensable in our society, it could become one of America's most attractive exports.

Some social inventions last a long time and others last only a short time. The historian Arnold Toynbee has shown us that the surviving institutions are generally those that contrive adaptive responses to challenge. This suggests what we must *not* do as a profession if we hope to continue our good works. Simply, we must not go on doing what we have done in the past.

To an extent that we need to consider critically, we seem still to be training professional psychologists as if their main job were to treat the posttraumatic stress disorders that preoccupied us in 1946. The last time I looked at time-in-function data, psychotherapy still topped the list of activities that engage the energies of professional psychologists. On the record, psychologists have done more to place psychotherapy on a firm scientific foundation than have the members of any other discipline. We have examined the theoretical bases of psychotherapy more closely than any others (e.g., Messer & Wachtel, 1992). We have been far more earnest in research on the processes and outcomes of psychotherapy than any others (e.g., APA Division 12, 1993; Strupp, 1992). But we are not the only ones who do it. Unlike the skills of medicine and law; unlike those of nursing, optometry, pharmacy, podiatry, and physical therapy for that matter, the skills of psychotherapy are neither clearly bounded nor legally monopolizable. By now, not only psychiatrists, psychologists, and social workers, but nurse practitioners, marriage and family therapists, "counselors" and "therapists" of every conceivable kind are ready to offer talk therapies that are not easily distinguished from those that psychologists provide. We may believe that our therapies are better, and they may actually be better, but so far nobody has been able to prove that we do the job better than others, and most of the subdoctoral people doing something like psychotherapy today are willing to offer it at lower cost than most psychologists would like to charge.

Furthermore, not all the psychotherapy going on today, even by the most extensively trained practitioners, can legitimately be defined as health care. Much of it can, but some of it cannot. It does not matter whether the provider holds an MD, a PhD, or a PsyD degree. It does not matter what kinds of "diagnoses" we stick on our "patients." Much of the "therapy" that psychiatrists and psychologists do, especially the long-term, psychodynamic kind, has nothing whatever to do with "illness" in any sensible definition of that term. We should continue to provide bona fide mental health care, and we deserve to be well paid for it. But we cannot expect Manhattan cab drivers to pay psychoanalysts large amounts of money to strengthen the ego boundaries of the Woody Allens of the world.

I am not opposed to the practice of psychotherapy. For the indefinite future, psychotherapy is likely to remain a prominent staple in the array of services that professional psychologists provide. We should continue to do it, continue to teach it, continue to examine it, and continue to improve it. But if psychotherapy is all we do, or even the main thing we do, our profession is in serious jeopardy.

Neither can we stake our future on our dubious distinction as a science. The argument that professional psychology is "based" in science has taken several forms over the years. Before World War II, in what I have called the preprofessional phase of our development (Peterson, 1991), science was all there was to psychology. The science might be applied, and more and more psychologists gained employment outside of the academy, but education for practice was scattered, and the cultural definition of the field exclusively as science prevailed both formally and politically. After the war, the Shakow Report (APA, 1947) and the Boulder conference (Raimy, 1950) defined the reciprocal relationship between science and practice that characterized the scientist–professional phase. As training conferences from Boulder to Gainesville (Belar & Perry, 1992) have affirmed and as I have agreed (e.g., Peterson, 1985, 1991) the scientist–practitioner concept has great power and needs to be sustained. However, when the argument for science in the education of professional psychologists is stated in a way that devalues professional work, disparages specific training for practice, and restricts the scope of professional service, it needs to be examined closely.

Students who come to our professional schools from the academic departments of research universities tell us how much "practice-bashing" goes on in the halls of academe. Some of that is just ignorant, spiteful muttering. Most students are smart enough to question the biases of their professors and find out for themselves what the profession can be and what professional schools have to offer. Sometimes, however, the derision of professional work and opposition to direct education for practice are raised above innuendo to reasoned argument. A particularly forceful argument has recently been advanced by Richard McFall (1991) in a "Manifesto for a science of clinical psychology" that he presented as his presidential address to Section III, the Society for a Science of Clinical Psychology of APA Division 12. McFall's argument is "objective" in the best Popperian sense. It is coherent, clear, and boldly expressed, "out there" where it can be examined critically. I single it out for discussion because it is the strongest statement I have seen of the proresearch, antipractice position in the debate that currently divides practitioners from researchers in psychology. It offers me an opportunity to restate some counter arguments that I will attempt to make equally clear, and thereby to bring our differences into the sharp relief required for respectful debate and possible resolution.

In his manifesto, McFall asserted one cardinal principle and two corollaries aimed at advancing clinical psychology as an applied science. The cardinal principle holds that scientific clinical psychology is the only legitimate and acceptable form of clinical psychology. As long as "science" is defined in a sufficiently comprehensive and flexible way to accommodate the problems with which professional psychologists are concerned, no one I know will disagree. Nor will anyone dispute McFall's insistence on quality assurance in justifying the services that psychologists offer to the public. The criteria he proposed for assuring quality, however, require careful scrutiny. In an adaptation of recommendations by Julian Rotter (1971a) McFall claimed as the first corollary of his cardinal principle that psychological services should not be administrated to the public, except under strict experimental control, until they have satisfied these four minimal criteria:

1. The exact nature of the service must be described clearly.
2. The claimed benefits of the service must be stated explicitly.
3. These claimed benefits must be validated scientifically.
4. Possible negative side effects that might outweigh any benefits must be ruled out empirically.

In imposing these restrictions, McFall appears to be reverting to the view of professional psychology as applied science that I assigned historically to the

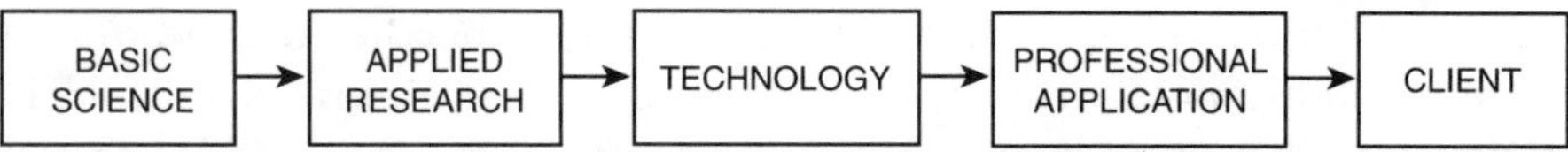

Figure 11.1. Professional activity as applied science. Reprinted from D. Peterson (1991), p. 425.

preprofessional phase of the devlopment of our discipline and represented graphically in Figure 11.1. According to this view, psychologists begin by discovering the basic laws of nature, which then leads to applied research, which produces a technology, which, as applied by professionals, finally makes it way over to the client. Attributions of value are clearly ordered from left to right. Basic science is more valuable than applied research, and applied research is more valuable than professional application. In fact, the practitioner is little more than a technician, and the client is little more than a passive recipient of all these labors. All the client has to do is swallow the pill.

The trouble with this view is that it is a grossly inaccurate representation of the kinds of problems professionals encounter, the kinds of services they offer, and the processes through which their clients are served. The concept of professional work as applied science depends on the doctrine of technical rationality, which Donald Schön (1983) demolished in his book *The Reflective Practitioner*. By examining the way master practitioners in architectural design, town planning, product engineering, industrial management, and psychotherapy actually think in action, Schön demonstrated that the problems professionals encounter in all these fields are not fixed but fluid, not general but unique, not precisely definable but uncertain in their nature. The task of the professional is not one of fitting predesigned solutions to fixed problems but one of artful inquiry, flexible problem setting, and disciplined but creative design. The professional is not a technician, routinely applying the proven techniques that science has provided, but a reflective investigator, constantly reformulating the problem with which each client is concerned, designing and testing the solutions that each new case may invite.

As a professional, the investigator is a scientist of sorts, but science itself could never grow within the bounds that Rotter and McFall place around it. As criteria for credible, constructive science, the restrictions implied by McFall's first corollary became philosophically indefensible with the publication of Karl Popper's *Logik der Forschung* in 1934. More recent developments in analytic philosophy and constructionist metatheory (cf. chap. 12 in this volume) have completely discredited the positivistic assumptions that underlie McFall's argument. As limits on a profession, the criteria he proposed would only assure that professional psychologists never do much of value.

As a researcher investigating a problem with which Professor McFall was also concerned, I would read his reports with interest and take care to find out what he was doing before undertaking any new studies of my own. As a journal editor, I have given special encouragement to the publication of his work. As a professional confronted with a client whose condition bore some resemblance to those McFall had studied, I would carry knowledge of his findings into my reflections and formulations. As an educator of scientists and practitioners in psychology I am ready to believe that he runs a fine research program, but I am disappointed by his misrepresentation of professional programs as lacking in scientific content, and concerned about the breach between educators in research-oriented programs and educators in practice-oriented programs that misunderstandings of this kind can foster. As a client, I would be hesitant to bring my problems to anyone who subscribed to the credo that McFall endorses. What if my condition isn't in his book? Will I be recruited as a subject in an experiment? Perhaps. But then I will expect him to pay me.

I will not quarrel with the basic intent of McFall's second corollary: The primary and overriding objective of doctoral training programs in clinical psychology must be to produce the most competent clinical scientists possible. McFall and I differ, however, in our defintions of acceptable science. He rejects idiographic investigation. I seek to advance it. The strategy of inquiry that I consider most useful for professional psychologists has essentially the same structure that Schön found common to all the "reflective professions" he examined. It resembles closely the strategy that Trierweiler and Stricker (1992) proposed in their conception of the practitioner as a "local scientist." I have called my version "disciplined inquiry" and summarized its main features graphically in Figure 11.2.

Neither scientific theory nor empirical research is excluded from the process. The "guiding conception" within which each inquiry is conducted includes the most powerful available theory as well as the epistemological and

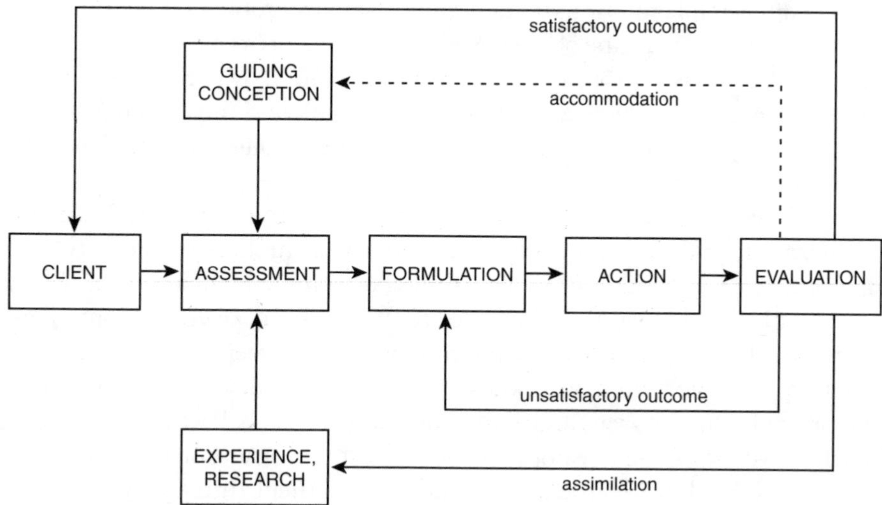

Figure 11.2. Professional activity as disciplined inquiry. Reprinted from D. Peterson (1991), p. 426.

axiological assumptions that underlie all professional work. The assessment through which a constructive formulation and a promising plan of action are derived is informed by any factual research that may have been done on problems of a similar kind as well as the personal and collective experience that any well-trained practitioner brings to the study. The most important characteristic of disciplined inquiry in professional practice, however, as contrasted with disciplined inquiry in nomothetic research, is that it begins and ends in the condition of the client, not in a body of general scientific knowledge. Occasionally, but not necessarily, an inquiry will contribute generalizable knowledge or broadly useful technique. Still more rarely, dramatic and unexpected results may require revision or amendment of a theory. In each and every case, however, the fundamental goal of the practitioner is to improve the functional effectiveness of the individual client, whether the client is a person, a family, a work group, an athletic team, a school system, a business organization, a governmental agency, or any other human entity. In the interest of our clients, we cannot start from science and apply only what we know for sure. We must start with the needs of the people who pay for our help, and apply all the useful knowledge we can find or create.

What are the most urgent needs that we see about us now? Does anybody have any trouble naming them? Preventive, cost-effective health care; alternatives to hospitalization for the severely mentally ill; reducing drug abuse, alcohol abuse, substance abuse of any kind; decent nurturance for children who lack stable families; strengthening families wherever that is possible; better schooling; more productive business practices; alternatives to violence on the street, in the home, wherever it happens; reducing the bigotry on which ethnic violence is based.

Has science told us how to solve these problems? Of course not. People hanker after simple solutions to immensely complex problems. Drugs? Say no. Crime? More prisons. One of the mistakes social scientists have made over the past few decades is to propose a simple solution of their own. Science. Give us plenty of money for our research (spoken message), and (unspoken message) we'll solve your problems. Of course we were doomed to fail, and our credibility has suffered for it.

We need to face the most serious problems confronting the people in our society now, but we need to do so in a spirit of intellectual modesty that approaches awe. We cannot all attack all of our problems all at once. Each of us can only do what we can where we are. We must not overreach ourselves. Emphatically, we must not make promises we cannot keep. But neither do we need to settle for what we "know for sure." We never know anything important for sure anyway, and neither does anybody else. If we do not know as much as we may some day hope to know about the conditions that threaten our society, we have learned a good deal about them through 100 years of scientific research and 50 years of large-scale professional work. Who knows more about effective methods for behavior change in preventive health care?

Who knows more about child development and the role of the family in rearing healthy children? Who knows more about human learning and the educational process? Who knows more about incentives, authority, communication, and effective organization in the workplace? Who knows more about conflict and its resolution? Who knows more about the origins of social prejudice and effective ways of reducing it? We need to meet our clients on their terms, attend to their needs. And then, in honest, respectful alliance with our clients, we must bring the knowledge and skills of our profession into their service.

The approach I propose has much in common with the "psychology as a means of promoting human welfare" that George Miller (1969) outlined in his presidential address to the APA 25 years ago. It also has much in common with the best of the community psychology that has developed since that time. As practitioners, however, we face some realities that neither Miller nor most academic community psychologists have had to consider. It is easy enough for a distinguished professor at Rockefeller University to "give psychology away." It is not so easy for a student coming out of the Antioch New England Graduate School with a PsyD degree and a $50,000 debt. Contemporary community psychology is rich in noble aims, but so far it has been seriously deficient in providing career paths for students. I do not see many ads for community psychologists in the *New York Times*. We who are educators of professional psychologists must prepare students to meet the most urgent needs of the public, but at the same time we ought to see that opportunities for a decent living are accessible to our graduates.

For all these reasons, we need to go beyond even the best of our individual efforts. We need to join in cooperative action to share the experiences we are gaining. I can show you the records of Rutgers professional school graduates who are helping the families of AIDS babies in Newark, organizing services for autistic children and their families in several regions along the East Coast, and transforming special services in the schools of one of the Appalachian states. All are well paid. I am sure you can show me similar kinds of work that the graduates of your schools are doing. I want to know about them. We need to form networks of practitioners working on comparable problems, and get the news to one another about the experiences we are gaining. We need to share reports of our failures as well as our successes. The traditional journals will not do the job for us. They are too slow and their editors are too commonly infected with outdated positivistic biases to encourage the free flow of information that we need. The systematic self-studies on which the member organizations of NCSPP are now embarking, especially detailed descriptions of the work our graduates are doing, are a start in the direction we should take. We need to continue those kinds of efforts, extend them, systematize them, and invite others, especially our colleagues in the research-oriented university programs, to join in the enterprise. At the same time, those of us who are engaged in more traditional forms of university research should maintain our involvement in the research networks already active in our field.

The information we collect can be used to show the public what we are doing in a graphic way that anyone can understand. Most nonpsychologists have very foggy ideas about the nature of our discipline. Many are still confused about the difference between psychologists and psychiatrists, and when they do find out they are all too likely to accept the negative definition that medicine has pinned on us. We are the ones who do *not* have MDs and cannot prescribe drugs. In groping for identity, we have contributed to the confusion.

Listen to us. "We're a profession, but we aren't really a profession, we're a science. We do research, but most of us don't actually do any research. We aren't really scientists, we aren't really professionals, we're scientist–professionals. We aren't exactly scientist–professionals, we're scholar–professionals. We're sort of like scientists, but we aren't general scientists, we're local scientists. What we do isn't exactly research, it's disciplined inquiry." We sound like Jackie Mason.

In our scholarly disputations, we need to refine these kinds of distinctions as sharply as we can, but in telling the public who we are and what we do, we need to simplify. Simplify to clarify, but never to deceive. I don't think that is so hard to do. "We are professional psychologists. Our profession is concerned with improving the effectiveness of human behavior. It is based on the science of psychology. Preparation for practice in psychology requires 5 years of graduate study that includes thorough scholarly education and extensive training in the skills of practice. Graduates hold the Doctor of Psychology degree. Here is what they do: case, case, case . . . "

We need to mount a massive public education campaign to get this message across, complete with television ads, brochures in professional waiting rooms and academic advisors' offices, notices on the bulletin boards of schools and colleges, everywhere we can get people to see them.

As a comprehensive discipline, we all need to work together. All of us, practitioners and researchers alike. We are all striving for excellence, but we are not in a race to see who wins. We msut all work together to meet the most urgent needs that the people of our land are facing today. If we fail to do this, if we just go on talking to the worried well or tell people we can't help them because we haven't done enough research yet, our society will find a way to get along without us. But if we wade right in, if we tackle the problems that matter most in today's world, if we join in partnership with one another and with those we are working to help, if we share our skills and knowledge in a coordinated way, if we finally get clear about who we are and show people what we can do, there is reason to foresee a profession so useful and so well known that anybody anywhere who wants to live a more effective life will think of us early, and nobody planning any kind of human service will dream of going ahead without us.

12

WAYS OF KNOWING IN A PROFESSION: TOWARD AN EPISTEMOLOGY FOR THE EDUCATION OF PROFESSIONAL PSYCHOLOGISTS

DONALD R. PETERSON AND ROGER L. PETERSON

On my desk are two papers. One is a newspaper article that appeared recently under the title "Psychologist Loses License for Exorcism." The article reports, "A state board revoked the Arizona license of a psychologist who says he successfully exorcised angry spirits from a 10-year-old boy with a Bible, holy water, crucifix, and prayer," and then billed the state $180 for the 2-hour procedure. The psychologist, a Lutheran minister who has practiced exorcism for 12 years, said he would perform an exorcism again if the need arose. "It's a sad state," he said, "when the board can't recognize prayer as treatment. . . . No one seems to care that the boy seems to be cured." When asked about the basis for their action, board members said that "exorcism is not recognized as a legitimate form of psychological treatment."

The second paper is an article titled "A Constructive Relationship for

---

This chapter was originally prepared for an NCSPP conference on Standards for Education in Professional Psychology: Reflection and Integration, in Cancún, Mexico, in January 1994. The various sections were written independently by the two authors and are often expressed in first-person form. Donald Peterson wrote the introduction, the section on analytic philosophies, and most of the postscript. Roger Peterson wrote the section that begins with "the reflective practice of professional psychology" and ends after "some proposals." Whenever either of us says "we," it usually means that we have discussed the matter between ourselves and agree fairly closely about it. Authors are listed alphabetically.

Religion With the Science and Profession of Psychology: Perhaps the Boldest Model Yet," that appeared in the March 1994 issue of the *American Psychologist*. The argument in the article goes beyond the scientist–practitioner model and even beyond the model of the psychologist as metaphysician–scientist–practitioner (O'Donohue, 1989) to call for an explicit and constructive relationship between psychology and religion. According to the abstract, "Psychology's previous noninteractive stance toward religion was premised on an outmoded understanding of science and an overly narrow professionalism. Contemporary philosophy of science breaks down the demarcation between science and other forms of human knowing and action, including religion" (Jones, 1994, p. 184). On this broader foundation, an interactive relationship among psychological science, psychological practice, and religion is proposed.

We face the core dilemma of professional psychology. As a profession, we have claimed as our purview no less than the assessment and improvement of psychological functioning (all kinds) at the biopsychological, individual, interpersonal, organizational, and community levels. At the same time, we insist that our methods be rigorous. If we aspire to meet the needs of the human community, how can we neglect the spiritual sphere of human existence? But how far can we go in broadening the base of our discipline? Shall we include discussion of the relationship between psychology and religion? The editors of the *American Psychologist* said yes. Shall we include exorcism as an acceptable form of psychological treatment? The Arizona licensing board said no. The conflict of rigor and relevance, of course, goes far beyond the location of boundaries between religion and psychology. The perennially vexing antinomies of research methodology and clinical experience and of multicultural content and the "canon" offer familiar examples. Where do we draw the lines, and what is the rational basis for drawing any lines at all?

The dilemma faced by every practitioner is sharpened for those of us who assume responsibility for educating professional psychologists. Not only must we decide what to include in our individual repertoires of skills and knowledge, we must also decide what to require in the preparation of generations of students. If we choose wisely and some of our students become teachers, the good we do will extend geometrically. If we get it wrong, we fail an obligation at best and at worst we exponentiate damage.

In efforts to resolve the dilemma, we are forced to consider the epistemological assumptions on which our work is based. Whether we examine them explicitly or not, the assumptions we make about our sources of knowledge permeate all our decisions and all our actions. Although scientific research and professional practice differ in crucial ways, they share a functional core. The central activity in both forms of enterprise is disciplined inquiry (D. Peterson, 1991). Of course educators must decide which techniques to teach their students (projective techniques? feminist psychotherapy?). We have to decide on the conceptions that guide our inquiries (psychodynamic? behavioral? an eclectic blend? of what? how combined?). We have to determine how much and what kinds of factual knowledge our students need to master. Choices in these decisions are neither easy nor obvious. Neither fact nor revelation can set our course, though facts are useful, and revealing insights too, wherever we can gain them. Ultimately we must examine the philosophical foundations of the entire enterprise.

Psychologists have done this all along, perhaps more earnestly than practitioners of any other science or profession. In this chapter, we consider some of these efforts, especially those of the past half century, to see where we might go now in the continuing struggle to develop an informative science and a useful profession and do our best to educate students responsibly. Our account begins with the work of some analytic philosophers whose ways of knowing dominated psychology until very recently, and many of whose ideas deserve a place in any sensible philosophy we may contrive today. We continue with a description of the problems those epistemologies got us into, less by faithful interpretation of the analytic philosophies than by distorted translation into restrictive methodological rules. We proceed to a discussion of some recent alternatives and amendments to analytic philosophy, especially those of a constructionist and pragmatic turn. We conclude with some proposals and questions that need to be considered by those of us who are especially concerned with standards for the education of professional psychologists.

THE ANALYTIC PHILOSOPHIES

Later in this chapter, we consider a set of philosophical views that are variously characterized as *postmodern*, *hermeneutic*, *interpretive*, *contextualist*, *constructionist*, or *social constructionist*. These views are often contrasted with alternative views, said to dominate psychology until the postmodern ideas came along, that are characterized as *modernist*, *empiricist*, and, especially, *positivistic*. In developing arguments of the postmodern kind, proponents frequently begin with a critique of positivistic science in which they outline and then repudiate a cluster of related propositions. The critiques vary in emphasis and tone, but they sound a common theme. The following extract is a composite of sentences that have appeared in critical summaries of modernist, positivistic, logical empiricism. In most cases, the sentences were transcribed literally from their sources. In a few cases, the sentences were paraphrased for logical and grammatical consistency. Here, according to some of the most influential postmodernists, is what positivistic science claims:

> This century has been characterized by a strong and pervasive belief in "certainty through science." It has been assumed that the logical–

> empirical system would provide a secure foundation for certain and indubitable knowledge. The positivist conception of science has its roots in a definition of knowledge that holds that only those things of which we are absolutely certain can be counted as knowledge. If a knowledge claim fails the test of certain truth, then it cannot be included within the body of scientifically approved statements.
>
> Objective science strives for decontextualized facts. It separates fact from value, detail from context, and observation from theory. In empiricist inquiry it is taken for granted that the world is made up of basic objects or elements that can be described in a manner that involves no interpretation. Experimental procedures with operationally defined variables are used to determine correlations and lawlike relationships among various aspects of the human realm. The laws are supposed to have universal validity. The positivistic researcher is only interested in discrete relationships which hold across individuals. On this view, case study is at best a limited, second-class way of seeking knowledge, not very different epistemologically from the personal or journalistic anecdote. (Fishman, 1993; Gergen, 1982; Messer, Sass, & Woolfolk, 1988; Packer & Addison, 1989; Polkinghorne, 1983)

Well. Any epistemology as restrictive as that is obviously unsuitable for a human science that aims to embrace the most interesting subtleties of personal experience and the unavoidable complexities of social behavior. As a "way of knowing" for professional psychologists, it is downright ridiculous. As practitioners, we are not paid to prove our theories. We are paid to help our clients. Case study is our main job. Our efforts are saturated with value. Whether we are treating a disturbed patient in psychotherapy or consulting with the officers of a failing business, our clients know, and we must too, the general directions change must take. We cannot decontextualize our clients, nor any of the "facts" we learn about them. They bring their histories with them. They live in indivestible environments before, during, and after any contact they may have with us. We cannot limit the information on which decisions are reached and actions are taken to "indubitable knowledge." We work in a sea of uncertainty. In every special case, we do well if we can bring some order out of confusion, replace an implausible construction with a more plausible one, contrive a more effective design than the one our client had to start with. In responsible service to those who seek our help and pay our bills, we are obliged to reject old ways of thinking and welcome the new. Goodbye positivism and logical empiricism. Hello hermeneutics and social constructionism.

Before dismissing the positivists and their descendants too quickly, however, it is prudent to consider what the best of them actually said, not what their critics or outdated proponents say they said. As most psychologists know, the term *positivism* was coined by the nineteenth-century French philosopher Auguste Comte, who aimed to replace theological and metaphysical philosophies with a unified philosophy of science. In 1924, a group of philosophers, mathematicians, and scientists in Vienna began to advance a comparable but more complex idea. The group was formed by Moritz Schlick, professor of philosophy at the University of Vienna, on the suggestion of two of his junior colleagues, Herbert Feigl and Felix Kaufmann. The group became known as the *Wiener Kreis*, the Vienna Circle. Prominent members included Rudolf Carnap, Philip Frank, Otto Neurath, Hans Hahn, Victor Kraft, Kurt Gödel, and Friedrich Waismann. Hans Reichenbach, Carl Hempel, Alfred Ayer, Ernest Nagel, Charles Morris, and Alfred Tarski were among the most important visitors. The early work of Ludwig Wittgenstein was very influential in the thinking of the group, as were the writings of Bertrand Russell and Albert Einstein. Wittgenstein himself, however, did not participate in the discussions. Neither did Karl Popper, although his first book was published in a series that the leaders of the Vienna Circle edited, and might never have been published at all, according to Popper's report, without the kind encouragement of Feigl. Feigl wrote the first paper on the Vienna Circle's views to be published in the English language, and it was he who invented the phrase *logical positivism*.

Although the group aimed for a philosophy that would unify all of science, their own views were far from homogeneous. A fairly vigorous rivalry developed between the Vienna group and a group in Berlin led by Hans Reichenbach and Carl Hempel. In Reichenbach's writings especially, the Vienna positivists were often treated as adversaries. Popper's philosophy deviated still more sharply from the views of many positivists, and he not only saw himself but was regarded by most members of the circle as the major opponent of orthodox positivism.

For all their differences, however, the analytic philosophers shared a common passion for separating fact from fiction and sense from nonsense. Most of them assumed that a real world existed before any human beings were around to think about it, that the world would continue independent of their ideas after they were gone, and that the main job of science was to understand the workings of the world as completely and as accurately as possible. This they proposed to do in large part through observation (empiricism) and rational (logical) analysis of concepts related to the observations. Hence *logical empiricism* is not an inappropriate title for the general line of philosophical thought that they developed, though many of them were touchy about the labels others attached to them, just as many clinical psychologists object to such lumpish groupings as *behavioral* or *psychodynamic*. In general, the analytic philosophers envisioned an ideal of apodictic truth, but few of them considered it fully attainable in any synthetic discipline, least of all the human studies, and none of them, except possibly in their earliest writings, suggested that only indubitable knowledge be entered in the book of science.

In the following remarks, I summarize some of the views of some of the analytic philosophers on some of the issues that concerned them. The issues I have chosen are those that continually engage me as I try to think sensibly about the work and education of professional psychologists. The views I present are mainly those of the logical empiricists after 1950 or thereabouts, and conspicuously, of Sir Karl Popper, who for reasons shown in the following sections, is more accurately described as a critical rationalist than as a logical empiricist. I refer to Popper's works more frequently than to those of any other analytic philosopher for several reasons: the depth and range of his conceptions, the vast influence he had on the field of metatheory, and the special relevance of his views to the problems facing professional psychology. I am also drawn to his writing by the clarity with which he expressed his ideas. In a sparkling little piece titled "Against Big Words," he wrote, "Anyone who cannot speak simply and clearly should say nothing and continue to work until he can do so" (Popper, 1984/1992, p. 83). His writings show that he meant what he said.

Critical Realism

The ancient arguments between realists and idealists, from Plato on, are metaphysical arguments. People of good will and sound intelligence have taken both sides. In some early formulations of the Vienna group, especially those of Rudolf Carnap, an idealistic or phenomenalistic view prevailed. According to this view, the only realities we can know are experienced phenomena. "Knowledge" can only mean logical constructions from sense data.

Popper (1970/1985 and elsewhere) disagreed. He regarded critical realism (not a naive realism that identifies the real with the phenomenally given) as the only sensible ontological basis on which science could proceed. The realist assumption—that a real world exists for science to discover—distinguishes between appearance and reality but cannot be demonstrated or proved. Neither can an idealist assumption be refuted. At the simplest level, the idealist says, "The world (including you, my friend) is just my dream." At a more complex level, the idealist says, "All we can reasonably talk about are our mental constructions." There is no factual or logical way to refute those arguments. If I try to convince the idealist of the reality of the world, say by throwing water in his face, the idealist can always counter that he is only dreaming that he felt the splash.

However, the idealist doctrine can be argued, and Popper, who decided early not to waste his time in scholastic verbal dispute, dismisses the argument quickly on grounds of common sense: the view that most people assume would be held by any sensible person free of encumbering philosophical obscurities. Popper also invoked the favored criterion of constructionists: agreement among rational people following informed consideration of the issue. He concluded one of his statements in support of critical realism by quoting Albert Einstein and Winston Churchill. After close analysis of a refutation of naive realism by Bertrand Russell, Einstein wrote, "I do not see any metaphysical danger in our acceptance of things—that is, the objects of physics . . . together with the spatiotemporal structures which pertain to them." In one of Churchill's autobiographical accounts, he wrote,

> Some of my cousins who had the great advantage of University education used to tease me with arguments to prove that nothing has any existence except what we think of it. . . . I always rested upon the following argument which I devised for myself many years ago. . . . [Here] is this great sun standing apparently on no better foundation than our physical senses. But happily there is a method, apart altogether from our physical senses, of testing the reality of the sun. . . . [A]stronomers . . . predict by [mathematics and] pure reason that a black spot will pass across the sun on a certain day. You . . . look, and your sense of sight immediately tells you that their calculations are vindicated . . . We have taken what is called in military map-making a "cross-bearing." We have got independent testimony to the reality of the sun. When my metaphysical friends tell me that the data on which the astronomers made their calculations . . . were necessarily obtained originally through the evidence of their senses, I say "No." They might, in theory at any rate, be obtained by automatic calculating-machines set in motion by the light falling upon them without admixture of the human senses at any stage. . . . I . . . reaffirm with emphasis . . . that the sun is real, and also that it is hot—in fact as hot as Hell, and that if the metaphysicians doubt it they should go there and see. (quoted in Popper, 1970/1985, pp. 224–225)

Of course Churchill had not proved realism, for the idealist could always argue that he or she was dreaming the debate, calculating machines and all. Yet this argument is silly (Popper's word) because of its universal applicability. To Popper, an assumption of reality is not only the most clearly defensible basis for scientific research, it is very like a minimum requirement for the adjudication of sanity.

Demarcation of Science From Nonscience

All psychologists, practitioners as well as researchers, have an interest in distinguishing sense from nonsense, rationality from irrationality. Insofar as they regard their discipline as a science, or as science-based, they have to be concerned about the boundaries between science and everything else. However rigid or relaxed the rules may be, some criteria must be established to mark off science from nonscience.

The boundaries set by the early positivists were closely restrictive. Like Comte before them, they wanted to exclude metaphysics, along with opinion and superstition, from scientific discourse, and a close definition of "factual meaning" gave them grounds for doing so. A sentence was regarded as scientifically meaningful if and only if there was some way to test it.

Very soon, however, they saw that a rigid demand for immediate testability would shut science off from the exploration of issues of great interest but for which no acceptable tests had yet been developed. They relaxed their criteria then and there. They also abandoned any delusion any of them might once have had about the practical attainability of certain truth. As early as 1936, Rudolf Carnap published an article on "Testability and Meaning," in which he wrote

> If by verification is meant a definitive and final establishment of truth, then no (synthetic) sentence is ever verifiable . . . We can only confirm a sentence more and more. Therefore we shall speak of the problem of *confirmation* rather than of the problem of verification. We distinguish the *testing* of a sentence from its confirmation, thereby understanding a procedure—e.g. the carrying out of certain experiments—which leads to a confirmation in some degree either of the sentence itself or its negation. We shall call a sentence *testable* if we know such a method of testing for it; and we call it *confirmable* if we know under what conditions the sentence would be confirmed. . . . [A] sentence may be confirmable without being testable; e.g. if we know that our observation of such and such a course of events would confirm the sentence, and such and such a different course would confirm its negation without knowing how to set up either this or that observation. (Carnap, 1936/1953, p. 47)

Some of the logical empiricists, however, saw even these conditions as unnecessarily confining. P. W. Bridgman's book, *The Logic of Modern Physics* (1927/1953), had had a powerful effect on scientific research in many fields, including psychology, and Bridgman's dictum on operational meaning was taken literally by many investigators. "In general, we mean by any concept nothing more than a set of operations; *the concept is synonymous with the corresponding set of operations* (1927/1953, p. 36). A rigidly confining corollary seemed to follow: Unless a concept can be operationally defined, it is factually meaningless and therefore unfit for scientific consideration.

Among other logical empiricists, Feigl questioned the prevailing positivistic, operationistic interpretation of the meaning of existential hypotheses, and on several grounds, including parsimony, heuristic value, and nomological coherence, justified the legitimacy of hypothetical construction in the development of scientific theory. Indirectly testable propositions, as well as those that were directly testable or might become so, could be subject to scientific investigation (Feigl, 1950).

Feigl's argument was inspired in part by MacCorquodale and Meehl's (1948) article, "On a Distinction Between Hypothetical Constructs and Intervening Variables." Constructs are not reducible to empirical laws. Their formulation involves surplus meaning, "something more" than the abstraction of empirical relationships that define intervening variables, and their elaboration was regarded by MacCorquodale and Meehl not only as scientifically permissible but heuristically desirable for the rapid advance of scientific knowledge. Among psychologists, the idea of "construct validity"

(Cronbach & Meehl, 1955) gained wide acceptance. In developing any means to examine human behavior, investigators need to consider the validity, or "truth value," of their instruments, but they are not restricted to the study of phenomena that are directly observable or quantitatively defined. Multiple, indirect means, progressively organized to form a coherent "nomological network," are also acceptable and useful.

Even Bridgman, in his later years, questioned his early suggestion that the problem of "understanding the process of understanding" could be solved by any such means as requiring operational definition of concepts. He wrote,

> In some of my early writings I spoke of the two-fold aspect of the problem of understanding—there was the problem of understanding the world around us, and there was the problem of understanding the process of understanding, that is, the problem of understanding the nature of the intellectual tools with which we attempt to understand the world around us. The implication in my early writings was that the latter is a closed problem which we may hope to solve . . . to a sufficient approximation. . . . Now this position may still be correct "in principle," although I am beginning to have my doubts. However, it is becoming more and more obvious that the problem of understanding the nature of our intellectual tools offers so many present complexities that it is not profitable to separate the one problem from the other the way I did. In fact, the problem of better understanding our intellectual tools would seem at present to have priority. . . . It is evident, as its critics have often pointed out and I myself have repeatedly stated, that the operational approach cannot be completely general and that it can by no means provide the basis for a complete philosophy. (Bridgman, 1959, pp. 1–2)

None of this intellectual liberalism, however, led Bridgman to soften his advocacy of operational analysis as a fruitful approach to scientific inquiry. Analyzing the world by examining what one *did* in the investigative process was to do something new and unusual, and this for Bridgman was a way to open new intellectual vistas. Far from closing the doors on study of the unknown, operational analysis was a powerful key to scientific discovery.

Other analytic philosophers (e.g., Pap, 1953; Waismann, 1945) also broadened the base of defensible scientific inquiry, but it was left to Popper to destroy the remaining bounds of primitive positivism entirely.

The Problem of Induction

Popper began his attack by disputing the positivistic assumption that scientific knowledge grows through the inductive accumulation of empirical facts. However simply or complexly the positivists might put it, their basic claim was that what elevated science over pseudoscience was the scientific method, and that this method was the method of induction. The basic idea of science as inductive accretion had been questioned by every philosopher since

Francis Bacon, except possibly John Stuart Mill, but according to Popper the logical positivists too had fallen into the inductivist trap. Carnap's statement, "We . . . confirm a statement more and more" typified their position. This, said Popper, is not the way science advances. The inductivist assumption is a case of common sense gone wrong. Popper called it the "bucket theory of mind" and illustrated it with a drawing of a human head shaped like a bucket, with handles that look like ears and informational droplets falling from eye-like holes into the intellectual slosh in the bottom of the pail.

In Popper's devastating simplification of the positivist view, what allegedly enters the mind are the elements of knowledge. Knowledge then consists of an accumulation, or at best a synthesis of, the elements brought in by the senses. The most important aim of science, however, is not the accumulation of facts but the development of ever more powerful ways of thinking about the world, the construction of enlightening theory. This Popper proposed to do by the general method of conjecture and refutation (Popper, 1934/1959, 1968, and elsewhere).

The Critical Scrutiny of Knowledge Claims

Scientific inquiry does not start in observation and end in certainty. It starts in conjecture about some problem with which the investigator is concerned and proceeds through an endless cycle in which the conjectures are examined both rationally and empirically, rejected when they fail, and continually replaced by better ideas. Like Kuhn (1970) and Polanyi (1958) after him, Popper insisted that all observations are "soaked in theory." The investigator starts where prior knowledge ends, proposes bold theories "held with a light hand," subjects them to the severest possible criticism, and replaces them, willingly and gratefully, with the better theories inquiry may suggest. The following quotations, originally published in 1934, capture the spirit of his approach:

> Science does not rest upon rock bottom. The bold structure of its theories rises, as it were, above a swamp. It is like a building erected on piles. The piles are driven from above into the swamp, but not down to any natural or "given" base; and when we cease our attempts to drive our piles into a deeper layer, it is not because we have reached firm ground. We simply stop when we are satisfied that they are firm enough to carry the structure, at least for the time being. (Popper, 1959, p. 111)

> *We do not know; we can only guess.* And our guesses are guided by the unscientific, the metaphysical (though biologically explicable) faith in laws, in regularities which we can uncover—discover. Like Bacon, we might describe our own contemporary science—"the method of reasoning which men now ordinarily apply to nature"—as consisting of "anticipations, rash and premature" and as "prejudices."
>
> But these marvelously imaginative and bold conjectures or "anticipa-

tions" of ours are carefully and soberly controlled by systematic tests. Once put forward, none of our "anticipations" are dogmatically upheld. Our method of research is not to defend them, in order to prove how right we were. On the contrary, we try to overthrow them. Using all the weapons of our logical, mathematical, and technical armory we try to prove that our anticipations were false—in order to put forward, in their stead, new unjustified and unjustifiable anticipations, new "rash and premature prejudices." (Popper, 1959, pp. 178–179)

> What the scientist's and the lunatic's theories have in common is that both belong to *conjectural knowledge*. But some conjectures are much better than others . . . We may *prefer* some competing theories on purely rational grounds. In the first place they are governed by the idea of truth. We want, if at all possible, theories which are true, and for this reason we try to eliminate the false ones.
>
> But we want far more than this. We want new and interesting truth. We are thus led to the idea of *the growth of informative content*, and especially of *truth content*. That is, we are led to the following *principle of preference;* a theory with a great informative content is on the whole more interesting, even before it has been tested, than a theory with little content. Admittedly, we may have to abandon the theory with the greater content, or as I also call it, the bolder theory, if it does not stand up to test. But even in this case we may have learned more from it than from a theory with little content, for falsifying tests can sometimes reveal new and unexpected facts and problems.
>
> Thus our logical analysis leads us directly to a theory of method, and especially to the following methodological rule: try out, and aim at, bold theories, with great informative content; and then let these theories compete, by discussing them critically and by testing them severely. (Popper, 1974, p. 1022)

Nowhere does Popper claim that science embodies truth, nor that only "true" statements be admitted to the body of scientific knowledge. He merely proposes that we seek truth as an ideal, that we examine the "verisimilitude" or truth-likeness of any claim to knowledge that we may make in the most stringent way we can manage.

The criterion for admission of a conjecture is its falsifiability. At first glance, falsifiability appears to be nothing more than the reverse of verifiability, but as Popper expands the idea, it conveys an entirely different attitude. Our job, as investigators, is not to confirm our prior beliefs. We should all know going in that ignorance vastly exceeds any provisional "knowledge" we may claim and that the object of inquiry is to eliminate our inevitable errors.

> What we should do, I suggest, is to admit that all knowledge is human; that it is mixed with our errors, our prejudices, our dreams, and our hopes; that all we can do is to grope for truth even though it be beyond our reach. We may admit that our groping is often inspired, but we must be on guard against the belief, however deeply felt, that our inspiration carries any

authority, divine or otherwise. If we thus admit that there is no authority beyond the reach of criticism to be found within the whole province of our knowledge, however far it may have penetrated into the unknown, then we can retain, without danger, the idea that truth is beyond human authority. And we must retain it. For without this idea there can be no objective standards of inquiry; no criticism of our conjectures; no groping for the unknown; no quest for knowledge. (Popper, 1943/1963, p. 132)

The Place of Values in a World of Facts

The writings of the logical positivists carried a strong reformist current. In advancing a unified science, they hoped to find a way of transcending parochial differences, reaching common ground, and promoting a better world. Many members of the Vienna Circle were Jewish. Although the group began to disperse before Hitler came to power, they saw the evils of the Nazi menace more quickly and more clearly than many others. Unlike Martin Heidegger, for example, they opposed Nazi despotism from the start on rational as well as political grounds. In *The Open Society and Its Enemies*, Popper (1943/1963) not only exposed the flaws (and concurrent cruelties) of Marxist political and economic theory; he wrote to oppose dogmatism in all its forms. His book, *In Search of a Better World* (Popper, 1984/1992), is a collection of lectures and essays over 30 years, all directed toward improving human society, not merely understanding it, though to Popper deep understanding was essential to any lasting good anyone might do, and the deliberate effort to make others happy—to create a heaven on earth, as heaven was envisioned by the helpers—could only lead to hell.

To be socially beneficial, scientific knowledge had to be valid and objective, but Popper did not mean by "objectivity" that the scientists stood aloof from the objects of inquiry or sought to understand them in some disembodied way. He distinguished between three phenomenal worlds. He called the world of things—of physical objects—the first world, the world of subjective experience the second world, and the world of statements in themselves the third world. To avoid confusion with the geopolitical "third world," he sometimes called the last realm "world 3."

As any constructionist might do, he regarded the third world as essentially the product of the human mind. What else could it be? In a general sense, all products of the human mind, such as tools, institutions, works of art, and myths, were included. The problems, theories, and critical arguments that preoccupy scientists were seen as inhabitants of the third world, but these had some special qualities, about which Popper wrote as follows:

I often find myself mistaken in the belief that . . . I have grasped an idea clearly: when trying to write it down I may find that I have not got it yet. This "it," this something which I may not have got, which I cannot be certain that I have got before I have written it down, or at any rate formulated it in language so clearly *that I can look at it critically from various sides*, this "it" is the thought in the objective sense, the third-world object which I am trying to grasp. The decisive thing seems to me that we can put objective thoughts—that is, theories—before us in such a way that we can criticize them, argue them. (Popper, 1974, p. 145)

The innermost nucleus of the third world is the world of problems, theories, and criticism. The nucleus itself is not a domain of values, but it is dominated by a value: of objective truth and the growth of objective truth. The reason few philosophers with scientific training write about values is not that science is value free. To quote Popper again,

The reason is simply that so much of the talk about values is just hot air. So many of us fear that we too would only produce hot air, or, if not that, something not easily distinguished from it . . . I shall therefore say nothing more than that values emerge together with problems; that values could not exist without problems; and that neither values nor problems can be derived or otherwise obtained from facts, though they often pertain to facts or are connected with facts . . . In a sense we can say that throughout [the] human intellectual third world this value [of objective truth and its growth] remains the highest value of all, though we must admit other values into our third world. For with every value proposed arises the problem: is it *true* that this is a value? And, is it *true* that it has its proper standing in the hierarchy of values: is it true that kindness has a higher value than justice, or even comparable with justice? . . .

It is one of the grave mistakes of contemporary philosophy not to recognize that these things—our children—though they are products of our mind, and though they bear upon our subjective experiences—also have an objective side. . . . [O]ur purposes and our aims, like our theories, may compete, and may be discussed critically. . . . Admitting that the third world originates with us, I stress its considerable autonomy, and its immeasurable repercussions on us. Our minds, our selves, cannot exist without it: they are anchored in the third world. We owe to the third world our rationality, the practice of critical and self-critical thinking and acting. We owe to it our relation to our task, to our work, and its repercussions upon ourselves. . . . If I am right in my conjecture that we grow, and become ourselves, only in interaction with the third world, then the fact that we can all contribute to it, if only a little, can give comfort to everyone who feels that in struggling with ideas he has found more happiness than he could ever deserve. (Popper, 1974, pp. 154–156)

Popper's comments on professional ethics deserve thoughtful consideration—I would say heartfelt absorption—by all practitioners of psychology and every one of their teachers.

The old imperative for the intellectuals is: Be an authority! Know everything in your field!

Once you are recognized as an authority, your authority will be protected by your colleagues; and you must of course protect the authority of your colleagues.

The old ethics I am describing leaves no room for mistakes. Mistakes are simply not allowed. Consequently, mistakes must not be acknowledged. I do not need to stress that this old professional ethics is intolerant. Moreover, it always has been intellectually dishonest: it leads (especially in medicine and in politics) to the covering up of mistakes for the sake of protecting authority.

This is why I suggest that we need a new professional ethics, mainly, but not exclusively, for scientists. I suggest that it be based upon the following twelve principles. . . .

1. Our objective conjectural knowledge goes further and further beyond what any one person can master. So there simply cannot be any "authorities." This holds true also within specialized subjects.
2. *It is impossible to avoid all mistakes,* or even all those mistakes that are, in themselves, avoidable. All scientists are continually making mistakes. The old idea that one can avoid mistakes and is therefore duty bound to avoid them, must be revised: it is itself mistaken.
3. *Of course it remains our duty to avoid mistakes whenever possible.* But it is precisely so that we can avoid them, that we must be aware, above all, of how difficult it is to avoid them and that nobody succeeds completely. Not even the most creative scientists who are guided by intuition succeed: intuition may mislead us.
4. Mistakes may be hidden even in those theories which are very well corroborated; and it is the specific task of the scientist to search for such mistakes. The observation that a well-corroborated theory or a technique that has been used successfully is mistaken may be an important discovery.
5. *We must therefore revise our attitude to mistakes.* It is *here* that our practical ethical reform must begin. For the attitude of the old professional ethics leads us to cover up our mistakes, to keep them secret and to forget them as soon as possible.
6. The new basic principle is that in order to learn to avoid making mistakes *we must learn from our mistakes.* To cover up mistakes is, therefore, the greatest intellectual sin.
7. We must be constantly on the look-out for mistakes. When we find them we must be sure to remember them; we must analyze them thoroughly to get to the bottom of things.
8. The maintenance of a self-critical attitude and of personal integrity thus becomes a matter of duty.

9. Since we must learn from our mistakes, we must also learn to accept, indeed accept *gratefully*, when others draw our attention to our mistakes. When in turn we draw other people's attention to their mistakes, we should always remember that we have made similar mistakes ourselves. And we should remember that the greatest scientists have made mistakes. I certainly do not want to say that our mistakes are, usually, forgivable: we must never let our attention slacken. But it is humanly impossible to avoid making mistakes time and time again.
10. We must be clear in our own minds that *we need other people to discover and correct our mistakes (as they need us)*; especially those people who have grown up with different ideas in a different environment. This too leads to toleration.
11. We must learn that self-criticism is the best criticism; but *criticism by others is a necessity*. It is nearly as good as self-criticism.
12. Rational criticism must always be specific: it must give specific reasons why specific statements, specific hypotheses, appear to be false, or specific arguments invalid. It must be guided by the idea of getting nearer to objective truth. In this sense it must be impersonal.

I ask you to regard these points as suggestions. They are meant to demonstrate that, in the field of ethics, too, one can put forward suggestions which are open to discussion and improvement. (Popper, 1984/1992, pp. 200–202)

ON CONSTRAINT AND INSPIRATION IN DISCIPLINED INQUIRY

Of course the development of analytic philosophy did not end with Popper. A younger generation, including Adolf Grünbaum, Imre Lakatos, Wesley Salmon, the younger Wilfred Sellars, and Grover Maxwell continued the discourse, and those who are alive continue it still. For psychologists, the contributions of Donald Campbell and Paul Meehl, both of whom write in the analytic empiricist tradition, have been particularly influential. Anyone who is tempted to float off into a world of entirely linguistic interpretation would do well to study Meehl's philosophical and methodological papers, some of which have been collected in a convenient volume (Meehl, 1991).

I have never found the injunctions of the analytic philosophers the least bit confining—not as a researcher, not as a practitioner, and not as an educator of professional psychologists. My book on the clinical study of social behavior (D. Peterson, 1968a) was primarily a design for the case study of individuals, groups, and organizations, and I have written on the role of case study in the construction of professionally useful theory (D. Peterson, 1993b). I have studied the intricacies of interpersonal process in close human relationships as a researcher and as a clinician (D. Peterson, 1979b, 1982, 1992b), as well as a conceptualizer (Kelley et al., 1983; D. Peterson, 1989) and theoretical critic (D. Peterson, 1993a). For several years now, I have spent most of my time as a professional psychologist studying social prejudice and its abusive consequences in the university community of which I am a part (D. Peterson, 1990a, 1990b). Nothing I learned from Feigl in the courses I took from him more than 40 years ago, from Feigl and Meehl in the seminars on the philosophy of psychology that Minnesota graduate students of my generation were privileged to attend, nor certainly anything I learned by reading Popper, has kept me from examining those topics.

Indeed, I have found the orientation to inquiry embodied in the analytic philosophies liberating and inspirational. They offer a framework for my thought and direction to my investigations. I think they have helped me avoid, or quickly dismiss, the worst of my irrationalities. They have also helped me appraise the rationality of the views of others; to distinguish, for example, between interpretations of the role of race in the sociopolitical formulations of Leonard Jeffries and Cornel West. The old positivist questions, "What do you mean?" and "How do you know?" are never far from my mind. Until I have a reasonably promising approach to answering those questions, I think some more about them. To me, the kind of thinking at the center of the analytic philosophies is the core of disciplined inquiry. I fail to see how any trained psychologist can object to it.

Still, to a degree that I find disturbing, research in psychology has been shackled by silly rules of "proper scientific method." Inappropriately universalized demands for quantification and experimental control have made it difficult for any study that was not empirical in substance and quantitative as well as experimental in design to gain approval as a doctoral dissertation or publication in a "prime" journal. In too many quarters, only experimental studies, with data obtained under closely controlled conditions and analyzed through elaborate statistical routines, are fully acceptable as "research." I think that is deplorable. I do not consider the analytic philosophers responsible for the condition, but I do not deny the pervasiveness of tne attitude, and I welcome any change that will free practitioners and researchers in psychology to conduct the inquiries that a responsible profession and a useful science demand.

The analytic philosophies were not designed to suit the issues that confront professional psychologists or their teachers. They were developed primarily as a foundation for advancing knowledge in science, and primarily the physical sciences at that. But every thoughtful person, including every sensible philosopher, acknowledges that the human sciences differ from the physical sciences in important ways, and at least in some regards must require different approaches to the acquisition and utilization of knowledge. Furthermore, the challenges of inquiry for professional psychologists differ from those of career researchers in important ways, as I have repeatedly argued (e.g., D. Peterson, 1968b, 1976a, 1991), and as others (e.g., Albee & Loeffler, 1971; Kanfer, 1990) have agreed. It is not reasonable to expect an epistemology that was designed primarily to encourage sound thinking about celestial mechanics and thermodynamics to offer the most powerful possible ways of thinking about the problems faced by a psychoanalyst or a community psychologist.

As educators of professional psychologists, we reach still another level of concern. Schön (1983) has identified a common structure in the problem-solving activities of "reflective practitioners" across a range of disciplines, from architectural design through product engineering and business management to psychoanalysis and town planning. The special characteristics of effective professional work carry important implications for the education of reflective practitioners, as Schön (1987) has also proposed. How can we examine the educational process through which professional psychologists are prepared for careers of practice in order to get rid of the worst of our mistakes and create ever better ways of teaching our students what they need to know?

Without ever intending to, the analytic philosophers have offered some useful approaches to that question, but that should not discourage us from seeking still more powerful ways of thinking about our own profession, the education of professional psychologists. Let us seek new insights wherever we can find them, but examine them closely as they are proposed: "I may be wrong and you may be right, and by an effort, we may get nearer to the truth" (Popper, 1974, p. 1086).

REFLECTIVE PRACTICE OF PROFESSIONAL PSYCHOLOGY

Schön (1983) and Polkinghorne (1992), among others, have pointed to the limitations of the traditional, modernist view of the professions—that researchers discover new knowledge in particular areas and the professionals, in the tradition of technical rationality, apply it to life situations. Instead, Schön (1983) has argued that practitioners continually respond to their experiences in practice with "reflection-in-action" to review and reconceptualize a specific professional situation. In this process, they gain access to a system of knowledge separate from the findings of traditional university science (Polkinghorne, 1992). R. Peterson (1992a), following Gergen (1982, p. 18), spoke of this process of reflexivity as a fundamental characteristic of human psychological activity in which "one can step out of the ongoing flux of living and by a reflective glance examine actions and behaviors in the past tense" in order to help direct new action (p. 31). R. Peterson (1992a) described reflexivity in a number of situations. *Personal reflexivity* examines personal life processes. *Personal–professional reflexivity* characterizes how personal issues are reflectively used to illuminate professional situations as they are in supervision, analysis of countertransference, and training experiences such as the integrative seminars that a number of professional psychology programs have (Singer, 1982; Singer, R. Peterson, & Magidson, 1992). Using a broader definition than in R. Peterson's earlier paper, *professional reflexivity* certainly refers, first, to the issues, situations, and sorts of knowledge explicated by Schön (1983) with regard to a specific practitioner in a specific professional situation and, second, to the whole array of ways the profession studies itself to learn from its own performance, including self-studies and book chapters like this one. Third, one could argue that almost all kinds of systematic disciplined inquiry, formal and informal, that develop from reflection on a professional issue are a product of professional reflexivity.

SOCIAL CONSTRUCTIONISM AND POSTMODERNISM

Imagine an empirically oriented professional psychology dedicated to solving the bona fide social problems of diverse groups of people as they appear in their local communities. Imagine that this broadly inclusive professional psychology, thoroughly suffused with the best of community psychology, would neither be controlled by the interests of academic psychology nor those of long-term individual psychotherapy. The resulting professional psychology would not be too far from one created to be relevant to the postmodern era as informed by social constructionist metatheory.

In this brief section, the task is to characterize social constructionism so that readers new to this perspective can understand it, so that it can be recognized by adherents, and so that pragmatic overlaps between it and traditional perspectives can be seen. In either criticizing or joining postmodern psychology (Kvale, 1992) and other social sciences (Rorty, 1991; Rosenau, 1992), it is important to remember that the array of positions taken by various authors may be even more diverse and inconsistent than the variations within, for example, cognitive psychology or psychodynamic psychology. Some may find this presentation unexpectedly congenial; others, familiar with extreme views, may see postmodern psychology as undermining the discipline or the professional enterprise.

Social constructionism (Gergen, 1982, 1985, 1991, 1992; Kvale, 1992) emphasizes the social basis of knowledge and sees our accumulated psychological knowledge as a product and creation of particular social contexts. Gergen (1982, 1985, 1992) has been among the most persuasive in showing how the social knowledge on which the science and ultimately the profession depend is embedded in a particular culture and history, influenced by the scientific "rules" that have been developed primarily in university contexts, formed by power relationships and economics, and based on value-laden foundations. In contrast to the traditional view of scientific production, this frame "removes knowledge from data-driven and/or cognitively necessitated domains and place[s] it in the hands of people in relationship" (Gergen, 1985, p. 272). Any particular piece of psychological research or practice is embedded in a particular *context*—its historical *time* and its *culture*. Specific influences on knowledge products include local, regional, national, ethnic, economic, gender-based characteristics. Although this view may seem quite different from the more extreme examples of positivist metatheory, it is familiar, even commonplace, to students of history and political science.

Remembering that professional psychology must be anchored in the world of day-to-day experience rather than the world of the laboratory, these developments in psychology may be viewed as a small part of a much larger and more significant change in the direction of our intellectual and cultural history (Gergen, 1991, 1992), from the romanticism of the past century through modernism to postmodernism (R. Peterson & Gold, 1992). In the broader culture, postmodernism is associated with the arguably extreme deconstructionist ideas of controversial intellectuals like Derrida (1978) and Foucault (1975). Within psychology Gergen's vision (1982, 1985, 1991, 1992) has been accompanied by variations in feminist psychology (e.g., Hare-Mustin & Maracek, 1990b; Hawkesworth, 1989), in the family therapy literature (Anderson & Goolishian, 1988; Hoffman, 1992; Lax, 1992; McNamee & Gergen, 1992), in the cognitive literature (Mahoney, 1991), and in professional psychology (e.g., R. Peterson, 1992a; R. Peterson & Gold, 1992; R. Peterson & Lax, 1993; R. Peterson & Stiglitz, 1991).

According to Gergen (1991), the *romantic* view attributes to the self personal depth, passion, soul, creativity, moral fiber, deeply committed relations, friendships, and life purposes (Gergen, 1991, p. 6). It is a "world of the *deep interior*" (Gergen, 1991, p. 20), one consistent with long-term intrapsychic psychotherapy. The *modernist* view emerged in the enlightenment and emphasizes beliefs, opinions, and intentions (Gergen, 1991, p. 6). People are "rational agents who examine facts and make decisions accordingly" (Gergen, 1991, p. 19). This view emphasizes knowledge and progress; human beings are knowable, and problems can be fixed. In this tradition are the generic university psychological science of this century, the idea of incremental truth through empiricism, and the straightforward but naively oversimplified idea that the profession simply applies the products of this science (R. Peterson & Gold, 1992).

The *postmodern* view is characterized "by a plurality of voices vying for the right to reality" in which our views of the world become a "product of perspective" (Gergen, 1991, p. 7). Persons, institutions, and cultures are to be examined in a historical context and are "in a state of continuous construction and reconstruction" marked by "reflexive questioning" and "irony" (Gergen, 1991, p. 7). Lyotard suggests that the "grand narratives of legitimation," such as the narratives of modernism, romanticism, or progress, are no longer credible (quoted in Fraser & Nicholson, 1990, p. 22). Instead, legitimation becomes "plural, local, and immanent" (p. 23) and theory becomes "pragmatic and fallibilistic" (p. 35). In psychology, postmodern views emphasize the importance of context, meaning as derived from context, and context-stripping; constructionism (e.g., Gergen, 1985; Mahoney, 1991; R. Peterson, 1992a); reflexivity (e.g., Singer, R. Peterson, & Magidson, 1992); multiculturalism and diversity (e.g., Stricker et al., 1990); the reflecting team and collaborative versus hierarchical interaction (Lax, 1992); and the legitimacy and value of narrative accounts (e.g., Bruner, 1990; Sarbin, 1986). In a sense, the postmodern view includes the perspectives and methods of modernism but does not privilege them. Much more simply, as Shotter (1993b) said, postmodernism is self-consciousness about modernism.

Pauline Rosenau made a useful distinction between "skeptical" and "affirmative" postmodernists that both provides a comparative intellectual context for the array of ideas about postmodernism and implicitly locates professional psychology squarely in the affirmative camp. Inspired by the Continental European philosophers, skeptical postmodernists offer a "pessimistic, negative, gloomy assessment [and] argue that the post-modern age is one of fragmentation, disintegration, malaise, meaninglessness, a vagueness or even absence of moral parameters and societal chaos" (1992, p. 15). It is this sort of postmodernism that Bernstein is characterizing as waiting to "see if something new comes along in order to throw it too in the same empty abyss" (1992, p. 838).

The affirmative postmodernists, often American, agree with some of the skeptical postmodernists' critique of modernism but have a more hopeful, optimistic view. There is an openness to creating new institutions and ways of being, and they affirm ethical positions, make normative choices, develop political coalitions, and argue that certain value choices are superior to others (Rosenau, 1992). Professional psychology postmodernists, unlike those pragmatic philosopher Richard Rorty has criticized, have not

> given up on the idea of democratic politics, of mobilizing moral outrage of the weak, of drawing on a moral vocabulary common to well educated and badly educated, of those who get paid for analyzing symbols and those who get paid for pouring concrete or dishing up cheeseburgers. (R. Rorty as quoted in Bernstein, 1992, p. 831)

Going further, one can easily argue for the importance of the roles of professional psychologists in light of the dilemmas of the postmodern age.

In an earlier paper, R. Peterson characterized what might be seen as an affirmative postmodern position relevant to professional psychology:

> The "scientific" and "empirical" context of the development of psychological knowledge is changed from the universal to the contextual, from the distant and objective to the close and engaged, from ivory tower isolation to community embeddedness. It illuminates the present, puts

> the past in context, is much more pragmatic, and obliges a systematic consideration of the moral standards inherent in our science and profession. We must situate "ourselves within a much more diffuse and flowing realm of activity; simply, we must begin from within our actual everyday life situation . . . whatever *that* is" (Shotter, 1985, p. 168). (R. Peterson, 1992a, p. 25)

Even without the nudge from social constructionist metatheory, professional psychology seems headed in precisely this direction.

Constructionism and Constructivism

In contrast to social constructionism's clear focus on the social world, constructivism emphasizes the constructive, meaning-creating elements of an individual organism with a focus on an individual nervous system and cognition (Mahoney, 1991). In the often confusing literature, these positions sometimes are presented as if they are identical; other times as if they are mutually exclusive. It seems to us that each position requires the other, and the issue is which is to be in the foreground and which in the background. The social constructionist position assumes a view of individuals who themselves create a constructed internal reality independent, at least to some degree, of stimuli in the physical and social environment. To say otherwise would turn constructionism into a complex cognitive variant of radical behaviorism where everything comes from the outside. Without constructionism, the constructivists' world would ignore the social and the cultural to become a postcognitive solipsism.

The Physical World, the Social World, and Empiricism

Most versions of constructionism find it necessary to distinguish between the physical and the social worlds. From the constructionist view, the meaning and even the memories you have about the fight you had with your partner last week have no doubt changed a number of times. But your car is probably in the same place in the parking lot where you left it this morning. Only those with the most extreme positions dispute whether the space shuttle actually goes up or whether smallpox has been eradicated. A more traditional critical realism is relevant to these kinds of phenomena. Constructionists would add, however, that the choice of what to study or develop, the sorts of theoretical words used to explain such events, the importance of such events to particular local groups, and the network of legitimating and value-attributing ideas are all social creations. In an interesting turn, Shotter (1993a) suggested that the physical world can be understood in terms of causes and the social world in terms of reasons with a "zone of uncertainty" in between.

There would be little disagreement with the idea that the great majority of professionally relevant studies in psychology examine cultural phenomena, with biology an important second. Contrary to more extreme versions of social constructionism, empirical research in the social sciences retains its value but comes to be seen as fundamentally nonobjective, and its context and interpretation are changed (Gergen, 1982, 1992). Given the content of the field of psychology, it is inevitable, even exciting, that conversation and debate should develop around what is biological–physical and what social–individual.

Some have argued that ideological interests of particular groups in the behavioral sciences are masked by laying claim to "objectivity" through empiricism, which in fact rationalizes an enhanced position of authority or power (Gergen, 1982; Hawkesworth, 1989). Some of our ways of talking silence other voices (Shotter, 1993b). Further, the value position inherent in the objective position suggests that knowledge is best gained from distant relationships rather than from trusting, intimate, or collegial ones (Gergen, 1982, pp. 32–33) and is in direct contrast to the sorts of empathic connection that an anthropologist such as Geertz (1983) sees as a necessity in the development of similar sorts of knowledge. Though the relationship between scientist and participant may have little to do with the study of the atmosphere on Mars, it is critical to the study of the atmosphere of a particular intimate relationship or race relations in a city. A purported objective standpoint that privileges only certain kinds of data may carry within it a strong, potentially self-serving and negative, almost antisocial bias that seems far away from an interpersonally connected professional psychology.

Foundationalism and Essentialism

Foundationalism is the idea that thought or inquiry can be a fundamentally grounded pre-given principle assumed to be true beyond personal belief and unexamined practice (Rosenau, 1992, p. xi). *Essentialism*, in the context of the study of people, is the idea that it is possible to discover universal human truths or transhistorically valid principles (Gergen, 1982). It is not too much of an oversimplification to suggest that essentialism depends on foundationalism.

Certainly, the general ideas of social constructionist metatheory presented so far (e.g., emphasis on the social nature of knowledge, the situatedness of the observer, the importance of context, and the like) are in direct contrast to foundationalism and essentialism. Further, the language of psychological description and research is rooted in a specific culture (Gergen, 1982, p. 30). Human behavior may be much more responsive to situations and less internally driven than commonly supposed, and therefore much less stable. Although research based on methodological foundationalism moves forward based on a "limited set of systematically constrained experiences," there is a "multitude of disordered and discontinuous events taking place outside the scientific sanctum" that more accurately reflect real human phenomena (Gergen, 1982, p. 2). The resulting importance of local knowledge, as it can be illuminated by a variety of methods, is discussed later in detail. Although the methods and techniques of traditional empiricism certainly can and should be used to explore the full array of phenomena relevant to professional psychology, social constructionism directs attention in a particularly social direction. Contemporary pragmatism might provide a common ground for reconciling these positions.

PRAGMATISM

In the late nineteenth and early twentieth centuries, Charles S. Peirce, William James, John Dewey, and George Herbert Mead developed similar, characteristically American philosophical positions. Labeled "pragmatism" by James, these men shared common criticisms of foundationalism, the fallibility of inquiry, reductivistic scientism, and mechanical determinism, and they embraced a vision of an open universe with irreducible novelty, chance, and contingency long before the postmodernists (Bernstein, 1992). They highlighted the "priority of the intersubjective, social and communal dimensions of experience, language, and inquiry" and "focused their attention on the community of inquirers" (Bernstein, 1992, p. 814). Prior to what Bernstein (1992) has called the "resurgence of pragmatism," the work of these early pragmatists became marginalized and viewed by American philosophy departments primarily as an anticipation of logical empiricism. Recently with the emergence of Richard Rorty, Donald Davidson, and Hillary Putnam, a "properly developed" pragmatic orientation sees analytic philosophy, particularly in its later developments, as "contributing to an ongoing pragmatic legacy" (Bernstein,1992, p. 823) in such a way that can "lead us beyond many of the sterile impasses of so-called 'modern-postmodern' debates" (p. 818).

As a metatheory, pragmatism has some clear advantages. First, it is concerned with activity in the world, with action, and therefore with practice. Second, it becomes possible to side-step—in an elegant fashion—epistemological differences such as are embedded in essentialism and foundationalism. Third, pragmatism contributes to the metatheoretical background for a focus on local knowledge. Fourth, if, as Shotter (1993b) suggested, the debate going on is indeed more metamethodological than metatheoretical, a pragmatic view of method becomes more relevant.

Building principally on the ideas of Dewey and Davidson, Richard Rorty has developed a pragmatist philosophy that provides "an account of how the marks and noises made by certain organisms hang together in a coherent pattern, one which can be fit into our overall account of the interaction between these organisms and their environment" (1991, p. 10). Knowledge is not a "matter of getting reality right" or adopting a particular method, "but rather . . . a matter of acquiring habits of action for coping with reality" (p. 1). "Reality," like "knowledge" and "truth," is a "compliment paid to the beliefs which we think so well justified that, for the moment, further justification is not needed" (p. 24).

As mentioned by Rorty himself, his pragmatism has been endearingly called by Clark Gilmour the "new fuzziness," because

> It is an attempt to blur just those distinctions between the objective and the subjective and between fact and value which the critical conception of rationality has developed. We fuzzies would like to substitute the idea of "unforced agreement" for that of "objectivity." (Rorty, 1991, p. 38)

Though within professions and disciplines there may be conventional ways of distinguishing between fact and value, the fuzziness of those distinctions is particularly apparent when the assumptions about reality of two different groups are put side by side.

This sort of constructionist pragmatism has been called *neopragmatism* by Polkinghorne (1992, following Margolis, 1986). Polkinghorne has suggested that the test for pragmatic knowledge "is whether it functions successfully to fulfill intended purposes" (p. 151). "The more open we are to increasing and revising our patterns, and the greater variety of organizing schemes we have at our command, the more likely we are to capture the diversity of organization that exists in the world" (p. 152). In a broad sense, science serves to "collect, organize and distribute the practices that have produced their intended results" (p. 152). This neopragmatic science is inherently reflective and requires that science be embedded in practice and vice versa.

So, then, to take an example, what about the hypothetical video taken of last week's argument between spouses, a client's early life with his or her abuser, or of a crime? Would not that video provide the God's-eye view, in a way analogous to scientific truth through method? Perhaps we might agree that the video showed what the couple did and said while the camera was focused on them, but it would leave out the previous day's context and the next day's apology. It would take 4 years to view the movie of the client's early life, and what would we do if the remembered incident did not appear? Remembering the varying interpretations of the crime video that showed Patty Hearst robbing a bank as an alleged member of a radical group, we realize immediately that visual records of these kinds show some things but not others. We know that video cameras are pointed one way and not another, that all important things are not necessarily visible, that the taped product is mediated in language and subject to interpretive schemes, and the like. Moreover, its relevance, and therefore its pragmatic significance, depends on the explicit and implicit questions we wish to ask of the video—a particular "we" acting at a particular place and time. Further, its significance, in turn, depends on a group of particular people coming to agree that a video "proves" something useful and "contains" that moment's reality. The issues of what is wanted, the agreeing group, and the limits of method never disappear. All are strongly dependent on people in local circumstances.

It follows that knowledge is the product of local groups in local communities. When Rorty argued that we must all necessarily be "ethnocentric," he emphasized the importance of the local. With some additions, he meant "that beliefs suggested by another [local] culture must be tested by trying to weave them together with [local] beliefs we already have" (p. 26). Following Rorty (1991), I am not presenting a relativistic view, as if the reality of the other group can ever be as real to us as our local reality. Our "ethnocentric" (Rorty, 1991) world is real, though it is for us socially beneficial to understand and perhaps to find some way to incorporate yours.

LOCAL KNOWLEDGE

Though one might question on philosophical grounds the general postmodern position that all reality is local (cf. Gergen, 1985, 1991), it is hard to imagine the day-to-day realities of professional psychology in any other fashion. As Trierweiler put it, "the domain of discourse for the clinician is fundamentally local, specific, and open (in the sense of uncontrollable) as opposed to universal, general, and closed" (1992, p. 9). Still such an assertion is open to empirical investigation to determine just how narrowly specific or how broadly generalizable any given set of propositions may be. We can choose to study how all plants are similar, or we can pay attention to how plants grow differently both in New Hampshire as compared to Florida (depending on where one lives) and on the sunny side as compared to the windy side of the house (depending on where one gardens). The accumulating research on the importance of ethnicity, culture, and gender all support this sort of notion, as well as the recognition of the embeddedness in social contexts of most psychological research, particularly that relevant to practice.[1]

Local knowledge, embedded in a local culture and a local community, supports "a distinctive manner of imagining the real" (cf. Geertz, 1983, p. 172). Conventional dictionary definitions of *local* are fundamentally spatial; *local* refers to a particular place or places. In the postmodern era, characterized by easy mobility and convenient communications, *local* can be seen as technologically expanded to refer to a shared language and meaning-making identifiable in a particular group and relevant to the particular area of concern

[1]The following discussion of local knowledge draws not only on conversations between the authors but also from R. Peterson's conversational and written collaborations with Bill Lax (R. Peterson & Lax, 1993), Steve Gold (R. Peterson & Gold, 1992), Jan Peterson, and Steve Trierweiler (e.g., Trierweiler, 1992).

(cf. Gergen, 1991). People are part of many local cultures, which generate an array of characterizing narratives (Bruner, 1990).

The defining element of a local culture is implicit or explicit sharing of a sense of assumptive reality in an area of shared concern or discourse. The actions people take within their personal and professional roles define their realities, sometimes exposing differences demanding action in the social world and making the assumptive reality visible even to oneself (R. Peterson & Lax, 1993). People tend to repeat actions that seem to them to work, therefore creating an accumulated pragmatic local reality. This sort of enactment of an array of social roles may be necessary to protect the diversity of imaginings, cultures, opinions, and individuals. I am *not* suggesting that an essential reality is distorted by each of these levels of local knowledge and culture. Instead, a perspective becomes reality as it is *enacted* in this manner.

At this point, at least seven classes of local knowledge that intersect in the professional psychology enterprise can be delineated. When a professional psychologist and a client enter into a therapeutic or consultative relationship, they become part of a shared, coconstructed, local community (even as small as two) (Anderson & Goolishian, 1988) that has implicitly agreed to develop a local reality via the methods, techniques, ideas, and narratives of the psychology of the day and the region as they understand them (cf. Geertz, 1983), with at best only very partial legitimation by university science (Trierweiler, 1992). Of course, at each level there remain differences among the views of individual participants. Depending on the issues or concerns that are part of a particular conversation or require action, we are each a member of an array of particular local communities that share a set of stories and a way of thinking and imagining in which we each can feel understood (cf. R. Peterson & Lax, 1993).

1. *Local Knowledge of Particular Events Through Experience*

The first class of local knowledge is composed of specific events with identifiable participants and observers in real time. Trierweiler (1992, p. 12) called this "space–time local," to capture the idea that the events in question happen at a particular historical time and place, are nonrepeatable, and do not have self-evident meanings. This kind of local knowledge is accessible only to those who were there, who had the experience, and who share in what Shotter (1993a) called the "joint action."

2. *Local Knowledge of Particular Situations Through Information*

The second class is the information gathered or brought together about particular situations, interactions, and events, perhaps beginning with personal experience, and including the results of observations, interviewing, testing, surveys, or other sorts of data collected more systematically. This information is presumably communicable such that it does not depend on having been there.

3. *Local Knowledge of Individual People*

The third class is the narratives of people and their lives, the local knowledge of clients and psychologists as individual people. In this class falls the implicit personal, but not the organizational, connections of individuals to others who are in some way similar, as in gender, age, occupation, or shared illnesses or disabilities.

4. *Local Knowledge of Regional, Ethnic, and Racial Groups*

The fourth class are narratives connected with groups of people such as those in specific locales and geographical regions and those with racial and ethnic connections and identifications.

5. *Local Knowledge of Organizations, Institutions, and Third Parties*

The fifth class are the narratives from organizations and institutions to which the participants are connected, the local knowledge of "third parties." This refers to such groups as compose universities or professional organizations as well as, in the case of professional services, the social and service delivery context and the ethics of particular professions. Sometimes local organizations may embody disparate psychological theories, such as the local realities of the psychoanalytic institute and the family therapy institute across town. Certainly, the culture of third-party payers as exemplified in many managed-care situations provides another example.

6. *Local Knowledge of a Discipline*

The sixth class is the local knowledge of a particular field of inquiry, such as psychology, which is gained, broadly speaking, from the study, research, and practice of the discipline. (Lawyers, too, for example, would have a particular local knowledge.) In psychology, this includes the narratives we teach as epistemology and as theory, perhaps for intervention or consultation, as well as the potentially incompletely remembered compendium of research information filtered initially through one's faculty and professional program and years of selective attention (or inattention).

Psychology, of course, contains a multiplicity of working local realities and epistemologies, many more than the two or three typically explicated. When 100 experimental psychologists implicitly agree to work on a problem they see in human cognition with similar methods, they too have developed their local vision of reality, which for them at the time becomes the "real" psychology. We know that the local realities even within our profession are often unshared, such as those based on differences in culture between experimental and professional psychology, or within professional psychology, between theoretical orientations, between areas of focus of psychological attention, or between genders (R. Peterson & Stiglitz, 1991). Psychologists may see one another as participating in activities without much meaning, thereby marginalizing them. Still, theories are intended to get us to attend to one set of local phenomena and ignore or minimize some other set. In this context, for example, it might be said that cognitive theories are narratives that emphasize ways of viewing the world over history or motivation. Object relations theories tell stories of childhood and attend more to early experience than to recent life. Other narratives focus attention on the individual self, on the developing person, on learning, on social relationships, on ethnic diversity, on culture, and so on. In addition to espoused positions, this pragmatic view of local reality includes the implicit local elements of psychological reports and the actual scholarly work of colleagues next door and of one's students.

In spite of their training to the contrary, many professional psychologists, perhaps like most other human beings, seem to be captured by one local narrative. It is commonplace to suggest that different members of a system have different experiences of reality, that people are not seen as having awareness of the causes of their behaviors (from both behavioral or psychoanalytic perspectives), and that people's descriptions of the world are influenced by those important to them (even their therapists). However, many still attempt the dangerous journey across local professional cultures, for example, to become an advocate for a certain version of the facts in the legal context (R. Peterson & J. Peterson, 1993).

It follows that differences between psychologists are seldom based on data or even differences in interpretation of data, but rather differences in local communities, their narratives, and their local realities. It is critical for all of us to recognize, regardless of orientation and perspective, that the entire enterprise of psychology itself and all the varied associated methods are only a local culture. In his writing, anthropologist Clifford Geertz (1983) often found elegant ways to remind us that the worlds of other cultures are no less real than our own. For this experience, we need not follow Geertz's steps all the way to Bali or Morocco; closer to home we might engage in regular conversations with lawyers, literary critics, or religious fundamentalists.

7. Local Knowledge Embedded in Grand Narratives

All of the preceding classes of local knowledge are situated in a seventh class of knowledge, the grander narratives of particular political, social, and historical contexts (Hawkesworth, 1989)—such as American gender narratives, the great narrative of progress, and religious beliefs.

The meaning of any particular aspect of experience in professional psychology can only be reliably understood as it is enacted as a local reality in this multilayered context. A systematic element of education, supervision, and training, therefore, must necessarily be to examine whatever a particular narrative illuminates and what it hides in the shadows, how they clash or fit together, and how they unfold in time (Trierweiler, 1992). If follows that there must be a multiplicity of methods of inquiry to study these classes of local knowledge and thereby support preparation for practice.

THE PEOPLE DOING RESEARCH AND PRACTICE IN PROFESSIONAL PSYCHOLOGY

In the original modernist view, the university researchers were to discover new knowledge and the technicians would apply it. The scientist–practitioner model proposed a more complex idea. Boulder-model professional psychologists were to do both. Instead, as is well known, three things happened: (a) the great majority of professional psychologists never did research beyond their dissertations, (b) the professionals seldom looked to traditional research to aid in solving their professional problems, (c) those who did research often engaged in minimal professional activity.

Explanations varied (R. Peterson, 1992a). One explanation is that American psychology has within it

> two cultures (Kimble, 1984) or two sorts of people (Dana, 1987) variously defined. One of these cultures is said to be inhabited generally by the sorts of faculty . . . which Sampson (1985) speaks of as dominated by "egocentric control," Shotter (1989) identifies as governed by the text of "possessive individualism," and Dana (1987) labels "alpha persons"—the bad (mostly) guys or the real scientists depending on one's perspective. The other culture, Sampson's "sociocentric" and Dana's "beta persons," is said to consist of the good guys, women, minorities, and creative–intuitive, humanistic types or soft-headed anti-scientists. (R. Peterson, 1992a, p. 26)

Although there may be some validity in the ideas of different cultures and personal dispositions, a more pertinent idea may be that professional psychology has been grounded so far in an inadequate conception of "science." We are advocating a rigorous professional psychology that demands a particular sort of contextual, engaged, related, committed science, *not* the elimination of science and substitution of a similarly valuable but substantially different humanism.

The second explanation for the limited link between science and practice in contemporary American psychology is that people create knowledge products consistent with who they are and the culture in which they find themselves—that is, participants in American university life (cf. R. Peterson, 1992a). Sarason (1981, 1982) suggested that traditional universities attract and select intellectual "rugged individualists," "assertive, ambitious prima donna types" who "go their own way and frequently clash" (1982, p. 222) and thereby develop a particular sort of competitive, though creative and productive, culture. The usually white-male faculties were influenced by contingencies that rewarded short, contained studies in the modernist tradition, not clinical activity. Indeed, it is not too much of an exaggeration to argue that professional psychology programs and schools were created as a response to this culture.

Although professional psychology succeeded in creating a culture focused on practice, at its best it was supported by the lore derived from disciplined, reflective practice. Three things were increasingly clear: First, the effectiveness of widely used interventions in their actual service-delivery context was not being systematically evaluated. This clinically relevant area demands substantial skill in outcome evaluation and accountability methodology. The effectiveness of the procedures used by professional psychologists as well as the effectiveness of the professional psychologists themselves are obvious matters of social responsibility.

Second, the broad array of issues embedded in local knowledge and directly relevant both to particular practice circumstances and to groups different from the dominant culture were not being subjected to disciplined inquiry.

Third, in a parallel way, the fashion in which the professional psychologist remained a scientist was not convincingly explicated. Trierweiler and Stricker (1992; Trierweiler, 1992) have been most persuasive in describing the way in which professional psychologists must be "local clinical scientists" who are

> critical investigators of local (as opposed to universal) realities (a) who are knowledgeable of research, scholarship, personal experience, and scientific methodology; and (b) who are able to develop plausible, communicable formulations for understanding essentially local phenomena using theory, general world knowledge including scientific research, and most important, their own abilities as skeptical scientific observers. (Trierweiler & Stricker, 1992, p. 104)

It follows that the acquisition of core professional skills and processes that will allow access to the necessary, locally relevant information may be more central to the profession than acquisition of supposedly general psychological knowledge (Trierweiler & Stricker, 1992). Therefore "skills in local investigation and in problem solving (thinking on one's feet) assume unusual importance" (Trierweiler, 1992, p. 10).

According to Trierweiler

> the guiding metaphor becomes a Sherlock Holmes or a Jane Marple standing in direct confrontation with the constraints, mysteries, banalities, and surprises of unique realities, rather than the distant, conserva-

> tive, skeptical, and abstractly speculative university-based scientist most of us have struggled with in our professional identities. (1992, pp. 10–11)

Training in critical thinking and the professional development of an investigative style become central to the solution of local problems.

The participants in the workgroup on theory, research, and methodology at the National Council of Schools and Programs of Professional Psychology (NCSPP) Midwinter Conference on Women in Professional Psychology (which included G. Edwall, N. Goldberger, L. Mangione, G. Stricker, S. Trierweiler, as well as the authors; Edwall & R. Peterson, 1991) had a series of particularly interesting ideas about the person of the local clinical scientist: The traditional definition of role of the scientist as the objective, disinterested observer who scrutinizes a subject seldom characterizes science as practiced. Local clinical scientists should be enthusiastic—even passionate—about their interests, just as university researchers actually are. In addition, there are a variety of other scientific roles available, for example, participant–observer, advocate, and representative. As one source of knowledge and ideas, one's own experience should be valued in a self-critical and self-reflective fashion, along with knowledge from other disciplines, from biology and physics to fiction and poetry. Of course, people should devote explicit attention to their own values, attitudes, and biases—their situatedness. The resulting knowledge products should value the experiences of participants reported in their natural languages and their own voices, including the different voices of gender and ethnicity. An important role of the researcher in real settings is that of facilitator of efforts to examine and solve problems in the local context. The products should serve the ends of empowerment, and the authors should be particularly sensitive to the ethics and impact of disclosure and reporting (Edwall & R. Peterson, 1991).

If the Boulder model means only that the practitioner needs to be a (local) scientist, then we have done little more than reinvent this model. Our version, though, emphasizing the priority of roles, is substantially different, more the *local practitioner–scientist-scholar* than university scientist–practitioner. Later, we shall have a few words to say about the creation of professional psychology cultures in which this sort of practice and disciplined inquiry would be possible, in which researchers could be meaningfully experienced in practice and practitioners would be able to do some relevant research with enthusiasm and passion.

MULTIPLICITY OF METHODOLOGIES

Central to our position is the idea that the problems and issues faced by professional psychologists should determine the methods of inquiry to be used rather than vice versa, as has so often been the case. Inquiry is necessarily disciplined, systematic, and scholarly. Methodological multiplicity is necessary to illuminate all the various levels of local knowledge, wherever the information necessary to understand and to influence the situation is primarily available. Of course, the professional psychologist should have access to all of the usual quantitative methods associated with psychological research as well as those associated with quasi-experiments and evaluation. In addition, disciplined inquiry should draw on new conceptual models, recently developed methodologies, and methodologies borrowed from other disciplines (Edwall & R. Peterson, 1991). For the sake of example, the following brainstormed list includes descriptive natural science observation, constructivist oral histories; anthropological methods, ethnographic methods, hermeneutics, an array of new qualitative methods to analyze interview data, the single-case and representative-case methods, "design models" from architecture and other disciplines, and biographical study (Edwall & R. Peterson, 1991). If, as Shotter (1993a) suggested, words do not map on the world but instead draw people's attention to things, qualitative methods are particularly important.

Following this line of thinking down a road often traveled by others, R. Peterson and Gold (1991) identified two cultures in psychology. On one hand is the romantic world of the deep interior—the world of personal depth and words, creativity, deeply committed relationships, the soft, the clinical, the interpersonal, the intuitive, the supportive, the qualitative, the circular, and the descriptive. On the other, there is the modernist world of the enlightment, which emphasizes beliefs, opinions, intentions, the quantitative, the linear, the causal—through knowledge and progress, problems can be solved. Disciplined inquiry necessarily blends both cultures. Methods, too, are situated. As Trierweiler (1992) pointed out, most traditional methods, drawn from modernism, focus on nomothetic concerns and work toward generating consensus among scientists regarding supposedly universal formulations—a different task than the local problem solving of professional psychologists. Whether the focus is on research problems or problems in a more general sense, different local cultures believe in and support different methods. If a culture does not accept the methods by which solutions are attempted, no outcome can be meaningful. Feminists have been particularly articulate in pointing out gender bias and how in traditional methodology empiricism tends to decontextualize phenomena (e.g., Belenky, Clinchy, Goldberger, & Tarule, 1986; Edwall & Newton, 1992; Hare-Mustin & Maracek, 1990b, 1990c; Hawkesworth, 1989).

There should be a continuity between research and professional life whereby methodologies are relevant to actual communities in solving the problems of interest. As Trierweiler said, at least some of the strategies for inquiry must fit "into the realities of professional practice" (1992, p. 8). In this sense, the methodologies should include the researcher as listener.

DIVERSITY

Clifford Geertz said a number of things in his comments on ethnography that help to characterize the sorts of attitudes necessary in working across the diversity of local cultures. Geertz argued that people need to avoid "the we-logical, you-confused provincialism" (1983, p. 149), remembering we "are all natives now, and everybody else not immediately one of us is an exotic" (p. 151). The goal is to try to figure out what people down the street think they are up to from their own perspective (p. 58), even as we advocate our own. As with lighting for a photograph, each local psychology and each diverse culture illuminates some population or problem or issue or phenomenon, while at the same time it throws others into the shadows. In the language of postmodernism, some elements in the clear light become dominant and privileged, others, hardly visible, are marginalized. Professionals need to understand these issues and be trained to deal with the differing local customs and reality—a combination of down-the-street diplomacy, ethnography, and systematic training and supervision relevant to local knowledge and local narratives.

As Rorty suggested, this sort of respectful empathic connection to the local realities of others is not always sufficient or available. Therefore, the moral tasks of a liberal democracy are "divided between the agents of love and the agents of justice[,] . . . connoisseurs of diversity [exemplified by Geertz] and guardians of universality" (1991, p. 206). Illuminating the dilemmas of professional psychologists, Rorty said:

> The former insist that there are people out there whom society has failed to notice. They make these candidates for admission visible by showing how to explain their odd behavior in terms of a coherent, if unfamiliar, set of beliefs and desires—as opposed to explaining this behavior with terms like stupidity, madness, baseness, or sin. The latter, the guardians of universality, make sure that once these people are admitted as citizens, once they have been shepherded into the light by the connoisseurs of diversity, they are treated just like all the rest of us. (1991, p. 206)

In Rorty's terms, professional psychologists, like anthropologists, are trained primarily as agents of love, but far less as agents of justice. The compassionate and interpretive connections along the dimensions of local knowledge seem all the more complex and critical when the differences are of gender, race, ethnicity, sexual orientation, and so forth, and are therefore regularly associated with power differentials, discrimination, and oppression. Historically, of course, the perspectives of women, people of color, gay men, and lesbians have been marginalized (Hare-Mustin & Maracek, 1990a, 1990b, 1990c) while the modernist white, upper–middle-class male remained in the spotlight. Even the enhancement of training of professional psychologists in this area does not lead to the understanding and attitudes necessary to becoming agents of justice. Though we may succeed as participants in a liberal democracy, as professionals we need to find a way to include both an appreciation for the marginalized individual and a sense of Justice, who with her blindfold, sees no differences.

In a similar way, the concerns of professional psychology can be seen as marginalized in organized psychology (R. Peterson, 1992a, 1992b; Weiss, 1992) just as issues surrounding family, from family theory to the family lives of faculty and students themselves, have been historically marginalized in clinical training programs (R. Peterson, 1992c). Perhaps just as professional psychologists are guardians of the individual and diversity, traditional academic psychologists, like lawyers, are guardians of universality.

SOME PROPOSALS

Following are four proposals that might help the various cultures in professional psychology work together.

An Inclusive Vision of Inquiry

It is critical that psychology as a whole and professional psychology in particular support the creation of a broad array of knowledge products (both formal and implicit), all associated with disciplined inquiry. Taking care not to exclude any viable method or psychological problem, four classes of inquiry can be delineated: (a) Although all the usual questions and quantitative methods associated with university psychological science have been less useful to practice than hoped, there remains a place for theory-driven, hypothesis-testing research. (b) Systematic ways of evaluating outcome and providing data both for accountability and for the improvement of psychological procedures will gain in importance in the era of national health insurance. (c) The local knowledge necessary for practice is often gained by recently developed methodologies (including qualitative as well as quantitative) and methodologies borrowed from other disciplines. (d) Skills in critical thinking and "in local investigation and in problem solving" (Trierweiler, 1992, p. 10) are probably used more often by practitioners than all the others sorts of inquiry.

Pragmatism

As exemplified above by the brief sketch, Rorty's neopragmatism (1991; see also Bernstein, 1992) or another similar frame provides a way of moving professional psychology forward. Including the pragmatic elements of local knowledge, there are many more similarities and areas of overlap between the sorts of information gained through varying epistemologies (e.g., logical empiricism, critical realism, social constructionism) than the divisive rhetoric would suggest. The dialogue about divergent epistemological views tends to take place around the extremes of position, whereas inquiry and practice usually take place toward the center. We can do the best we can to take to heart the later logical empiricist concerns relevant to clear reasoning, and at the same time continue to be responsive to the needs of our clients and our society.

Training for Disciplined Inquiry

In light of the arguments presented in this chapter, it follows that there should be training in all four areas of disciplined inquiry for all professional psychologists, whether from Boulder model or professional programs. The anticipated career paths of the students, not the espoused orientation of the program, should lead to the relative emphases. The methods of university science should be primarily for those who expect university careers. Training in the other areas of inquiry should take precedence for professional goals. The training should include a broad and diverse presentation of epistemologies, including critical thinking, relevant to professional psychology, as supported, for example, by the book by Trierweiler and Stricker (in press) on the local clinical scientist. Methodological training should explicitly lead to the development of critical thinking and an investigative temper and style. In spite of historical rhetoric to the contrary, training in the methodologies on which traditional university science is based does not provide these basic, relevant skills nor prepare professional psychologists for the sorts of inquiry they are more likely to do. If the training in disciplined inquiry is done well, the possibilities for relationship between inquiry and professional practice will seem synergistic, not contradictory.

Doctoral training ought to involve the production of some sort of scholarly, professionally relevant knowledge product in a way employing any of the modes of inquiry. This work need not be original knowledge in the classic sense of the arts and sciences PhD dissertation but rather a demonstration of doctoral-level competence in professionally relevant local investigation. The scholarly product should be to disciplined inquiry what internship is to professional practice. Work toward the dissertation should have person-centered research supervision, designed to help both women and men develop and find their professional voices. In explicit contrast to the rugged individualist's supposed independent creation of knowledge, this sort of training in inquiry involves a collaborative vision, rather than one glorifying primarily individual efforts. These projects should be seen as the product of a collaboration between the student researchers, an appropriately constituted group of advisors, and the participants (Edwall & R. Peterson, 1991).

Creation of Professional Psychology Cultures

Attainment of the sorts of educational cultures for professional psychology programs that support these sorts of activities and values will not be easy. Certainly it means surmounting the classic research versus teaching and clinical work split that has been so damaging to our profession. Understanding that people have different interests and abilities, departmental contingencies must be such that researchers do some meaningful clinical work and teachers and clinicians are expected to engage in some aspect of professional development, understood broadly (including all sorts of inquiry, leadership in psychological organizations, organization of service delivery systems, and so on). Because all professional psychologists will not be faculty at doctoral programs, faculty must model the array of activities in which graduates will ultimately find their professional lives. Training and the modeling must be consistent with careers actually available to graduates with large school debts, which is a potentially more difficult task.

R. Peterson and Gold (1992) described the two cultures of clinical training as illuminated by the discussion of romanticism and modernism. They argued that the professional elements of doctoral education require greater collegiality between faculty and students than has been historically associated with the modernist tradition.

> A major element of this collegiality is the legitimacy of both the modernist and romantic perspectives as well as even broader theoretical diversity in professional psychology, included within an atmosphere of respect and open discussion. A second major element of the collegiality is the willingness of both students and faculty in their different roles to model cooperation with and responsiveness to evaluation. . . . Collegiality demands that we treat one another, faculty and student alike, with a particular sort of mutual respect. . . . Essential to creating a multicultural and multitheoretical collegial culture is open-mindedness, in Jerome Bruner's words "a willingness to construe knowledge and values from multiple perspectives without a loss of commitment to one's own values" (Bruner, 1990, p. 30). (R. Peterson & Gold, 1992, p. 25–26)

This sort of postmodern culture (R. Peterson & Lax, 1993) is also critical to the integrated group practice settings if professional psychology is to survive and prosper through managed care and national health insurance.

POSTSCRIPT: COMMON GROUND, UNCOMMON GROUND, AND SOME QUESTIONS

The issues we have addressed are not just relevant to those who work within professional programs but also to all those who train doctoral-level psychologists who will engage in professional practice. It is time to find a way to work together to serve the urgent needs of our clients and our culture without wasting time in philosophical warfare. Once epistemological argument moves beyond a match between straw opponents, much of modern analytic philosophy and postmodern constructionism can be seen to stand on common ground. When Rorty denied the availability of "skyhooks" on which to hang certain knowledge, and Popper likened the construction of scientific knowledge to driving piles into a swamp, they used different metaphors to illustrate comparable antifoundationalist assumptions. Rorty and Gergen inveigh against essentialism, but it was Popper who invented the term *essentialism* and advocated his own form of *antiessentialism* when he was working on *The Poverty of Historicism* in 1935 (Popper, 1974). Many arguments about the "objectivity" of knowledge can be reduced to semantic disagreements about the meaning of the term. Practically speaking, does any of this make any difference to professional psychologists and their teachers?

Well, yes, it does. Maybe the positivists and their descendants did not *prohibit* inquiry into the domains that most concern practitioners, but as (wrongly) interpreted by many academicians, the "rules of method" that took hold in organized, academically institutionalized psychology clearly *inhibited* systematic exploration of issues that could not be studied empirically, defined quantitatively, and controlled experimentally. Responsible practitioners could not possibly limit their studies to so small and barren a domain, so they went ahead anyway, "science" be damned. Many of them felt uneasy about that decision, or if they appeared to grow comfortable in their clinical forays, the academicians were quick to tell them that they *ought* to feel uneasy. Whatever careful reading and coherent logic *might* have allowed within the modernist tradition, the more vigorous arguments of the postmodern philosophers seem to have been required to legitimate the local inquiries with which professional psychologists are predominantly concerned. Instead of restricting practice to an impossibly narrow "science," the constructionist and pragmatist arguments vigorously encourage expanding science to embrace the kinds of phenomena with which practitioners are continually and unavoidably concerned.

But in the process of expansion, do we not risk a new flood of irrationality? If logical positivism was so badly distorted by the academicians, is there no danger that the postmodern views will be twisted another way by practitioners? Demands for proof, for documentation, both logical and empirical, can all too easily be swept aside by inappropriate extension of the obvious truth that all knowledge is a human construction.

Despite similarities, important philosophical issues remain unsettled in the dialogue between critical rationalists and pragmatic constructionists. Practically as well as philosophically, it makes a mighty difference whether the ultimate grounds for accepting a knowledge claim is that it works, that informed critics agree about it, or that it is true. The choice between inclusiveness and comprehensiveness on the one hand and precision on the other—between "something more" and "nothing but"—is one that researchers in psychology can legitimately shade on the side of precision. However, the eternal search for responsible balance can never be abandoned by practitioners. What are the most powerful guidelines for disciplined inquiry in the practice of psychology? How can we teach those to our students? Should something akin to the philosophy of psychology be included in the training of professional psychologists? Should it be required? If so, how should it be incorporated into the curriculum, and what else do we leave out? These and other questions of a similar kind are among those that anyone who presumes to set standards for education in professional psychology must ultimately address.

We cannot expect agreement. The logical empiricists excluded metaphysics from the domain of scientific inquiry as factually meaningless. Popper included metaphysics as subject to rational criticism. Popper considered both Freudian and Adlerian psychoanalytic theories as pseudoscience because their tenets could never be falsified. Meehl, who professes strong neo-Popperian sympathies, not only practices psychoanalysis professionally but regards psychoanalytic theory as a fit subject for metatheoretical scrutiny, and he has written incisively about it.

The guiding conception that every professional psychologist follows in framing disciplined inquiry inevitably contains not only theoretical and epistemological content but axiological assumptions as well. How closely do we agree about any of those, even at the extremes? Consider the example with which this chapter began, there representing the dilemmas of rigor versus relevance, here representing the problems we face in defining moral foundations for the practice of psychology. The contemporary practice of exorcism is not limited to one psychologist in Arizona; it is common in several forms of pastoral counseling. What is our stand in matters of this kind? The article on religion and psychology cited near the beginning of this chapter was written by a representative of an institution that was recently approved for associate membership in NCSPP. The school's motto is, "Since 1860 for Christ and His Kingdom." Several other member institutions teach a professional psychology that is grounded in Christian beliefs and moral principles. The rest of our programs are not free of axiology. Most of them seem to rest on the ethical and moral foundations of some kind of secular humanism, or possibly a liberal Judaism, that is never made explicit.

Are we all of one mind about these matters? Surely not. But surely we can discuss the issues, particularly in conferences working toward the development of standards for professional education. We are increasingly convinced that we need to bring the sorts of issues explored in this chapter into the education of professional psychologists. As scientists, we might be able to set aside these questions. As teachers of professional psychologists, we cannot.

13

THE REFLECTIVE EDUCATOR

Education for practice has concerned psychologists for many years. The dominant corporate response to this concern has been to talk about professional training in conferences. The Boulder conference on training in clinical psychology (Raimy, 1950), the Chicago conference on the professional education of clinical psychologists (Hoch, Ross, & Winder, 1966), and the Vail conference on professional training in psychology (Korman, 1976) were specifically devoted to issues in the preparation of psychologists for professional careers. Even those conferences more generally concerned with graduate education in psychology (Bickman, 1987; Roe, Gustad, Moore, Ross, & Skodak, 1959) directed more attention to professional training than to any other issues. With the development of professional schools and establishment of the National Council of Schools and Programs of Professional Psychology (NCSPP), conference activities were intensified. Already, NCSPP has sponsored nine conferences in which participants have scrutinized various aspects of the educational system (Peterson, Peterson, & Abrams, in press). Further conferences have been proposed. Another is scheduled as I write.

This chapter was originally prepared for an NCSPP conference on Standards for Education in Professional Psychology II: Implementation and Dissemination, in New Orleans, LA, in January 1995. From *American Psychologist*, 50, 975–983.

All of this work—all the preconference papers, all the planning and management of the meetings themselves, all the talk, all the resolutions, all the reports—is based on the assumption that the practice of psychology requires extensive training. How disquieting it is then, or at least how disquieting it ought to be, to consider data relating effectiveness in the practice of psychology to training for practice and find nothing to suggest that training helps at all. The assumptions underlying education for practice in psychology have recently been challenged by several critics (e.g., Christensen & Jacobson, 1994; Dawes, 1994). Dawes's critique is the most comprehensive to date, and its central conclusion—that the profession to which many of us have devoted our careers is a "house of cards"—the most disturbing.

Dawes's review begins with an examination of relationships between efficacy in psychotherapy, the single activity to which practitioners devote most of their time (Garfield & Kurtz, 1976; Moldawsky, 1990; D. R. Peterson, Eaton, Levine, & Snepp, 1982), and training for the practice of psychotherapy. Early in the account, he cites the study by Strupp and Hadley (1979) that compared the therapeutic effectiveness of well-credentialed psychologists with university professors who had no training in psychology. Clients in the study represented the range of problems usually seen in outpatient settings: mainly anxiety and depression, with obsessional trends and borderline personality common among the clientele. Cases were randomly assigned to "trained" and "untrained" therapists. Outcomes were gauged by several acceptably reliable measures. With all their training and experience, with all their licenses and diplomas, the professionals did not do one bit better than the professors.

The review continues with summaries of related research. All support similar conclusions. Professionals and "paraprofessionals" do not differ in effectiveness of treatment (Berman & Norton, 1985). Efforts to show unique therapeutic effectiveness for trained professionals have failed (Lambert, Shapiro, & Bergin, 1986). The level of experience of professional psychotherapists is unrelated to their efficacy (Stein & Lambert, 1984).

Anyone who has done a great deal of psychotherapy will remember early mistakes, no longer repeated, and will find it difficult to believe that experience has nothing to do with expertise. Anyone who has supervised generations of trainees will have trouble believing that nothing can be taught by listening to all those tapes, examining episodes where things went wrong, and figuring out better ways to help people understand themselves and behave more effectively. Maybe the studies were flawed, the controls uneven, or the measures insufficiently subtle. Surely, we say, something has been left out.

Indeed, anyone who examines the original studies cited by Dawes will find that they provide a fragile foundation for the strong proposition that training and effectiveness of treatment are unrelated. Many of the studies resemble the one by Strupp and Hadley (1979) in that the treatment at issue is some kind of conversational counseling. In these, the modal therapeutic transaction has one person, socially defined as a "therapist," talking with another person, socially defined as a "client," about the client's psychosocial condition, with the primary aim of relieving the client's distress. In this situation, it is not entirely surprising to find that anybody who has a good brain, a kind heart, and the psychological knowledge that has become part of the popular culture and who is, if nothing else, someone other than the client and presumably an expert, can help most people feel better about themselves.

Another group of studies in the summaries Dawes cites involve relatively simple, repetitive forms of behavioral treatment. There is no reason to suppose that residency training in psychiatry or doctoral education in clinical psychology is needed to learn when and how to spoon ice cream into the mouths of autistic children or provide social reinforcement for adaptive behavior among hospitalized psychotic adults. Adequately refined studies of various forms and levels of training related to more complex patterns of learning-based treatment, such as the cognitive–behavioral therapies and the multimodal approaches of Arnold Lazarus (1989), have yet to be done. To many thoughtful scholars (e.g., Beutler & Kendall, 1995), the case for training in the provision of psychological therapy remains an open question.

But Dawes does not attempt to prove (although he implicitly accepts) the null hypothesis that trained and untrained psychotherapists are the same. What he does show, convincingly, is that a large number of studies designed to examine associations between training for psychotherapy and effectiveness of treatment have failed to show any positive relationships. Results as substantial and consistent as these cannot be explained away, and they cannot responsibly be ignored.

Dawes then turns his baleful glare on some assumptions about clinical skills in prediction and diagnosis that many practitioners appear to harbor. He begins with a review of the studies of clinical versus actuarial prediction that were first summarized by Paul Meehl in 1954. As Meehl noted, the distinction between clinical and actuarial methods does not reside in the kinds of information on which predictions are based but on the way information is used to predict behavior—the way test scores, interview impressions, observer ratings, performance records, and similar kinds of data are combined to predict which students will succeed in college, which parolees will commit further crimes, which outpatients will go crazy enough to require hospitalization, and other long-term, socially important outcomes. In clinical prediction, an "expert" examines all available information, integrates it in whatever way his or her own understanding of the measures and the individual case may suggest, and offers a judgmental forecast. In actuarial prediction, research is done to determine which variables in a predictor set are actually correlated with the outcome and how the predictors should be weighted to maximize predictive accuracy. The best predictions are usually derived from linear combinations of a few variables.

At the time Meehl published his first review, some 20 studies comparing clinical and actuarial prediction had been done. Not one showed clinical prediction to be conclusively superior to actuarial prediction. Within the ensuing 12 years, an additional 25 studies had piled up. Jack Sawyer (1966) reviewed them and reported the same result. However appealing it might be to believe that sensitive, trained experts would beat the formulas, all analyses showed the opposite. Actuarial methods did better, often by wide margins and with near perfect consistency. Still later, Dawes, Faust, and Meehl (1989) summarized the ever-growing body of research, made up by then of about 100 studies, in an article in *Science*. Nothing had changed, nor were there any good reasons to expect clinical methods to forge ahead. Human judgment is simply not as good a tool as systematic research in selecting predictors and optimizing weighted combinations of those in forecasting behavioral outcomes.

Dawes continues his critique by showing that judgmental accuracy, the correct inference of facts about the past or current state of an individual, is no more related to experience than is the prediction of behavioral outcomes. Nobody, but nobody can tell for sure what happened in the mind of a killer when he or she pulled the trigger. There is no sure way to tell whether an adult, now "remembering" abuse as a small child, actually suffered the abuse, and the methods commonly used by "experts" to attempt a determination, such as retrospective interviews and hypnosis, are so flagrantly prone to distortion that we would all be better off without them. Forensic psychologists who bring Rorschach protocols into court to support or refute legal claims are ignoring mountains of negative evidence on the validity of the test and are subject to challenge on ethical grounds. Display of credentials and a long history of professional experience may impress a gullible jury, but neither qualification has withstood the test of scientific evaluation.

Neither, says Dawes, will our claims of special expertise survive public scrutiny. E. Lowell Kelly, one of the pioneers in developing the scientist–practitioner model that placed research first among the functions of clinical psychologists, was honored late in his career for his many contributions to the field. Firm in his belief that research was the only uniquely valuable service that psychologists could offer to the public and mindful of the discouraging findings from his own classic studies of Veterans Administration (VA) trainees in clinical psychology (Kelly & Fiske, 1950; Kelly & Goldberg, 1959), Kelly deplored the increasing professionalization of psychology that had taken place after the VA program brought large numbers of clinicians into the field. In his last speech to the American Psychological Association (APA), Kelly expressed his grave concerns. Unfortunately, however, he misjudged the time allotted to his talk, and his last words, "Soon the bubble will burst," were lost to the audience.

Sadly, Dawes believes, they were also lost to the field at large. As Dawes sees it, the bubble *has* burst. The subtitle of his book is *Psychology and Psychotherapy Built on Myth*. The current practice of psychology, as he describes it, is at best a well-intentioned mistake and at worst an outright fraud. He clearly regards the development of professional schools and the Doctor of Psychology (PsyD) degree as unmitigated disasters. He is not alone in his views. The dust jacket of his book displays prototypic comments by sympathetic colleagues. Our idols have "clay feet." "Dawes adds his voice to a chorus of concern [about the scientifically unsupported myths of professional psychology]." "This book speaks for all of us who have watched in distress as the profession of psychology ran roughshod over the science of psychology."

Dawes is crankier than most critics of professional psychology, but his is not an isolated complaint. It is the voice of the scientists in psychology, who are now outnumbered and feel overpowered by a burgeoning, often irresponsible professional guild. The voice is angry, but there is anguish in it too. Those of us who are dedicated to the responsible education of professional psychologists need to hear it.

RESPECT FOR RESEARCH IN THE EDUCATION OF PROFESSIONAL PSYCHOLOGISTS

I hold as reasonable principles in education for the practice of psychology that procedures shown by careful research to be useful should be taught, that procedures that have been extensively tested through rigorous research and have failed to show any utility should not be taught, and that claims of utility for evidently useless procedures are unethical. I therefore agree with Dawes that the currently common emphasis on training for conventional, conversational psychotherapy is unjustified because a large body of research has failed to show any relationship between training and effectiveness of performance. I also agree that efforts to improve clinical "sensitivity" are misdirected because a large body of evidence has failed to show that training improves predictive success or inferential accuracy. And I agree emphatically with Lee Sechrest (in Hayes, 1989) that we must show the courage to acknowledge what we cannot do and to desist from claims of expertise that we do not possess. Anyone who argues that "the empirical evidence is all negative, but my experience tells me otherwise, so I'm still sure I know what I'm doing and refuse to change my practice," will get no sympathy from me.

Another argument that troubles me is the one that goes, "my practice is successful, I get more referrals than I can handle, so I don't see any reason to change." I hear this frequently from practitioners, including some who serve as part-time faculty of our professional school at Rutgers. In fact, one of our visiting professors has published the argument. Stanley Moldawsky (1990) surveyed 237 licensed psychologists in New Jersey to find out whether they were in group or individual practice, how much psychotherapy they were doing, how their referral rates were holding up, and where their referrals came from. He received 137 replies and found that the large majority of respondents were still in solo practice, they still devoted most of their time to psychotherapy, their referral rates had either increased or remained stable over the preceding 3 years, and their main referral sources were, in order, former patients, other psychologists, physicians, and schools. Moldawsky concluded that "Solo practice is healthy, viable, and growing in New Jersey" (p. 546) and urged increasingly forceful political action to maintain public access to appropriate psychotherapeutic services.

I sympathize strongly with this aim. Preserving public access to useful, cost-effective psychological services, whether they take a long time or a short time, is advantageous to the public and profession alike, and Moldawsky rightly asserts the need for political action to maintain access. One suspects, however, that the guild interests of psychologists whose main stock in trade is long-term, psychodynamically oriented psychotherapy also come into play in actions of this kind. To any extent that they do, to any extent that practitioners' interests in their own status and financial well-being take precedence over true concern for their clients, their political actions are not only inimical to the public good but ultimately damaging to the profession itself.

As I have argued at length elsewhere (D. R. Peterson, 1996), the survival of our profession requires us to direct our energies toward meeting the most fundamental needs of our society, often by creating new services, not toward preserving the status quo or enhancing advantages to our own professional establishment. Educators of future generations of practitioners bear special responsibilities in this regard. Educators need to see that students are trained in procedures likely to offer demonstrable utility in the long, *long* run. To demonstrate the value of any class of procedures, psychoanalytic or any other, it is not enough to show that the procedures are widely practiced and commercially salable. So are the casting of Tarot cards and the reading of horoscopes.

In pondering decisions about these matters, I align myself with Dawes, McFall (1991), and others who insist that "scientific" professional psychology is the only legitimate and acceptable form of professional psychology. To me, inclusion of a procedure as "scientific" need not require rock-hard prior proof of effectiveness, but it does require that the procedure be subject to systematic scientific inquiry and that large bodies of sound research do not indicate persuasively that the procedure fails to do what it is purported to do.

For any procedure as complex as psychoanalytic treatment, I consider the case still open, but possibly closing. Paul Meehl, a trained psychoanalyst who still puts some of his patients on the couch but offers his own variety of rational–emotive therapy to most of the people he sees, notes that divergences in theory and technique among therapists in a broadly "psychoanalytic" tradition are ". . . vast, increasing, and show little or no signs of the sort of cumulative, self-corrective, convergent development characteristic of post-Galilean science" (Meehl, 1993, pp. 321–322). If, as Meehl appears to suspect, the research program centered on the study of psychoanalysis is "degenerating" in the sense defined by Lakatos (1970) and Meehl (1990), educators need to consider very carefully how much of psychoanalytic theory and technique to include in their programs.

Clearly, educators cannot responsibly ignore procedures that *are* documentably effective. By now, psychologists have developed a substantial body of methods, both for assessment and change, that do work. Many of the statistically derived, empirically validated tests that psychologists have developed in their psychometric tradition are demonstrably valuable. The approach to functional assessment that I described in *The Clinical Study of Social Behavior* (1968a) has shown its power. The field has advanced impressively since (though I do not claim because) I wrote that book. As examples, Dan Fishman and I have presented a wide range of more recent assessment systems, along with their common developmental structure, in our book, *Assessment for Decision* (D. R. Peterson & Fishman, 1987). As to treatment, researchers have made considerable progress in sorting out which treatments work for which people with which problems (see especially Wilson, 1995). Available to us now is a reasonably sturdy empirical base for the flexible approaches to treatment conspicuously represented in the multimodal therapy of Arnold Lazarus (1989, 1990) and clearly visible in the approaches of many others. Martin Seligman (1993) has summarized some useful reasearch on *What You Can Change and What You Can't*. Barlow, Hayes, and Nelson (1984), among others, have shown how the work of practitioners can be made more rigorous than it usually is and thereby begin to bridge the gap that currently divides research from practice in our field. The several task forces on assessment and intervention activated by recent leaders of the APA Division of Clinical Psychology (APA Division 12) are beginning to issue their reports (APA Division of Clinical Psychology, 1995). As these reports appear, all of us educators are obliged to study them carefully and review our programs in light of the findings.

Responsible, open-minded practitioners will attend to these reports too. Seeking always to provide the best available services to their clients, studiously critical of their own practices, and eager to acquire more effective ways to examine and improve human functioning, they will want to add the best of the new methods to their technical repertoires. If the research community and the professional community in psychology cross the gulf that now separates them, if they stop scolding each other, open themselves to alternative views, and begin to work cooperatively, the flow of effective methods for attacking truly important human problems will swell beyond anything the Division 12 task forces can find to recommend today. Sensible practitioners will want to learn these methods, not only in a spirit of responsibility but as a matter of simple self-interest.

As our educational system currently functions, however, they will have no place to go. Resources for continuing education and postdoctoral training, as they stand in psychology today, are not a "system" at all. They are a chaotic disgrace, consisting for the most part of a potpourri of ill-conceived, empirically untested workshops. Responsible educators, mindful of the neglect of continuing education and postdoctoral training that has accompanied our early preoccupation with predoctoral education, will begin to recognize that our own graduates constitute an important clientele and will develop the organized opportunities for lifelong education that a constantly improving profession requires.

We need to evaluate our educational programs far more thoroughly than we have done to date. An initial plan for doing so was proposed more than 10 years ago by an APA task force on the evaluation of education, training, and service in psychology (APA, 1982). I was a member of that group. The others were Sol Garfield, Ronald Kurz, Neal Miller, and Janet Spence, with Lee Sechrest as chair. In our report, we examined the assumptions on which an evaluation program should be based (e.g., more than skills and technique are involved in education and training for a profession; we do not have a very good understanding of what actually occurs in clinical training), determined what questions should be addressed (e.g., what kinds of students enter what kinds of programs and what is the normal progression during training; what are the typical career patterns of clinical psychologists), and then outlined an initial research program that would begin to answer some of the questions.

I left the meetings of the task force with considerable hope that some comprehensive evaluation research would actually be done through APA, but so far as I know, nothing has come of our work. At the time, APA was financially strapped and in no position to support our project. Lee Sechrest tried to get some external funding, but none was forthcoming. To my best knowledge, our proposal, now known wistfully as the "tee-feets report" after the acronym for the task force, lies moldering in the APA archives.

I do not know what the other members of the task force have done to advance the plan we laid out, but I know what I did. When I became President of NCSPP, I proposed the self-studies that began with the La Jolla report (Callan, Peterson, & Stricker, 1986) and continue in the activities currently underway in NCSPP. Several of us have tried several times to encourage comparable studies of PhD scientist–practitioner programs through the Council of University Directors of Clinical Training, but so far we have met a cool reception. I will not speculate on the reasons for that, but I find it interesting to note that some of those who are loudest in proclaiming the virtues of science have not seen fit to join the leaders of professional schools in subjecting their programs to systematic evaluative research.

RESPECT FOR PRACTICE IN THE EDUCATION OF RESEARCHERS IN PSYCHOLOGY

Dawes's book is smashing in every sense of the term. For all his scholarship, however, the author shows no sign of familiarity with the history of direct education for the practice of psychology, no understanding of the model of education to which all of us in NCSPP have subscribed, and no knowledge of the work we have done to examine and improve our educational practices. He treats the development of PsyD programs as the precipitous action of a professional guild. "In 1971 the APA made a momentous decision. As evidence indicated that training in theory and research were unrelated to effectiveness as a psychotherapist, the association recognized a new degree, the doctorate of psychology without research training" (Dawes, 1994, p. 15). That, of course, is not how it happened (D. R. Peterson, 1992c). To tell even a short story of the development of the professional doctorate in psychology without mentioning the deliberations of the Clark Committee (APA, 1967), the Chicago conference (Hoch, Ross, and Winder, 1966), the rationale for the first program (D. R. Peterson, 1968b), or the Vail conference (Korman, 1976) is not merely incomplete. It is historically vacant and misleading in its implications. A thorough historical account would have to include the century-long tale of hopeful unions, schismatic separations, and uneasy alliances that have marked the course of psychology as a science and as a profession from the beginning to the present time. Anyone who dismisses practitioner programs as "psychology without research training" either has not read or has grossly misinterpreted the reports of the NCSPP conferences at Mission Bay (Bourg et al., 1987) and San Antonio (R. L. Peterson et al., 1992), not to mention the reports that preceded and followed those conferences. In deriding professional schools and the professional degree, Dawes does not appear to acknowledge that the vast majority of the practitioners he indicts were trained in academic, departmental scientist–practitioner programs and hold the PhD degree. One suspects that critics who think this way are operating less from observation and documented fact than from hearsay and presumption, "in a vacuum" as Dawes would say. I encourage them to visit a fair sample of our schools, to read what some of us have written about the approach to professional education that we are developing, and to join us in the empirical studies of our operations that we are currently undertaking.

The model of practice to which we in NCSPP have collectively subscribed has been summarized in several catch phrases, but I think the essence of it is captured best in Donald Schön's (1983, 1987) concept of the "reflective practitioner." "What is the kind of knowing in which competent practitioners engage?" Schön asks. "How is professional knowing like and unlike the kinds of knowledge presented in academic textbooks, scientific papers, and learned journals? In what sense, if any, is there intellectual rigor in professional practice?" (1983, p. viii).

Like Dawes, Schön rejects the common reply of the practitioner to his or her academic colleague, "I do not accept your view of knowledge, but my own is so complex, so fraught with ineffable mysteries, that I cannot describe it." Like Dawes, Schön seeks to examine the "effable" in practice, though he finds that skilled practitioners know more than they can say, that they carry tacit knowledge, born of experience, into their work.

When Schön studies the way experienced professionals in architectural design, town planning, product engineering, business management, and psychotherapy actually grapple with the problems that confront them, he does not find them simply "applying science." The problems they face are not easily defined problems that lend themselves to fixed solutions. The most interesting situations are uncertain, unstable, and complexly contextualized. Each is unique in some regard. The intellectual process that goes on in the work of skilled professionals can be described as "reflection-in-action."

> When someone reflects-in-action, he becomes a researcher in the practice context. He is not dependent on the categories of established theory and technique, but constructs a new theory of the unique case. His inquiry is not limited to a deliberation about means which depends on a prior agreement about ends. He does not keep means and ends separate, but defines them interactively as he frames a problematic situation. He does not separate thinking from doing, ratiocinating his way to a decision which he must later convert into action. Because his experimenting is a kind of action, implementation is built into his inquiry. (Schön, 1983, p. 68)

Schön's observations and analyses lead him to reject the currently dominant epistemology of practice, which he calls "technical rationality." According to the doctrine of technical rationality, professional activity consists of instrumental problem solving made rigorous by the application of scientific theory and technique. But this is not the way professional activity, at its best, actually goes. As an epistemological framework for practice, technical rationality is unacceptable because it fails to embody the essential features of skilled professional work. It is unacceptable because it creates a hierarchy of values in which research is glorified and practice is demeaned. It is unacceptable because, despite the appearance of linkage between research and practice, it actually separates research from practice. It sends the scientists, thinking positivistically, off in one direction, and the practitioners, thinking artistically, off in another, with neither well prepared for the challenges they will encounter. Finally, technical rationality is epistemologically unacceptable because it limits the purview of professional work to those areas that have been scientifically examined and for which well-tested techniques are available. When carried to its logical extreme, as Rotter (1971b) and McFall (1991) have done, technical rationality prohibits professional application of any procedure that has not been carefully tested through rigorous, preferably experimental, research. But in all professions, much of the domain of greatest concern is unexplored. In psychology, most of it is. And it is exactly in the unexplored areas, the huge *terra incognita* of psychology, that society's most important problems and, potentially, psychology's most important contributions are likely to be found.

> The dilemma of "rigor or relevance" arises more acutely in some areas of practice than in others. In the varied topography of professional practice, there is a high, hard ground where practitioners can make effective use of research-based theory and technique, and there is a swampy lowland where situations are confusing "messes" incapable of technical solution. The difficulty is that the problems of the high ground, however great their technical interest, are often relatively unimportant to clients or to the larger society, while in the swamp are the problems of greatest human concern. Shall the practitioner stay on the high, hard ground where he can practice rigorously, as he understands rigor, but where he is constrained to deal with problems of relatively little social importance? Or shall he descend to the swamp where he can engage the most important and challenging problems if he is willing to forsake technical rigor? (Schön, 1983, p. 42)

Schön, well aware of the danger and discomfort that lie before him, chooses the swamp. So do I (e.g., D. R. Peterson, 1968a, 1979a, 1990b, 1996). In "forsaking technical rigor," however, neither of us has considered it necessary to fly off into an intuitive never-neverland. Reflection in action draws on past research and documented theory wherever pertinent research has been done and well-tested theories are available. Wherever high ground appears, we need to seize it, hold it, and work from it in the public benefit. But, inevitably, the most effective professional work goes beyond formal research to critical, often inventive study of the novel case. In my own conception of psychology as a profession, the central function of the practitioner is neither psychotherapy nor traditional psychodiagnosis, though both are included, but disciplined inquiry, systematic assessment linked with change in individuals, groups, and organizations (D. R. Peterson, 1968a, 1991, 1996).

Now, suppose an academician learns something about the Schönian idea of practice that NCSPP has embraced. Will he or she respect it, in the sense of valuing practice for its own sake? Not necessarily. Anybody who hangs on to a positivist epistemology of science and a technically rationalist view of practice as applied science will still regard professional service as inherently less valuable than research, just as they will see the PhD degree as inherently superior to the PsyD, or for that matter the MD, DDS, or any other professional degree. I cannot think of much to do about those attitudes, except to affirm our own values and hope that some who disparage us will examine our viewpoint and our practices directly, rather than rejecting them out of hand.

THE REFLECTIVE EDUCATOR

In my view, development of a more useful profession of psychology requires fundamental revision of our epistemology to systematize the many ways of knowing required for a comprehensive profession (cf. Peterson &

Peterson, 1994) and redirection of the profession itself beyond historic emphases on psychodiagnosis and psychotherapy toward meeting the most pressing needs of the larger society through disciplined inquiry (cf. D. R. Peterson, 1996). Fulfillment of these grand visions, of course, is a task for future generations and requires a spirit of cooperation between scientists and practitioners that has been ebbing dangerously in recent years, though some signs of revival are beginning to appear.

As educators, our path is clear. Specifically, we need to treat the education of professional psychologists not as science, not as art, and certainly not as an annoying distraction from research-as-the-source-of-all-that-is-good-and-true, but as a profession in itself. Full acceptance of our professional responsibilities as educators requires us to subject our educational process to the kind of analysis that Schön has described as reflective practice and I have described as disciplined inquiry (D. R. Peterson, 1991, in press). Examining the profession of educating professional psychologists as a form of disciplined inquiry requires us all to abandon doctrinaire presumptions about the "best" form of education for practice. Neither the scientist–practitioner model nor the practitioner model of professional education can be demonstrably sustained as superior to the other, though rhetorical arguments have been presented for each. As practitioners of disciplined inquiry, we approach the problem of education for practice empirically. We ask, who are our clients, and what do they seek from us? To whom are we accountable? What are the guiding conceptions within which our educational practices are framed? What kinds of research might inform our efforts? How can our programs be evaluated and improved?

As reflective educators, every one of us needs to engage in a continuing process of reflection-in-action as we go about our educational duties. The substance of our cognitive dialogues will surely differ from one educator to another, but in all cases we need to take a close, critical look at our programs, to question everything about them, and to come as near as we can to rational answers to the questions before inserting, removing, or sustaining various features of our programs. Maybe you would like to come in on a sample of the internal conversation that went on between the critic and the educator in me as I studied Dawes's *House of Cards*.

Critic. Dawes says that all or most of the projective tests that psychologists use, like the Rorschach, are worthless. Do you agree?

Educator. I'm still not absolutely sure about that, but in general yes, I agree. I have said so in print on several occasions.

Critic. You claim that procedures that have been thoroughly examined through sound research and have failed to show any utility should not be taught in professional schools. Do you teach the Rorschach in your school?

Educator. I couldn't teach it myself with any conviction, but one of our faculty members does. So yes, the Rorschach is included in our assessment series.

Critic. How do you justify that?

Educator. That's a long story. When I was directing the clinical PhD program at the University of Illinois, we were acutely aware of the accumulating negative evidence on the Rorschach and most other projective tests. Some of the sentence completion devices might have been exceptions, but the negative evidence on the major projectives, like the Rorschach, finally got so strong that we decided to stop teaching it. That left us feeling virtuous, but farther down the line our students began to get into trouble when they went on internships. The internship supervisors had all been trained in these wonderfully rigorous scientist–practitioner PhD programs, many of them psychoanalytic in orientation, places like Michigan and NYU. The supervisors didn't seem to be reading the same journals we were. They were busy writing elaborate projective concoctions in their own practices, and they insisted that our students do the same. In evaluations, they told us we weren't training our students properly. So we began to advise our PhD students to sign up for a course in projective techniques that was offered in the counseling program in the College of Education, and when we designed the PsyD program we included brief technical training in the administration and interpretation of the Rorschach as a requirement. We didn't spend hundreds of hours of the students' time on it. When I came to Rutgers, projective techniques were already part of the program, and I didn't see any wisdom in fighting with the faculty about that particular issue. There were lots of others I considered more important. Today at Rutgers, projective techniques are taught by Louis Sass, a literate, critical scholar, with the blessing of the chair of our clinical department, Stanley Messer, another fine scholar and a highly responsible administrator. I respect Sass and Messer thoroughly, although I differ with them on this issue, as do several other faculty members in our school. In matters of this kind, we are likely to have Messer and Sass on one side, Arnold Lazarus and Terry Wilson on the other, and Sandra Harris, as dean, mediating a yeasty discussion. This is not a bad way to reach decisions in a school like ours, and maybe not such a bad way to reach decisions nationally. I would like to see the less useful parts of our programs reduced and the more useful parts expanded, but I see that as a dialectical, developmental process. The education of professional psychologists, like most other professional activities in psychology, takes place in a complex cultural context. Our accountabilities are mixed. Cultural change takes time.

That is a snatch of one little reflective conversation. Dawes's book inspired or revived many others. If I agree, and I do, that research on actuarial prediction is as convincing as Dawes says it is, how come we don't use actuarial methods in selecting students for admission to our program? If the main problem in the cognition of professional psychologists is that they separate practice from research, how can we teach them to do otherwise? If the main problem with programs designed to prepare psychologists for careers of clinical research is that most of their graduates never publish any research, what might we do to change that? The questions abound. They all require reflective attention, though most of the answers are far longer than the one about the Rorschach.

Beyond continuing reflection, the self-studies currently underway in NCSPP, and the kind of evaluative research proposed in the TFEETS report, there is much more that we can do, and professional schools provide ideal settings for the needed inquiries. We do not have to wait for knowledge about the study and improvement of human behavior to trickle down from the ivory towers. There is plenty of applied research that we in the professional schools are in the best of all possible positions to do. The kinds of case studies that Davison and Lazarus (1994) have described and the kinds of evaluative research that Gene Pekarik (1995) and others are doing offer ready examples. Protocol analyses of the kind Schön has done, not just with one psychotherapist and his or her supervisor but with many professional psychologists and their teachers in many different situations, can begin to map the structure (or structures?) of reflective practice in our field. Taxometric studies of the kind Meehl (1993) has considered for psychoanalysis, over the full range of roles that professional psychologists now occupy, can begin to show what kinds of unity, if any, prevail among those who are licensed under the rubric "psychologist." The kind of longitudinal, observational research that the distinguished medical sociologist, Reneé Fox, has done in her studies of medical training (Fox, 1959, 1988, 1989) could be translated readily to professional training in psychology. As a participant observer, Fox watched medical students go through all the agonies and satisfactions that come with dissecting human cadavers, learning the absurdly large amount of scientific and technical content embodied in modern medical education, enduring the rigors and acquiring the skills that are the soul of internship and residency training, and watching some patients live and others die. She talked with students all along the way. It is significant that none of her works could be called, "How Doctors Learn to Be Absolutely Sure of Everything They Do." Some of her most compelling essays appear under the title, "Training for Uncertainty." Fox's work was done in a spirit inspired by the first teacher of practitioners in medicine, and I leave you with some of Hippocrates's aphorisms.

Life is short
And the art long
The occasion instant
Experiment perilous
Decision difficult

Our experiment is perilous, but we cannot stop it now. We must continue, with all the care that responsible experiment requires.

14

DARK CONCERNS AND RAYS OF HOPE: SEMIRANDOM RECOLLECTIONS AND OBSERVATIONS ON THE EDUCATION OF PROFESSIONAL PSYCHOLOGISTS

When Paul Meehl invited a hesitant young English major into his office in the spring of 1947, he could scarcely have imagined that he was entering a relationship that would still be going strong 50 years later. Besides my continuing to read a considerable share of Meehl's voluminous published works and his reading papers I send to him from time to time, we have maintained a sporadic correspondence over the years. I do not know how many people Paul writes to, but the number must be large. His speed notes are legendary. The ones he sends to me usually go, "DRP . . . (observation, usually trenchant, often funny; information, always pertinent, often surprising; provocative question) . . . PEM." Mine to him are not so telegraphic, but also, far from e-mail, are not even run through a typewriter. We once wondered together whether we were the only people alive who still wrote letters by hand. Throughout my work life, Meehl's ideas have continued to challenge and inform me. A few years ago, he sent me a kindly inscribed copy of a book containing some of his philosophical and methodological papers (Meehl, 1991). When *History of Psychotherapy* (Freedheim, 1992) appeared, I sent a copy to Meehl "in gratitude for a lifelong education."

A couple of years before that, the student editors of our school newsletter had asked several faculty members to comment on experiences outside the classroom that had influenced our careers. The section in which the responses appeared was headed, "The Training That Taught Me Most," and my contribution went as follows:

> My personal relationship with Paul Meehl. Meehl not only led me into clinical psychology, but was mentor and model to me throughout my graduate study. He was my advisor, so naturally he helped me plan my coursework, complete my dissertation, and meet all the other demands of the rigorous Minnesota PhD program, but he did far more than that. He always greeted me warmly. When I came in the door of his office, he would say, "Donald Robert Peterson!" and I would say "Paul Everett Meehl!" and then our conversation would begin, a respectful discussion often punctuated by laughter, between two people interested in the same topic. We were never close, equal friends. To this day, I feel that he is the professor and I am the student. But by prizing me, he helped me learn to prize myself. I have never written an article, chapter, or book without thinking, at some point, "What would Paul Meehl say about that?"

Shortly afterward, I heard that Meehl had retired, and I sent him a copy of the newsletter, with a cover note assuring him that he was not the only teacher and critic who inhabited my brain, only the most persistent, and reminding him that I didn't always agree with my critics. I was juggling several deadlined projects at the time and I sent the note and newsletter to him in haste. I did not read the copy in the newsletter when it appeared nor when I mailed it off to Meehl. Several weeks later, with leisure at last to idle through an accumulation of material that had piled up on my desk, I finally read the statement as it was printed in the newsletter. To my horror, I saw that the graduate student who had typed my handwritten comment about Meehl had mistaken the letter "h" for a "k," so my tribute came out saying that the training that had taught me most was "my personal relationship with Paul Meekl" and that even now, nearing retirement, I found myself asking what "Paul Meekl" would say about something I was writing.

I was embarrassed to the point of audible, repeated groans not only by my typographical carelessness but even more by the harsh realization that at least one of the students in the Rutgers Graduate School of Applied and Professional Psychology did not recognize Meehl's name. I wrote to Paul about that. He consoled my regret about the typographical matter by sending me one of his own papers on taxometrics in which he had failed to notice that the term "Hitmax" in a running head had come through as "Hitman." Paul wondered whether readers might suspect a connection with the Mafia.

His note continued.

> Remember old (Name Name) at VA? Before arriving, he sent request for two reprints, got titles as '*Private* [for Profile] analysis of the MMPI, etc.' and "The K factor as a *suppository* [for suppressor] variable, etc.' I sent them, mentioned the parapraxes and jokingly added 'Perhaps you are

thinking these results won't replicate and you can stick them up your ass.' If I'd known him I'd never have done that. He was one of the half dozen most anxious people I've ever known outside a mental hospital. Died very young of Ca. I'll bet stress played a part. Do not fret over "Meekl." Gave us excuse for a little exchange, hah? Re student not recognizing my name, we had an APA *site visitor* on our clinical program who clearly didn't recognize it. Such is fame! . . . I'm still puzzled by your interest in hermeneutics in psy. How is it different from interpretation? Or mebbe that's too long for letters. Requires talk?"

Meehl's question about hermeneutics got me to rereading Popper, Carnap, and Feigl, along with Gergen, Bernstein, and Rorty. Some of the effects appear in this book. The whole episode led me to place the following notice in our student newsletter.

ATTENTION ALL STUDENTS

Perhaps it is not quite as important for you in your time to know as much about profile analyses and suppressor variables as it was for me in my time, but I hereby declare any student in our school who does not recognize the name of Paul Meehl, and who cannot write a thoroughly informed statement about clinical vs. actuarial prediction, construct validity, and the other issues in clinical psychology that Meehl has so brilliantly elucidated, to be psychologically illiterate and undeserving of the Doctor of Psychology degree.

I am deeply concerned about the education our students are receiving and fearfully sympathetic with Lee Sechrest's wry remark that we are not so much educating too many psychologists as turning out too many people who are "peripherally acquainted with psychology." The problem is not limited to professional schools. In recruiting faculty for a line vacated when Peter Nathan left Rutgers to become vice president for academic affairs at the University of Iowa, we searched aggressively for candidates with strong research potential but at the same time the clinical skills and knowledge needed to prepare students for careers of practice. In the current buyer's market, we received applications from many of the best known scientist–practitioner programs in the country. One after another, candidates came and went, often showing that they knew everything about whatever area they had chosen for their dissertation research but not enough beyond that to meet our needs. I remember one candidate in particular, about to receive a PhD from one of the most famous clinical programs in the country, who had never heard of G. Terence Wilson or Arnold Lazarus. I could forgive the lapse on Wilson, I guess. On my scale, Terry is still young, and maybe not everybody needs to know the best work going on substance abuse and eating disorders—but Arnold Lazarus? One of the most frequently cited clinicians since Freud? It turned out that the candidate confused Arnold Lazarus with Richard Lazarus of Berkeley, and then, on inquiry, knew next to nothing about Richard Lazarus's work either. What are professional psychologists learning these days?

This whole book says what I think they ought to be learning, but I am not at all sure that they are. As I have indicated in several sections of the book, I am equally concerned about the risks to quality brought on by the rapid expansion of professional schools and programs over the past 25 years. When we were planning the first PsyD program at Illinois, there was reason to hope that comparable programs might be established in other strong universities; NYU, Minnesota, Tennessee, even Harvard. With a few exceptions, it didn't happen. To their own advantage, the research faculties stuck with their research programs and left the education of practitioners to small colleges and freestanding professional schools. In many of these, standards for admission were relaxed. At Rutgers and several other schools I know, the ratio of admissions to applications is even more stringent than in the scientist–practitioner programs of most other universities, but that level of selectivity does not hold for practitioner programs nationwide. Not long ago, clinical psychology was a harder profession to get into than medicine. No doubt that condition excluded many fine clinicians, but most of the people who did get in were very good at mastering cognitively complex material. If that changes we all will lose. For this and other reasons, I am painfully worried about the expansion of PsyD programs in institutions where the general standard of academic quality is— how can I say this—less than lofty.

Once a poor Doctor of Psychology program is established, it is next to impossible to abolish it. Those in charge of the program can usually demonstrate that their program is no worse in preparing psychologists for practice than the accredited PhD programs in neighboring research universities. If I were incautious about libel, I could name a half dozen clinical programs in Class I (Carnegie Foundation ratings), AAU (the elite, highly selective Association of American Universities) research universities to whose graduates I would not refer my worst enemy, let alone my dearest friend. I could name an equal number of programs in small but excellent institutions to whose graduates I would entrust any of my beloved sons or daughters. For me, that is the bottom line of quality. Ultimately each program must be judged on its own merits rather than by the reputation of the institution in which it is housed.

Early in development of the PsyD program at the University of Illinois, I worried about blurring the distinction between PhD and PsyD programs. As the dissertation requirement for the PsyD degree was first imposed by the Graduate College, and then progressively "scientized" by the Illinois faculty, I foresaw death of the program by cancer-like growth of inappropriate research demands. As PsyD programs have formed in institutions that lack strong research traditions, however, my concerns have taken a different turn. I now fear that standards of scholarship will not be as strict as they need to be. Preserving the scope of disciplined inquiry over the entire terrain of professional psychology, and at the same time insisting that rigorous scholarly standards be maintained, is a difficult act to balance, but balanced it must be if truly vital issues are to be addressed in the most productive possible ways.

I hope small colleges and freestanding schools can afford the critical masses of teachers and scholars needed to prepare practitioners for one of the most difficult professions imaginable and at the same time contribute in their own diverse ways to advancing knowledge in the field. I am not sure how many can manage that now. In early meetings of the National Council of Schools and Programs of Professional Psychology (NCSPP) I was depressed by the realization that not more than two or three of the people in the room could qualify by scholarly contributions of any kind for tenure at a major university. As my own views have changed and as NCSPP has developed, my concerns have lightened somewhat. More and more schools and programs are recruiting faculty who not are only equipped to prepare psychologists for practice but also to do the kinds of research a developing profession needs. Several schools and programs have developed research centers to provide the institutional encouragement, the mutually inspiring group of collaborating scholars, and the administrative supports needed to develop and sustain active research programs. Some of the schools are already hotbeds of intellectual ferment and technical innovation.

I hope more universities will develop supradepartmental organizations—professional schools, centers, or institutes—for the education of professional psychologists. A full-scale professional school in a research university is in the best position of any organization to conduct the entire range of inquiries a science-based profession requires. Faculty in the schools are as well qualified as those in any academic department to do the carefully controlled research that appears in our most distinguished journals and thereby to help solidify the base of knowledge needed for an empirically sturdy profession. But faculty and students in professional schools are also free to address the broader range of issues that our profession needs to confront if we are ever to engage the most pressing problems in our society. They can undertake the important but risky studies that would be unsafe for faculty and students in most academic departments to consider but that can provide ever more systematic knowledge about the manifold tribulations and opportunities of the human condition.

Throughout our profession, we must grow beyond the limited kinds of practice we happened to learn in graduate school, move to meet the most challenging needs of our society, and bring to those needs the comprehensive, disciplined, self-correcting, progressively more effective forms of human service that constitute psychology's unique way of improving the human condition. We need to define our profession clearly and let the public know what we can do. We have a long way to go in that regard. When U.S. Sen. Daniel Inouye casually asked some of his colleagues what kind of education psychologists received, he found several unsure whether the master's or the bachelor's level was more common. When Rep. Henry Waxman was approached by a contingent of psychologists offering to provide expert knowledge about the addictive properties of tobacco, he took them at first to be social workers. My wife and I have gotten friendly with the staff of several restaurants in Manhattan. The last time we were in one of our favorites, the manager, a well-educated, cultured woman about 40 years old, asked me to remind her what kind of work I did. I told her I was a psychologist. What kind? Clinical. "Oh," she said, "I think clinical psychiatry is a fascinating field. Scott Peck's *Road Less Traveled* changed my life."

I hope faculties in the research universities will begin to value professional service for its own sake. I have not heard much of that yet. Mostly what I hear is contempt for practitioners—the very students the professors have trained. The contempt was there all along, but expressions seem to have become more strident lately, spurred no doubt by the sense of shrinking opportunities and stiffening competition that many of us experience, but exacerbated, I fear, by the militancy of some leaders of the scientific societies that formed when efforts to reorganize the APA foundered among our collective confusions of identity. All too often, leaders of those groups have felt impelled to disparage the pursuits of others in a misguided and unnecessary effort to justify their own pursuits.

In its nature, psychology is a pluralistic discipline. We are not one but many. The primary reference group for many APA members is not the APA, nor even one of the ever-growing numbers of divisions of the APA, but one of the several sections of one of those divisions. For many practitioners, the group that provides the most vital support and direction is neither the national association nor any part of it but the state or local psychological association closest to their practice. The basic fault line that divides psychology into distinct cultures is the line that divides practice from research. The two are related. The two are interdependent. But the cultures of science and practice are not the same, and no monistic ideology can make them the same. The claim that all psychology, including all of its practices, are and must be forms of science, cannot be sustained politically, because it cannot be sustained logically or morally. Logically, monism fails because it denies fundamental, irreconcilable differences in the aims and modes of inquiry of science and practice. Morally, monism fails because it traps its adherents into vicious dilemmas. Academicians eager to draw students into their popular clinical programs then condemn graduates who actually go into practice and treat practitioners in general like an inferior race. Students who want to become practitioners are forced to lie about their intentions to get into research-oriented scientist–practitioner programs, do no research after they get out, and find their sole claim to distinction in a bogus PhD.

These dilemmas cannot be reconciled by attempts to assimilate all psychologists into one monolithic culture. Efforts by one constituency to dominate the other merely drive the other away. At this stage in our development, the best hope for our future does not lie in exclusion of one group by another as some might prefer, nor in assimilation of all groups into a homogeneous whole as many might wish, but in a thorough-going pluralistic integration as originally defined by William James (1909/1977), as advocated by the historian John Higham (1984) for the human community as a whole, and as I have proposed (Peterson, 1995) as an ethos for psychology.

Pluralism is above all a philosophy of minority rights. It calls first for the consolidation of strength within each group. It opposes assimilation because that threatens group survival. But it also opposes separatism because that shuts each group off from the others and prohibits the larger unities the groups can form together. In our society, pluralistic integration welcomes the assertion of Black political power, the continuing pressures of the women's movement, and the demand for gay rights, but not violent expressions that harm innocent others. In our universities, it welcomes multicultural education but retains the best of Eurocentric thinking, seeking not to replace one with the other but to bring their best expressions and the conflicts between them into the same classrooms. In psychology, pluralistic integration welcomes the establishment of distinctive societies for scientists and practitioners but opposes exclusionary separations between them and vigorously opposes any attempt by one group to dominate the other. By unrelenting search for common ground and patient quest for civil conversation, it calls for the development of relationships among discrete groups that are at least mutually tolerable and at best actively cooperative in the larger societies in which the groups reside.

The pluralistic way is not an easy way. It offers less of stability than the incessant flux of an open society. It does not provide the assurance of certain truth but carries always an uneasy ambiguity. It does not offer the comfort of sameness and agreement. Instead it brings the turbulence of difference and dispute. But in the uncertainty and fluidity of pluralistic integration lie the grounds for constructive change. Through the bold assertions of its constituents, the disagreements and confrontations that follow, and the creative resolutions that can then emerge, come the gifts of diversity. Sameness can only breed more of the same. All creation comes of combining different elements. Pluralistic integration requires us all, above all, to open ourselves to those who are different from us and may oppose us. It requires us to honor the identities of others and to hear their claims but also to press our own claims, and beyond our differences to find the common values that bind us all together.

Lately, I have seen a few signs that leaders in our distinctive cultures are ready to form new links over their divides. Here and there, faculties in research universities and faculties in professional schools are starting to listen to each other, in the open, respectful exchange that offers our only chance of finding common ground. More and more have seen that the challenge for science and practice in psychology is not for one to depose or absorb the other but rather to find new ways of working together against the human problems that threaten our society. Here lies the direction for our discipline that can bring the best we have to offer into the public benefit. Scientists and practitioners alike, we must never forget that the reason many of us came into this field in the first place was to find out how we could help people of all kinds, in all conditions, live better lives.

REFERENCES

Aiken, L. S., West, S. G., Sechrest, L., Reno, R. R., Roediger, H. L., Scarr, S., Kazdin, A. E., & Sherman, S. T. (1990). Graduate training in statistics, methodology, and measurement in psychology: A survey of PhD programs in North America. *American Psychologist, 45*, 721–734.

Albee, G. W. (1966). Psychological center. In E. L. Hoch, A. O. Ross., & C. L. Winder (Eds.), *Professional preparation of clinical psychologists* (pp. 140–142). Washington, DC: American Psychological Association.

Albee, G. W. (1970). The uncertain future of clinical psychology. *American Psychologist, 25*, 1071–1080.

Albee, G. W., & Loeffler, E. (1971). Role conflicts in psychology and their implications for a reevaluation of training models. *Canadian Psychologist, 4*, 465–481.

Allport, G. W., & Odbert, H. S. (1936). Trait-names: A psycholexical study. *Psychological Monographs, 29*, (1, Whole No. 211).

American Psychological Association. (1982). *Report of the APA Task Force on Education, Training, and Service in Psychology*. Washington, DC: Author.

American Psychological Association, Central Office. (1970). APA accreditation: A status report. *American Psychologist, 25*, 581–584.

American Psychological Association, Commission on Accreditation. (1969). *Report*. Washington, DC: Author.

American Psychological Association, Committee on Accreditation. (1996). *Site visitor workbook: Guidelines for the review of doctoral and internship programs*. Washington, DC: Author.

American Psychological Association, Committee on Training in Clinical Psychology. (1947). Recommended graduate training program in clinical psychology. *American Psychologist, 2*, 539–558.

American Psychological Association, Committee on Scientific and Professional Aims of Psychology. (1967). The scientific and professional aims of psychology. *American Psychologist, 22*, 49–76.

American Psychological Association, Division of Clinical Psychology, Task Force on Promotion and Dissemination of Psychological Procedures. (1995). Training in and dissemination of empirically validated psychological treatments: Report and recommendations. *The Clinical Psychologist, 48*, 3–24.

American Psychological Association, Division 12, Task Force on Promotion and Dissemination of Psychological Procedures. (1993). *A report to the Division 12 Board*. Washington, DC: Author.

American Psychological Association, Task Force on the Evaluation of Education, Training, and Service in Psychology. (1982). *Report*. Washington, DC: Author.

American Psychological Association, Section on Clinical Psychology, Committee on the Training of Clinical Psychologists. (1935). The definition of clinical psychology and standards of training for clinical psychologists. *Psychological Clinic, 23*, 1–8.

American Psychological Association and American Association for Applied Psychology, Subcommittee on Graduate Internship Training. (1945). Graduate internship training in psychology. *Journal of Consulting Psychology, 9*, 243–266.

Anderson, H., & Goolishian, H. (1988). Human systems as linguistic systems. *Family Process, 27*, 371–395.

Ax, A. F. (1953). The physiological differentiation between fear and anger in humans. *Psychosomatic Medicine, 15*, 433–442.

Ayllon, T., & Azrin, N. H. (1968). *The token economy: A motivational system for therapy and rehabilitation*. New York: Appleton-Century-Crofts.

Bandura, A. (1969). *Principles of behavior modification*. New York: Holt, Rinehart, & Winston.

Bard, M. (1970). *Training police as specialists in family crisis intervention* (Report No. PR 70-1). Washington, DC: U.S. Government Printing Office.

Barlow, D. H., Hayes, S. C., & Nelson, R. O. (1984). *The scientist–practitioner: Research and accountability in clinical and educational settings*. New York: Pergamon Press.

Belar, C. D., & Perry, N. W. (1992). National conference on scientist–practitioner education and training for the professional practice of psychology. *American Psychologist, 47*, 71–75.

Belenky, M. F., Clinchy, B. M., Goldberger, N. R., & Tarule, J. M. (1986). *Women's ways of knowing: The development of self, voice, and mind*. New York: Basic Books.

Bergin, A. E., & Garfield, S. L. (Eds.). (1971). *Handbook of psychotherapy and behavior change*. New York: Wiley.

Berman, J. S., & Norton, N. C. (1985). Does professional training make a therapist more effective? *Psychological Bulletin, 98*, 401–407.

Bernstein, R. J. (1992). The resurgence of pragmatism. *Social Research, 59*, 823–840.

Beutler, L. E., & Kendall, P. C. (1995). Introduction to the special section: The case for training in the provision of psychological therapy. *Journal of Consulting and Clinical Psychology, 63*, 179–181.

Bickman, L. (1987). Graduate education in psychology. *American Psychologist, 42*, 1041–1047.

Bijou, S. W. (1966). A functional analysis of retarded development. In N. R. Ellis (Ed.), *International review of research in mental retardation* (Vol. 1). New York: Academic Press.

Blank, L., & David, H. P. (1963). The crisis in clinical psychology training. *American Psychologist, 18*, 216–219.

Bloom, B. (1970). Current issues in the provision of campus community mental health services. *Journal of the American College Health Association, 18*, 257–265.

Bloom, B. (1971). A university freshman preventive intervention program: Report of a pilot project. *Journal of Consulting and Clinical Psychology, 37*, 235–286.

Bourg, E. F., Bent, R. J., Callan, J. E., Jones, N. F., McHolland, J., & Stricker, G. (Eds.). (1987). *Standards and evaluation in the education and training of professional psychologists: Knowledge, attitudes, and skills*. Norman, OK: Transcript Press.

Bridgman, P. W. (1927/1953). The logic of modern physics (excerpt). In H. Feigl & M. Brodbeck (Eds.), *Readings in the philosophy of science* (pp. 34–46). New York: Appleton-Century-Crofts.

Bridgman, P. W. (1959). *The way things are*. Cambridge, MA: Harvard University Press.

Bruner, J. (1990). *Acts of meaning*. Cambridge, MA: Harvard University Press.

Caddy, G. R., & LaPointe, L. L. (1984). The training of professional psychologists: Historical developments and present trends. In G. S. Tryon (Ed.), *Professional practice of psychology*. Norwood, NJ: Ablex.

Callan, J., Peterson, D. R., & Stricker, G. (Eds.). (1986). *Quality in professional psychology training: A national conference and self-study*. Washington, DC: American Psychological Association.

Carnap, R. (1953). Testability and meaning. In H. Feigl & M. Brodbeck (Eds.), *Readings in the philosophy of science* (pp. 47–92). New York: Appleton-Century-Crofts. (Original work published 1936)

Carnegie Council on Policy Studies in Higher Education. (1976). *A classification of institutions of higher education*. Berkeley, CA: Author.

Carson, R. C. (1969). *Interaction concepts of personality*. Chicago: Aldine.

Cattell, J. McK. (1937). Retrospect: Psychology as a profession. *Journal of Consulting Psychology, 1*, 1–3.

Christensen, A., & Jacobson, N. S. (1994). Who (or what) can do psychotherapy: The status and challenge of nonprofessional therapies. *Psychological Science, 5*, 8–14.

Conference Board of Associated Research Councils. (1983, March). Research programs preserve reputations, national survey finds. *APA Monitor*, 7.

Council of Graduate Schools in the United States, The. (1969). *The nature and naming of graduate and professional degree programs* (policy statement). Washington, DC: Author.

Cowen, E. L. (1973). Social and community interventions. *Annual Review of Psychology, 24*, 423–472.

Cowley, W. H. (1960). *An overview of American colleges and universities*. Unpublished manuscript, Stanford University, Stanford, CA.

Crane, L. (1925). A plea for the training of professional psychologists. *Journal of Abnormal and Social Psychology, 20*, 228–233.

Cronbach, L. J., & Meehl, P. E. (1955). Construct validity in psychological tests. *Psychological Bulletin, 52*, 281–302.

Dana, R. H. (1987). Training for professional psychology: Science, practice, and identity. *Professional Psychology: Research and Practice, 18*, 9–16.

Davies, A. E. (1926). An interpretation of mental symptoms of dementia praecox. *Journal of Abnormal and Social Psychology, 21*, 284–295.

Davison, G. C. (1986). Elimination of a sadistic fantasy by a client-controlled counterconditioning technique. *Journal of Abnormal Psychology, 73*, 91–99.

Davison, G. C., & Lazarus, A. A. (1994). Clinical innovation and evaluation: Integrating practice with inquiry. *Clinical Psychology: Science and Practice, 1*, 157–168.

Dawes, R. M. (1994). *House of cards: Psychology and psychotherapy built on myth*. New York: Free Press.

Dawes, R. M., Faust, D., & Meehl, P. E. (1989). Clinical versus actuarial judgment. *Science, 243*, 1668–1674.

Derner, G. F. (1959). The university and clinical psychology training. In M. H. P. Finn & F. Brown (Eds.), *Training for clinical psychology*. New York: International Universities Press.

Derner, G. F. (1975). Professional excellence and graduate education. *Clinical Psychologist, 29*, 1–3.

Derrida, J. (1978). *Writing and difference*. Chicago: University of Chicago Press.

Dollard, J., & Miller, N. E. (1950). *Personality and psychotherapy*. New York: McGraw-Hill.

Dörken, H., & Cummings, N. A. (1977). A school of psychology as innovation in professional education: The California School of Professional Psychology. *Professional Psychology, 8*, 129–148.

Ducker, D. (1980, September). *Survey of dissertations in clinical and professional psychology programs*. Paper presented at the 88th Annual Convention of the American Psychological Association, Montreal, Canada.

Edwall, G. E., & Newton, N. (1992). Women and the core curriculum. In R. L. Peterson, J. McHolland, R. J. Bent, E. Davis-Russell, G. E. Edwall, E. Magidson, K. Polite, D. L. Singer, & G. Stricker (Eds.), *The core curriculum in professional psychology* (pp. 141–146). Washington DC: American Psychological Association & National Council of Schools of Professional Psychology.

Edwall, G. E., & Peterson, R. L. (January, 1991). *Women in professional psychology: Theory, research, and methodology*. Work group summary prepared for the National Council of Schools of Professional Psychology Midwinter Conference on Women in Professional Psychology "Raising the Roof," Tucson, AZ.

Endler, N. S., Hunt, J. McV., & Rosenstein, A. J. (1961). An S-R inventory of anxiousness. *Psychological Monographs, 76* (17, Whole No. 536).

Ericksen, S. C. (1966). Responsibilities of psychological science to professional psychology. *American Psychologist, 27*, 950–953.

Eysenck, H. J. (1949). Training in clinical psychology: An English point of view. *American Psychologist, 4*, 173–176.

Eysenck, H. J. (1952). The effects of psychotherapy: An evaluation. *Journal of Consulting Psychology, 16*, 319–324.

Fairweather, G. W., Sanders, D. H., Maynard, H., Cressler, D. L., & Black, D. J. (1969). *Community life for the mentally ill: An alternative to institutional care*. Chicago: Aldine.

Feigl, H. (1950). Existential hypotheses: Realistic versus phenomenalistic interpretations. *Philosophy of Science, 17*, 35–62.

Fiedler, F. E. (1965). Engineer the job to fit the manager. *Harvard Business Review, 43*, 115–122.

Fishman, D. B. (1993). Introduction to the symposium: "Rally 'round the research case study: A postmodernist perspective." *International Newsletter of Uninomic Psychology, 13*, 5–6.

Flexner, A. (1915). Is social work a profession? In *Proceedings of the National Conference of Charities and Corrections*. Baltimore: Social Work.

Flexner, A. (1925). *Medical education: A comparative study*. New York: Macmillan.

Forbes, W., Dutton, M. A., Farber, P. D., Polite, K., & Tan, S. Y. (1994). *Clinical training in professional psychology: The National Council of Schools and Programs of Professional Psychology Second La Jolla Conference, 1993*. Paper presented at NCSPP conference on "Standards for Education in Professional Psychology: Reflection and Integration," Cancún, Mexico.

Foucault, M. (1975). *The archeology of knowledge*. London: Tavistock.

Fox, R. C. (1959). *Experiment perilous: Physicians and patients facing the unknown*. Glencoe, IL: Free Press.

Fox, R. C. (1988). *Essays in medical sociology: Journeys into the field*. New Brunswick, NJ: Transaction Books.

Fox, R. C. (1989). *The sociology of medicine: A participant observer's view*. Englewood Cliffs, NJ: Prentice-Hall.

Fox, R. E. (1986). Building a profession that is safe for practitioners: A personal perspective. *Psychotherapy in Private Practice, 4*, 3–12.

Fox, R. E., Barclay, A. G., & Rogers, D. A. (1982). The foundations of professional psychology. *American Psychologist, 37*, 306–312.

Frank, G. (1984). The Boulder Model: History, rationale, and critique. *Professional Psychology: Research and Practice, 15*, 417–435.

Franks, C. M. (Ed.). (1969). *Behavior therapy: Appraisal and status*. New York: McGraw-Hill.

Fraser, N., & Nicholson, L. J. (1990). Social criticism without philosophy: An encounter between feminism and postmodernism. In L. J. Nicholson (Ed.), *Feminism/postmodernism* (pp. 19–38). New York: Routledge.

Freedheim, D. K. (Ed.). (1992). *History of psychotherapy: A century of change*. Washington, DC: American Psychological Association.

Freud, S. (1927). *The problem of lay analysis*. New York: Brentano's.

Funkenstein, D. H. (1955). The physiology of fear and anger. *Scientific American, 192*(5), 74–80.

Gaddy, C. D., Charlot-Swilley, D., Nelson, P. D., & Reich, J. N. (1995). Selected outcomes of accredited programs. *Professional Psychology: Research and Practice, 26*, 507–513.

Garfield, S. L., & Kurtz, R. (1976). Clinical psychology in the 1970s. *American Psychologist, 31*, 1–9.

Geertz, C. (1983). *Local knowledge: Further essays in interpretive anthropology*. New York: Basic Books.

Gergen, K. J. (1982). *Toward transformation in social knowledge*. New York: Springer-Verlag.

Gergen, K. J. (1985). The social constructionist movement in modern psychology. *American Psychologist, 40*, 266–275.

Gergen, K. J. (1991). *The saturated self: Dilemmas of identity in contemporary life*. New York: Basic Books.

Gergen, K. J. (1992). Toward a postmodern psychology. In S. Kvale (Ed.), *Psychology and postmodernism* (pp. 17–30). London: Sage.

Glaser, B. C., & Strauss, A. L. (1967). *The discovery of grounded theory: Strategies for qualitative research*. New York: Aldine.

Gough, H. G., & Peterson, D. R. (1952). The identification and measurement of predispositional factors in crime and delinquency. *Journal of Consulting Psychology, 16*, 207–212.

Grip, J. C. (1994). *Evaluation in professional psychology: The National Council of Schools and Programs of Professional Psychology Bahamas Conference, 1992*. Paper presented at NCSPP conference on "Standards for Education in Professional Psychology: Reflection and Integration," Cancún, Mexico.

Halstead, W. C. (1947). *Brain and intelligence: A quantitative study of the frontal lobes*. Chicago: University of Chicago Press.

Halstead, W. C., & Wepman, J. M. (1949). The Halstead-Wepman Aphasia Screening Test. *Journal of Speech and Hearing Disorders, 14*, 9015.

Hare-Mustin, R., & Marecek, J. (1990a). Gender and the meaning of difference: Postmodernism and psychology. In R. T. Hare-Mustin & J. Marecek (Eds.), *Making a difference: Psychology and the construction of gender* (pp. 22–64). New Haven, CT: Yale University Press.

Hare-Mustin, R., & Marecek, J. (1990b). *Making a difference: Psychology and the construction of gender*. New Haven, CT: Yale University Press.

Hare-Mustin, R., & Marecek, J. (1990c). On making a difference. In R. T. Hare-Mustin & J. Marecek (Eds.), *Making a difference: Psychology and the construction of gender* (pp. 1–21). New Haven, CT: Yale University Press.

Hawkesworth, M. E. (1989). Knowers, knowing, known: Feminist theory and claims of truth. *Signs: Journal of Women in Culture and Society, 14*, 533–557.

Hayes, S. C. (1989). An interview with Lee Sechrest: The courage to say, "We do not know how." *APS Observer, 2*(4), 8–10.

Hebb, D. O. (1949). *The organization of behavior*. New York: Wiley.

Hickson, D. J., & Thomas, M. W. (1969). Professionalisation in Britain: A preliminary measurement. *Sociology, 3*, 37–53.

Higham, J. (1984). *Send these to me: Immigrants in urban America*. Baltimore: Johns Hopkins University Press.

Hoch, E. L., Ross, A. E., & Winder, C. L. (Eds.). (1966). *Professional preparation of clinical psychologists*. Washington, DC: American Psychological Association.

Hodson, W. (1925). Is social work professional? A re-examination of the question. *Proceedings of the National Conference of Social Work* (Denver, CO).

Hoffman, L. (1992). A reflective stance for family therapy. In S. McNamee & K. J. Gergen (Eds.), *Therapy as social construction* (pp. 7–24). London: Sage.

Holt, R. R. (Ed.). (1971). *New horizons for psychotherapy: Autonomy as a profession*. New York: International Universities Press.

Homans, G. C. (1961). *Social behavior: Its elementary forms*. New York: Harcourt, Brace & World.

Hoshmand, L. T. (1994). *Orientation to inquiry in a reflective professional psychology*. Albany, NY: SUNY Press.

James, W. (1977). *A pluralistic universe: Hibbert lectures at Manchester College on the present situation in philosophy*. Cambridge, MA: Harvard University Press. (Original work published 1909).

Joint Council on Professional Education in Psychology. (1990, August). In T. T. Stigall. (Chair), *Report*. Symposium conducted at the 98th Annual Convention of American Psychological Association, Boston.

Jones, S. L. (1994). A constructive relationship for religion with the science and profession of psychology: Perhaps the boldest model yet. *American Psychologist, 49*, 184–199.

Kahn, M. W., & Santostefano, S. (1962). The case of clinical psychology: A search for identity. *American Psychologist, 17*, 185–190.

Kaiser, H. F. (1958). The varimax criterion for analytic rotation in factor analysis. *Psychometrika, 23*, 187–200.

Kanfer, F. H. (1990). The scientist–practitioner connection: A bridge in need of constant attention. *Professional Psychology: Research and Practice, 21*, 264–270.

Kanfer, F. H., & Phillips, J. S. (1970). *Learning foundations of behavior therapy*. New York: Wiley.

Kelley, H. H., Berscheid, E., Christensen, A., Harvey, J. H., Huston, T. L., Levinger, G., McClintock, E., Peplau, L. A., & Peterson, D. R. (1983). *Close relationships*. New York: Freeman.

Kelly, E. L., & Fiske, D. W. (1950). The prediction of success in the VA training program in clinical psychology. *American Psychologist, 5*, 395–406.

Kelly, E. L., & Goldberg, L. R. (1959). Correlates of later performance and specialization in psychology: A follow-up study of the trainees assessed in the VA Selection Research Project. *Psychological Monographs, 3* (12, Whole No. 482).

Kelly, G. A. (1955). *The psychology of personal constructs*. New York: Norton.

Kimble, G. A. (1984). Psychology's two cultures. *American Psychologist, 39*, 833–839.

Kopplin, D. A. (1986). Curriculum and curriculum review. In J. Callan, D. R. Peterson, & G. Stricker (Eds.). *Quality in professional psychology training: A national conference and self-study*. Washington, DC: American Psychological Association.

Korman, M. (1974). National conference on levels and patterns of professional training in psychology: The major themes. *American Psychologist, 29*, 441–449.

Korman, M. (Ed.). (1976). *Levels and patterns of professional training in psychology*. Washington, DC: American Psychological Association.

Kostlan, A. (1954). A method for the empirical study of psychodiagnosis. *Journal of Consulting Psychology, 18,* 83–88.

Kuhn, T. (1970). *The structure of scientific revolutions* (2nd ed.). Chicago: University of Chicago Press.

Kvale, S. (Ed.). (1992). *Psychology and postmodernism.* London: Sage.

Lacey, J. J. (1967). Somatic response patterning and stress: Some revisions of activation theory. In M. H. Appley & R. Trumbull (Eds.), *Psychological stress: Issues in research.* New York: Appleton-Century-Crofts.

Lacks, P. B., Colberg, J., Harrow, M., & Levine, J. (1970). Further evidence concerning the diagnostic accuracy of the Halstead organic test battery. *Journal of Clinical Psychology, 26,* 480–481.

Lakatos, I. (1970). Falsification and the methodology of scientific research programmes. In I. Lakatos & A. Musgrave (Eds.), *Criticism and the growth of knowledge* (pp. 91–195). Cambridge: Cambridge University Press.

Lambert, M. J., Shapiro, D. A., & Bergin, A. E. (1986). The effectiveness of psychotherapy. In S. L. Garfield & A. E. Bergin (Eds.), *Handbook of psychotherapy and behavior change* (3rd ed., pp. 157–212). New York: Wiley.

Lax, W. D. (1992). Postmodern thinking in clinical practice. In S. McNamee & K. J. Gergen (Eds.), *Therapy as social construction* (pp. 69–85). London: Sage.

Lazarus, A. A. (1971). *Behavior therapy and beyond.* New York: McGraw-Hill.

Lazarus, A. A. (1989). *The practice of multimodal therapy*. Baltimore: Johns Hopkins University Press.

Lazarus, A. A. (1990). Can psychotherapists transcend the shackles of their training and superstitions? *Journal of Clinical Psychology, 46,* 352–358.

Leitenberg, H. (1974). Training clinical researchers in psychology. *Professional Psychology, 5,* 59–69.

Levitt, E. E. (1957). The results of psychotherapy with children: An evaluation. *Journal of Consulting Psychology, 21,* 189–196.

Levy, L. H. (1962). The skew in clinical psychology. *American Psychologist, 17,* 244–249.

Levy, L. H. (1984). The metamorphosis of clinical psychology: Toward a new charter of human services psychology. *American Psychologist, 39,* 486–494.

Little, K. B., & Schneidman, E. S. (1959). Congruencies among interpretations of psychological test and anamnestic data. *Psychological Monographs, 73* (6, Whole No. 476).

Lovaas, O. I. (1968). Some studies on the treatment of childhood schizophrenia. In J. M. Shlien (Ed.), *Research in psychotherapy*. Washington, DC: American Psychological Association.

Lovaas, O. I., Schaeffer, B., & Simmons, J. Q. (1965). Building social behavior in autistic children by use of electric shock. *Journal of Experimental Research in Personality, 1,* 99–109.

Luria, A. R. (1966). *Higher cortical functions in man*. New York: Basic Books.

Lykken, D. (1974). Psychology and the lie detector industry. *American Psychologist, 29*, 725–739.

MacCorquodale, K., & Meehl, P. E. (1948). On a distinction between hypothetical constructs and intervening variables. *Psychological Review, 55*, 95–107.

Magidson, E., Edwall, G. E., Kenkel, M. B., & Jackson, J. (1994, January). *Women's issues in professional psychology: The National Council of Schools and Programs of Professional Psychology Tucson conference, 1991*. Paper presented at National Council of Schools and Programs of Professional Psychology conference on "Standards for Education in Professional Psychology: Reflection and Integration," Cancún, Mexico.

Maher, B. A. (1965). The clinician as research-psychopathologist. In *Preconference materials* (Prepared for the Conference on the Professional Preparation of Clinical Psychologists). Washington, DC: American Psychological Association.

Mahoney, M. J. (1991). *Human change processes: The scientific foundations of psychotherapy*. New York: Basic Books.

March, J. G. (Ed.). (1965). *Handbook of organizations*. Chicago: Rand McNally.

Marcia, J. E., Rubin, B. M., & Efran, J. S. (1969). Systematic desensitization: Expectancy change or counterconditioning? *Journal of Abnormal Psychology, 74*, 382–387.

Margolis, J. (1986). *Pragmatism without foundations: Reconciling realism and relativism*. Chicago: University of Chicago Press.

Marwit, S. J. (1983). Doctoral candidates' attitudes toward models of professional training. *Professional Psychology: Research and Practice, 14*, 105–111.

Masters, W. H., & Johnson, V. E. (1970). *Human sexual inadequacy*. Boston: Little, Brown.

Mayne, T. J., Norcross, J. C., & Sayette, M. A. (1994). Admission requirements, acceptance rates, and financial assistance in clinical psychology programs. Diversity across the practice–research continuum. *American Psychologist, 49*, 806–811.

McFall, R. M. (1991). Manifesto for a science of clinical psychology. *The Clinical Psychologist, 44*, 75–88.

McFall, R. M. (1996). Making psychology incorruptible. *Applied and Preventive Psychology, 5*, 9–15.

McFall, R. M., & Twentyman, C. T. (1973). Four experiments on the relative contributions of rehearsal, modelling, and coaching to assertion training. *Journal of Abnormal Psychology, 81*, 199–218.

McNamee, S., & Gergen, K. J. (Eds.). (1992). *Therapy as social construction*. London: Sage.

Meehl, P. E. (1946). Profile analysis of the MMPI in differential diagnosis. *Journal of Applied Psychology, 30*, 517–524.

Meehl, P. E. (1954). *Clinical versus statistical prediction: A theoretical analysis and review of the literature*. Minneapolis: University of Minnesota Press.

Meehl, P. E. (1971). A scientific, scholarly nonresearch doctorate for clinical practitioners. In R. Holt (Ed.), *New horizons for psychotherapy: Autonomy as a profession*. New York: International Universities Press.

Meehl, P. E. (1978). Theoretical risks and tabular asterisks: Sir Karl, Sir Ronald, and the slow progress of soft psychology. *Journal of Consulting and Clinical Psychology*, *46*, 806–834.

Meehl, P. E. (1979). *The seven sacred cows of academia: Can we afford them?* Unpublished manuscript, University of Minnesota, Minneapolis.

Meehl, P. E. (1984). *Are faculty salaries held down by faculty dogmas?* Unpublished manuscript, University of Minnesota, Minneapolis.

Meehl, P. E. (1990). Appraising and amending theories: The strategy of Lakatosian defense and two principles that warrant using it. *Psychological Inquiry*, *1*, 108–141, 173–180.

Meehl, P. E. (1991). *Selected philosophical and methodological papers*. Minneapolis, University of Minnesota Press.

Meehl, P. E. (1993). If Freud could define psychoanalysis, why can't ABPP do it? *Psychoanalysis and Contemporary Thought*, *16*, 299–326.

Meichenbaum, D. (1973). Cognitive factors in behavior modification: Modifying what clients say to themselves. In C. M. Franks & G. T. Wilson (Eds.), *Annual review of behavior therapy: Theory and practice* (pp. 416–431). New York: Bruner/Mazel.

Meltzoff, J. (1984). Research training for clinical psychologists: Point-counterpoint. *Professional Psychology: Research and Practice*, *15*, 203–209.

Meltzoff, J., & Kornreich, M. (1970). *Research in psychotherapy*. Chicago: Aldine-Atherton.

Messer, S. B., Sass, L. A., & Woolfolk, R. L. (Eds.). (1988). *Hermeneutics and psychological theory: Interpretive perspectives on personality, psychotherapy, and psychopathology*. New Brunswick, NJ: Rutgers University Press.

Messer, S. B., & Wachtel, P. L. (1992). Overview, theoretical perspectives in psychotherapy. In D. K. Freedheim (Ed.), *History of psychotherapy: A century of change* (pp. 105–108). Washington, DC: American Psychological Association.

Miller, G. A. (1969). Psychology as a means of promoting human welfare. *American Psychologist*, *24*, 1063–1075.

Miller, J. G. (1978). *Living systems*. New York: McGraw-Hill.

Mischel, W. (1968). *Personality and assessment*. New York: Wiley.

Mitchell, D. (1920). The clinical psychologist. *Journal of Abnormal Psychology*, *14*, 325–332.

Moldawsky, S. (1990). Is solo practice really dead? *American Psychologist*, *45*, 544–546.

Moore, D. L. (1992). The Veterans Administration and its training program in psychology. In D. K. Freedheim (Ed.), *History of psychotherapy: A century of change* (pp. 776–800). Washington, DC: American Psychological Association.

Mowrer, O. H. (Ed.). (1950). *Learning theory and personality dynamics*. New York: Ronald Press.

Nunnally, J., & Kittros, J. M. (1958). Public attitudes toward mental health professions. *American Psychologist, 13*, 589–594.

Oakland, T. (1994). Issues of importance to the membership of the American Psychological Association: Implications for planning. *American Psychologist, 49*, 879–886.

O'Donohue, W. (1989). The (even) bolder model: The clinical psychologist as metaphysician-scientist-practitioner. *American Psychologist, 44*, 1460–1468.

Packer, M. J., & Addison, R. B. (Eds.). (1989). *Entering the circle: Hermeneutic investigation in psychology*. Albany: State University of New York Press.

Pap, A. (1953). Reduction sentences and open concepts. *Methodos, 5*, 3–30.

Parsons, T. (1959). Some problems confronting sociology as a profession. *American Sociological Review, 24*, 547–556.

Patterson, G. R. (1971). Behavioral intervention procedures in the classroom and in the home. In A. E. Bergin & S. L. Garfield (Eds.), *Handbook of psychotherapy and behavior change*. New York: Wiley.

Paul, G. L. (1966). *Insight versus desensitization in psychotherapy. An experiment in anxiety reduction*. Stanford, CA: Stanford University Press.

Paul, G. L. (1969). Behavior modification research: Design and tactics. In C. M. Franks (Ed.), *Behavior therapy: Appraisal and status* (pp. 29–62). New York: McGraw-Hill.

Paul, G. L., & Lentz, R. J. (1976). *Psychosocial treatment of chronic mental patients: Milieu versus social-learning programs*. Cambridge, MA: Harvard University Press.

Pekarik, G. (1995). Training practitioner-scholars to do applied clinical research: An integrated model of coursework and supervised practice. In *Standards for education in professional psychology: Where are we?, Where are we going?, and How do we let people know?* (pp. 181–194). Washington, DC: National Council of Schools and Programs of Professional Psychology.

Penfield, W., & Rasmussen, T. (1950). *The cerebral cortex of man*. New York: Macmillan.

Perry, N. W. (1979). Why clinical psychology does not need alternative training models. *American Psychologist, 34*, 603–611.

Peterson, D. R. (1954a). Predicting hospitalization of psychiatric outpatients. *Journal of Abnormal and Social Psychology, 49*, 260–265.

Peterson, D. R. (1954b). The diagnosis of subclinical schizophrenia. *Journal of Consulting Psychology, 18*, 198–200.

Peterson, D. R. (1960). The age generality of personality factors derived from ratings. *Educational and Psychological Measurement, 30*, 461–474.

Peterson, D. R. (1965). Scope and generality of verbally defined personality factors. *Psychological Review, 72,* 48–58.

Peterson, D. R. (1966). Professional program in an academic psychology department. In E. L. Hoch, A. O. Ross, & C. L. Winder (Eds.), *Professional preparation of clinical psychologists* (pp. 143–146). Washington, DC: American Psychological Association.

Peterson, D. R. (1968a). *The clinical study of social behavior*. New York: Appleton-Century-Crofts.

Peterson, D. R. (1968b). The Doctor of Psychology program at the University of Illinois. *American Psychologist, 23,* 511–516.

Peterson, D. R. (1969). Attitudes concerning the Doctor of Psychology program. *Professional Psychology, 1,* 44–47.

Peterson, D. R. (1971). Status of the Doctor of Psychology program, 1970. *Professional Psychology, 2,* 271–275.

Peterson, D. R. (1976a). Need for the Doctor of Psychology degree in professional psychology. *American Psychologist, 31,* 792–798.

Peterson, D. R. (1976b). Is psychology a profession? *American Psychologist, 31,* 572–581.

Peterson, D. R. (1979a). Assessing interpersonal relationships by means of interaction records. *Behavioral Assessment, 1,* 221–236.

Peterson, D. R. (1979b). Assessing interpersonal relationships in natural settings. *New Directions for Methodology of Behavioral Science, 2,* 33–53.

Peterson, D. R. (1982). Functional analysis of interpersonal behavior. In J. C. Anchin & D. J. Kiesler (Eds.), *Handbook of interpersonal psychotherapy* (pp. 149–167). New York: Pergamon Press.

Peterson, D. R. (1983). *The case for the PsyD*. Unpublished manuscript, Rutgers University, New Brunswick, NJ.

Peterson, D. R. (1985). Twenty years of practitioner training in psychology. *American Psychologist, 40,* 441–451.

Peterson, D. R. (1989). Interpersonal goal conflict. In L. A. Pervin (Ed.), *Goal concepts in personality and social psychology* (pp. 327–362). Hillsdale, NJ: Erlbaum.

Peterson, D. R. (1990a). *Students speak on prejudice: A survey of intergroup attitudes and ethnoviolence among undergraduate students at Rutgers University*. New Brunswick, NJ: Rutgers University.

Peterson, D. R. (1990b). Working against prejudice in a large state university. In G. Stricker, E. Davis-Russell, E. Bourg, E. Duran, W. R. Hammond, J. McHolland, K. Polite, & B. E. Vaughn (Eds.), *Toward ethnic diversification in psychology education and training* (pp. 43–54). Washington, DC: American Psychological Association.

Peterson, D. R. (1991). Connection and disconnection of research and practice in the education of professional psychologists. *American Psychologist, 46,* 422–429.

Peterson, D. R. (1992a). Accreditation in psychology: A historical view. In P. D. Nelson (Ed.), *Perspectives, responsibilities, and challenges in accreditation: A national forum*. Washington, DC: American Psychological Association.

Peterson, D. R. (1992b). Interpersonal relationships as a link between person and environment. In W. B. Walsh, R. L. Price, & K. Craik (Eds.), *Person-environment psychology: Models and perspectives* (pp. 127–155). Hillsdale, NJ: Erlbaum.

Peterson, D. R. (1992c). The Doctor of Psychology degree. In D. K. Freedheim (Ed.), *History of psychotherapy: A century of change* (pp. 829–849). Washington, DC: American Psychological Association.

Peterson, D. R. (1993a). Fewer bricks; better buildings: Comment on C. Hazan & P. Shaver, Attachment as an organizational framework for research on close relationships. *Psychological Inquiry, 3*, 56–58.

Peterson, D. R. (1993b). Case study as a vehicle for theory construction in soft psychology. *International Newsletter of Uninomic Psychology, 13*, 13–21.

Peterson, D. R. (1995, August). *The gift of diversity*. Second annual Rosalee G. Weiss lecture, presented at APA convention, New York.

Peterson, D. R. (1996). Making psychology indispensable. *Applied and Preventive Psychology, 5*,1–8.

Peterson, D. R., & Baron, A., Jr. (1975). Status of the University of Illinois Doctor of Psychology program, 1974. *Professional Psychology, 6*, 88–95.

Peterson, D. R., & Bry, B. H. (1980). Dimensions of perceived competence in professional psychology. *Professional Psychology, 11*, 965–971.

Peterson, D. R., Eaton, M. M., Levine, A. R., & Snepp, F. P. (1982). Career experiences of Doctors of Psychology. *Professional Psychology, 13*, 268–277.

Peterson, D. R., & Fishman, D. B. (1987). *Assessment for decision*. New Brunswick, NJ: Rutgers University Press.

Peterson, D. R., & Knudson, R. M. (1979). Work preferences of clinical psychologists. *Professional Psychology, 10*, 175–182.

Peterson, R. L. (1992a). Social construction of the core curriculum in professional psychology. In R. L. Peterson, J. McHolland, R. J. Bent, E. Davis-Russell, G. E. Edwall, E. Magidson, K. Polite, D. L. Singer, & G. Stricker (Eds.), *The core curriculum in professional psychology* (pp. 23–36). Washington DC: American Psychological Association & National Council of Schools of Professional Psychology.

Peterson, R. L. (1992b). The social, relational, and intellectual context of the core curriculum and the San Antonio Conference. In R. L. Peterson, J. McHolland, R. J. Bent, E. Davis-Russell, G. E. Edwall, E. Magidson, K. Polite, D. L. Singer, & G. Stricker (Eds.), *The core curriculum in professional psychology* (pp. 3–12). Washington DC: American Psychological Association & National Council of Schools of Professional Psychology.

Peterson, R. L. (1992c, August). The marginalization of family theory, family therapy, and family issues in clinical training programs. In S. S. Lee & C. Thompson (Co-chairs), *Family issues in clinical psychology training*. Symposium conducted at the meeting of the American Psychological Association, Washington, DC.

Peterson, R. L. (1995, Summer). What I've learned as an NCSPP liaison. *NCSPP Newsletter, 13,* pp. 3, 6.

Peterson, R. L., & Gold, S. N. (1992, January). *Evaluation and the romantic and modernist cultures in clinical training programs: Toward collegiality.* Paper presented at the National Council of Schools of Professional Psychology Midwinter Conference on Evaluation in Professional Psychology, Bahamas.

Peterson, R. L., & Lax, W. D. (1993, January). *Toward theoretical and supervisory multiplicity.* Paper presented at the National Council of Schools of Professional Psychology Midwinter Conference on Training in Professional Psychology, La Jolla, CA.

Peterson, R. L., McHolland, J. D., Bent, R. J., Davis-Russell, E., Edwall, G. E., Magidson, E., Polite, K., Singer, D. L., & Stricker, G. (Eds.) (1992). *The core curriculum in professional psychology.* Washington DC.: American Psychological Association & National Council of Schools of Professional Psychology.

Peterson, R. L., & Peterson, J. S. (1993, June). *Reality and local cultures with examples from psychology and law.* Paper presented at the conference Inquiries in Social Construction, University of New Hampshire, Durham.

Peterson, R. L., Peterson, D. R., & Abrams, J. (in press). *Standards for education in professional psychology.* Washington, DC: American Psychological Association and National Council of Schools and Programs of Professional Psychology.

Peterson, R. L., Peterson, D. R., Abrams, J. C., & Stricker, G. (in press). The National Council of Schools and Programs of Professional Psychology educational model. *Professional Psychology: Research and Practice.*

Peterson, R. L., & Stiglitz, E. (1991, January). *Relationships between male faculty and female students in professional psychology training programs: Monitoring, sex, and empowerment.* Paper prepared for the National Council of Schools of Professional Psychology Midwinter Conference on Women in Professional Psychology, Tucson, AZ.

Pinard, R. P. A. (1967). A professional and an academic degree offered in the same department of psychology. In E. C. Webster (Ed.), *The Couchiching Conference on Professional Psychology.* Montreal: Canadian Psychological Association.

Polanyi, M. (1958). *Personal knowledge: Towards a post-critical philosophy.* Chicago: University of Chicago Press.

Polkinghorne, D. (1983). *Methodology for the human sciences: Systems of inquiry.* Albany: State University of New York Press.

Polkinghorne, D. E. (1992). Postmodern epistemology of practice. In S. Kvale (Ed.), *Psychology and postmodernism* (pp. 146–165). London: Sage.

Popper, K. R. (1959). *Logik der Forschung* [The logic of scientific discovery]. New York: Basic Books. (Original work published 1934)

Popper, K. R. (1963). *The open society and its enemies.* Princeton, NJ: Princeton University Press. (Original work published 1943)

Popper, K. R. (1968). *Conjectures and refutations: The growth of scientific knowledge.* New York: Harper & Row.

Popper, K. R. (1970/1985). Realism. In D. Miller (Ed.), *Popper selections* (pp. 220–225). Princeton, NJ: Princeton University Press.

Popper, K. R. (1974). Autobiography and replies to my critics. In P. A. Schilpp (Ed.), *The philosophy of Karl Popper* (pp. 3–181; 961–1197). LaSalle, IL: Open Court Trade and Academic Books.

Popper, K. R. (1992). *In search of a better world.* London: Routledge. (Original work published 1984)

Price, D. J. de S. (1965). Networks of scientific papers. *Science, 149,* 510–515.

Raimy, V. C. (Ed.). (1950). *Training in clinical psychology.* Englewood Cliffs, NJ: Prentice-Hall.

Raush, H. L., Dittman, A. T., & Taylor, T. J. (1959). Person, setting, and change in social interaction. *Human Relationships, 12,* 361–378.

Reisman, J. M. (1966). *The development of clinical psychology.* New York: Appleton-Century-Crofts.

Reisman, J. M. (1991). *A history of clinical psychology* (2nd ed.). New York: Hemisphere Publishing.

Reitan, R. M. (1966). Diagnostic inferences of brain lesions based on psychological test results. *Canadian Psychologist, 7,* 368–383.

Reitan, R. M. (1967). Psychological assessment of deficits associated with brain lesions in subjects with and without subnormal intelligence. In J. L. Khanna (Ed.), *Brain damage and mental retardation: A psychological evaluation.* Springfield, IL: Charles C Thomas.

Reppucci, N. D., & Saunders, J. T. (1974). Social psychology of behavior modification: Problems of implementation in natural settings. *American Psychologist, 29,* 649–660.

Roe, A., Gustad, J. W., Moore, B. V., Ross, S., & Skodak, M. (Eds.). (1959). *Graduate education in psychology.* Washington, DC: American Psychological Association.

Rorty, R. (1991). *Objectivity, relativism, and truth: Philosophical papers* (Vol. 1). Cambridge, England: Cambridge University Press.

Rosenau, P. M. (1992). *Post-modernism and the social sciences: Insights, inroads, and intrusions.* Princeton, NJ: Princeton University Press.

Rosenzweig, M. R. (1982). Trends in development and status of psychology: An international perspective. *International Journal of Psychology, 17,* 117–140.

Rotter, J. B. (1971a, September). *The future of clinical psychology.* Presidential address to the Division of Clinical Psychology, presented at the meeting of the American Psychological Association, Washington, DC.

Rotter, J. B. (1971b). On the evaluation of methods of intervening in other people's lives. *The Clinical Psychologist, 24,* 1–2.

Routh, D. K. (1994). *Clinical psychology since 1917: Science, practice, and organization.* New York: Plenum Press.

Russell, E. W., Neuringer, C., & Goldstein, G. (1970). *Assessment of brain damage*. New York: Wiley.

Sampson, E. E. (1985). The decentralization of identity: Toward a revised concept of personal and social order. *American Psychologist, 40*, 1203–1211.

Sarbin, T. R. (1986). (Ed.). *Narrative psychology: The storied nature of human conduct*. New York: Praeger.

Sarason, S. (1974). *The psychological sense of community: Prospects for a community psychology*. San Francisco: Jossey-Bass.

Sarason, S. B. (1981). An asocial psychology and a misdirected clinical psychology. *American Psychologist, 36*, 827–836.

Sarason, S. B. (1982). Individual psychology: An obstacle to understanding adulthood. In S. B. Sarason, *Psychology and social action: Selected papers* (pp. 211–231). New York: Praeger.

Sawyer, J. (1966). Measurement and prediction, clinical and statistical. *Psychological Bulletin, 66*, 178–200.

Schneidman, E. S., Farberow, N. L., & Litman, R. E. (1970). *The psychology of suicide*. New York: Science House.

Schön, D. A. (1983). *The reflective practitioner: How professionals think in action*. New York: Basic Books.

Schön, D. A. (1987). *Educating the reflective practitioner: Toward a new design for teaching and learning in the professions*. San Francisco: Jossey-Bass.

Sears, R. R. (1946). Graduate training facilities. I. General information. II. Clinical psychology. *American Psychologist, 1*, 135-143.

Sears, R. R. (1947). Clinical training facilities: 1947. *American Psychologist, 2*, 199–205.

Seligman, M. E. P. (1993). *What you can change and what you can't: The complete guide to successful self-improvement*. New York: Knopf.

Sells, S. B. (1963). *Stimulus determinants of behavior*. New York: Ronald Press.

Shapiro, A. E., & Wiggins, J. G. (1994). A PsyD degree for every practitioner: Truth in labeling. *American Psychologist, 49*, 207–210.

Shemberg, K. M., & Leventhal, D. B. (1981). Attitudes of internship directors toward pre-internship training and clinical training models. *Professional Psychology, 12*, 639–646.

Sherman, A. R. (1972). Real-life exposure as a primary therapeutic factor in the desensitization treatment of fear. *Journal of Abnormal Psychology, 2*, 19–28.

Shoben, E. J., Jr. (1949). Psychotherapy as a problem in learning theory. *Psychological Bulletin, 46*, 366–392.

Shotter, J. (1985). Social accountability and self specification. In K. J. Gergen & K. E. David (Eds.), *The social construction of the person* (pp. 167–188). New York: Springer-Verlag.

Shotter, J. (1989). Social accountability and the social construction of "you." In J. Shotter & K. J. Gergen (Eds.), *Texts of identity* (pp. 133–152). London: Sage.

Shotter, J. (1993a). *Conversational realities.* London: Sage.

Shotter, J. (1993b, December). *Conversational realities.* Continuing education workshop presented at Antioch New England Graduate School, Keene, NH.

Silverman, L. H. (1959). A Q-sort study of the validity of evaluations made from projective techniques. *Psychological Monographs, 73,* (7, Whole No. 477).

Singer, D. (1982). Professional socialization and adult development in graduate professional education. In B. Menson (Ed.), *New directions for learning: Building on experiences in adult development, No. 16* (pp. 45–63). San Francisco: Jossey-Bass.

Singer, D. L., Peterson, R. L., & Magidson, E. (1992). The self, the student, and the core curriculum: Learning from the inside out. In R. L. Peterson, J. McHolland, R. J. Bent, E. Davis-Russell, G. E. Edwall, E. Magidson, K. Polite, D. L. Singer, & G. Stricker (Eds.), *The core curriculum in professional psychology* (pp. 134–139). Washington DC: American Psychological Association & National Council of Schools of Professional Psychology.

Snepp, F. P., & Peterson, D. R. (1988). An evaluative comparison of PsyD and PhD students by clinical psychology internship supervisors. *Professional Psychology: Research and Practice, 19,* 180–183.

Snepp, F. P. (1983). *Attitudes toward training and the efficacy of the scientist-practitioner and professional models of training in clinical psychology.* Unpublished doctoral dissertation, Rutgers University, New Brunswick, NJ.

Snow, C. P. (1959). *The two cultures.* Cambridge: Cambridge University Press.

Snow, C. P. (1964). *The two cultures and a second look.* London: Cambridge University Press.

Stampfl, T. G., & Levis, D. J. (1967). Essentials of implosive therapy: Learning theory based on psychodynamic behavioral therapy. *Journal of Abnormal Psychology, 72,* 496–503.

Stein, D. M., & Lambert, M. J. (1984). On the relationship between therapist experience and psychotherapy outcome. *Clinical Psychology Review, 4,* 127–142.

Stern, S. (1984). Professional training and professional competence: A critique of current thinking. *Professional Psychology: Research and Practice, 15,* 230–243.

Stricker, G. (1975). On professional schools and professional degrees. *American Psychologist, 30,* 1062–1066.

Stricker, G. (1986). Admissions to professional schools. In J. Callan, D. R. Peterson, & G. Stricker (Eds.), *Quality in professional psychology training: A national conference and self-study.* Washington, DC: American Psychological Association.

Stricker, G., & Cummings, N. A. (1992). The professional school movement. In D. K. Freedheim (Ed.), *History of psychotherapy: A century of change* (pp. 801–828). Washington, DC: American Psychological Association.

Stricker, G., Davis-Russell, E., Bourg, E., Duran, E., Hammond, W. R., McHolland, J., Polite, K., & Vaughn, B. E. (Eds.). (1990). *Toward ethnic diversification in psychology education and training.* Washington, DC: American Psychological Association.

Stricker, G., & Keisner, R. H. (Eds.). (1985). *From research to clinical practice: The implications of social and developmental research for psychotherapy*. New York: Plenum Press.

Strupp, H. H. (1992). Overview, psychotherapy research. In D. K. Freedheim (Ed.), *History of psychotherapy: A century of change* (pp. 307–308). Washington, DC: American Psychological Association.

Strupp, H. H., & Hadley, S. W. (1979). Specific versus nonspecific factors in psychotherapy. *Archives of General Psychiatry, 36*, 1125–1136.

Stuart, R. B. (1969). Operant interpersonal treatment for marital discord. *Journal of Consulting and Clinical Psychology, 33*, 675–682.

Thibaut, J. W., & Kelley, H. H. (1959). *The social psychology of groups*. New York: Wiley.

Thorndike, R. L. (1955). The structure of preferences for psychological activities among psychologists. *American Psychologist, 10*, 205–207.

Trexler, L. D., & Karst, T. O. (1972). Rational-emotive therapy, placebo, and no-treatment effects on public-speaking anxiety. *Journal of Abnormal Psychology, 79*, 60–67.

Trierweiler, S. J. (1992, August). *The local clinical scientist: A model for integrating training in research and practice*. Paper presented in G. Stricker (Chair), *Research training in clinical psychology*. Education Miniconvention Symposium conducted at the 100th annual meeting of the American Psychological Association, Washington, DC.

Trierweiler, S. J., & Stricker, G. (1992). Research and evaluation competency: Training the local clinical scientist. In R. L. Peterson, J. McHolland, R. J. Bent, E. Davis-Russell, G. E. Edwall, E. Magidson, K. Polite, D. L. Singer, & G. Stricker (Eds.), *The core curriculum in professional psychology* (pp. 103–113). Washington DC: American Psychological Association & National Council of Schools of Professional Psychology.

Trierweiler, S. J., & Stricker, G. (in press). *Toward the scientific practice of professional psychology: Methodology for the local clinical scientist*. New York: Plenum.

Tryon, R. C. (1963). Psychology in flux: The academic-professional bipolarity. *American Psychologist, 18*, 134–143.

Ullmann, L. P., & Krasner, L. (1969). *A psychological approach to abnormal behavior*. Englewood Cliffs, NJ: Prentice-Hall.

Vernon, P. E. (1965). Ability factors and environmental influences. *American Psychologist, 20*, 723–733.

Waismann, F. (1945). Verifiability. *Proceedings of the Aristotelian Society, 19* (Suppl.), 119–150.

Wallin, J. E. W. (1911). The new clinical psychologist and the psycho-clinicist. *Journal of Educational Psychology, 2*, 121–132, 191–210.

Watson, C. G., Thomas, R. W., Anderson, D., & Felling, J. (1968). Differentiation of organics from schizophrenics at two chronicity levels by use of the Reitan-Halstead organic test battery. *Journal of Consulting and Clinical Psychology, 32*, 679–684.

Watson, R. J. (1953). A brief history of clinical psychology. *Psychological Bulletin, 50,* 321–346.

Webster, E. C. (Ed.). (1967). *The Couchiching Conference on Professional Psychology.* Montreal: Canadian Psychological Association.

Wiens, A. N. (1986). Public (legislative) expectations regarding quality control in the education and practice of professional psychology. In J. E. Callan, D. R. Peterson, & G. Stricker (Eds.), *Quality in professional psychology training: A national conference and self-study.* Washington, DC: American Psychological Association.

Wilson, G. T. (1995). Empirically validated treatments as a basis for clinical practice. In S. C. Hayes, V. M. Follette, T. Risley, R. M. Dawes, & K. Grady (Eds.), *Scientific standards of psychological practice: Issues and recommendations* (pp. 163–196). Reno, NV: Context Press.

Witmer, L. (1907). Clinical psychology. *Psychological Clinic, 1,* 1–9. (Original work published 1896)

Wolfle, D. (1946). The reorganized American Psychological Association. *American Psychologist, 1,* 3–6.

Wolpe, J. (1958). *Psychotherapy by reciprocal inhibition.* Stanford, CA: Stanford University Press.

INDEX

ABOUT THE AUTHOR

Donald R. Peterson received his BS, MA, and PhD degrees from the University of Minnesota and went on to teach at the University of Illinois at Urbana-Champaign such courses as introductory psychology and graduate seminars in behavior disorders and clinical assessment. He became director of the Illinois Psychological Clinic in 1963 and director of clinical training in 1964. In the latter position, he organized the first doctor of psychology program in the nation, which first admitted students in 1968. He later became the first dean of the Graduate School of Applied and Professional Psychology at Rutgers University, where he has remained as Professor, Emeritus.

Dr. Peterson has reported research data in various journal articles on a spectrum of topics, but he is best known for his definitional statements on the education of professional psychologists. He has also written or edited several books, including *The Clinical Study of Social Behavior* (1968), *Close Relationships* (written with H. L. Kelley et al., 1983), and *History of Psychotherapy: A Century of Change* (edited with D. K. Freedheim et al., 1992). In 1983, he received the American Psychological Association (APA) Award for Distinguished Professional Contributions to Applied Psychology as a Professional Practice, and in 1989, the APA Award for Distinguished Career Contributions to Education and Training in Psychology. His unique achievement in directing a research-oriented scientist–practitioner program, a professional program in an academic department, and a professional school in a major research university has left an influential mark on the enterprise of educating professional psychologists.

ABOUT THE AUTHOR